Walking In The Light of God's Greatness

The Breaths of Life

If it's NOT about you...who did Jesus die for?

The opinions expressed in this manuscript are solely the opinions of the author and do not represent the opinions or thoughts of the publisher. The author has represented and warranted full ownership and/or legal right to publish all the materials in this book.

Walking In The Light of God's Greatness
The Breaths of Life If it's not about you...who did jesus die for?
All Rights Reserved.
Copyright © 2011 The Bondsman
v3.0 r1.0

Cover Photo © 2011 The Bondsman

This book may not be reproduced, transmitted, or stored in whole or in part by any means, including graphic, electronic, or mechanical without the express written consent of the publisher except in the case of brief quotations embodied in critical articles and reviews.

ISBN: 978-1-7351260-0-5

PRINTED IN THE UNITED STATES OF AMERICA

Thank you

My thanks to Jerime
Who told me I should write this book.
His help in the development of the Faith in Actions
And
His continual encouragement, not to quit
Were invaluable.

My thanks to Star
Who, though no income was coming in,
While grieving the loss of both her parents,
Used part of her inheritance to pay the rent
And other bills
While this book was being written.

And to Barbara and Livia of Mobile, Alabama.

Without any of these people, their care and love,
these pages would not have been written.

May the writings of this book honor those,
who walk in the valley of the shadow of death
In the Light of God's Greatness.

Contents

Foreword vii

Intro xi

Quiz xvii

1. A Burning Light…Breath of Faith 1
   (He was in flames, literally, and sitting right next to me.)

2. Door of Death…Breath of Love 25
   (When he opened the door, he was shot dead.)

3. Held For Ransom…Breath of Greatness 45
   (The parents were frightened. Their son had been kidnapped…)

4. The Run…Deep Breath 69
   (He was running and I was chasing him.)

SECTION TWO

5. Homeward Bound…Breath of a Moment 93
   (There I stood. I was homeless…)

6. An Appointment…Breath of Warmth 111
   (It was the Lord's appointment, not mine.)

7. Sing a Song…Breath of Song 131
   (The most beautiful sound of singing…)

8. Vanished...Breath of Prayer 149
   (As I pulled off the exit ramp...)

9. Brothers...Breath of Brotherhood 171
   (One of my favoritte times as a homeless one...)

10. One Eyed Jack...Breath of Fire 191
    (He had been air lifted to a local hospital)

11. The Voyage...Breath of Hope 213
    (I slept the night on the ground by an exit ramp)

SECTION THREE

12. Out of Control...Eternal Breath 241
    (The were out of control, brandishing guns...)

This is the Only the BEGInnIng!..273

Prayer of Salvation..277

Resources Used 285

Foreword

This is not a work of fiction
All people in this book are real
All events in this book actually happened

In life, we sometimes become lost and confused.

Waking up, we cannot remember where we are.

Panicking, we become short of breath.

Our eyesight is weak, and we can no longer focus.

Our passing life fades before our eyes, and we tremble.

*A nightmare of emptiness and lost hope haunts
our every waking moment.*

The light grows dim...it is over.

If you have opened the pages of this book, then I would like to assure you, that it is not over for you yet.

I would like to let you know that this is only the beginning. Your age or life circumstances do not matter. It makes no difference whether you are male or female. It does not matter if you are lying on death's bed. It is not over. This is only the beginning.

It may be hard for you to see that right now…
But that's OK.

Perhaps you need to borrow someone else's eyesight. Another's eyesight, and a few lessons in breathing.

If your life has been a sleepwalk through Christianity, maybe you belong to a Secret Christian Sleeper Cell and require an activation signal. Why? God designed you for greatness, not for sleep!

Scripture says that God gives *The Breath of Life*.
"God breathed into Adam and he became a living soul!"
Genesis 2:7

Our every breath comes from God.

For in Him we live, and move, and have our being.
Acts 17: 28

So let us share 12 days of life, and move and have our being, in Him, in the breaths of life He gives, in each of those days.

One breath for each day, for the next 12 days.
Or …one breath each week, for the next 12 weeks.

For those days or weeks, we will journey through life
and death on the streets of America and abroad.

As we journey, we will look at life through the eyes of
others. We will use the eyesight of those who live and
die on the Streets of Mean.

We will rest our eyes and look at life through theirs,
to see what they see.

While resting our eyes, we will practice breathing.

After those days, with the proper breathing,
our focus will improve.
We will see life more clearly.
We will see that we are all called to walk in the
Light of God's Greatness.
And seeing, we will walk.

You are on the edge of God's Greatness…

No, this is NOT a magic book.
Just a book about walking in the Light of Gods Greatness

The Lord says, In the world you will have troubles

But Fear not, for I have over come the world.

In Him, you too can overcome the world.

It is not too late.

While there is yet, breath…there is yet, hope!

Intro

If you do it for the least of these my brethren, you do it for me.
Jesus

As we traveled through Nevada, we exited the highway at the southern tip of Las Vegas, right off Highway 15. The driver crossed Las Vegas Boulevard and pulled into a gas station.

When he stopped next to the pump, he told me we needed to panhandle some money for gas. Perhaps I should have done as he requested, but for some reason I decided not to. I did hitch the ride, but did not feel obligated to panhandle, as it was his choice to offer me a lift. Having no money to give, I left the man and his car.

I walked away with all of my gear, my backpack, and a suitcase with a broken wheel.

I began hitching again, walking up Las Vegas Boulevard. For the most part, although I was able to catch one short ride, I walked from the southern part of Las Vegas Boulevard all the way through the strip.

I walked past the gamblers and glitzy gambling halls, the small tourist shops and tourists strolling around, sightseeing. The streets of the hopeful, all wanting to taste the glory of Vegas and be clothed in its dazzling aura.

The last time I was there, I was able to stay at one of the nicer hotels and enjoy the food fare at one of their great all-you-can-eat buffets. This time, however, all I could afford was a dollar-menu item at the local McDonald's I walked by. And I just kept on walking.

It took me an entire day to go from the southern most spot in Las Vegas to the northern tip. Arriving in the evening, I made my way to an exit ramp. There, in the darkness of the night, I hid my belongings and walked back to some well-lit businesses.

The area I had ended up in appeared to be a gang banger neighborhood. I walked to a 7 11 and had to bang on the door. The neighborhood was so bad, that the local shops had their doors locked. You had to knock on the door to get in.

A young man came to the door and opened it.

I just need some water, I told the young man. My throat was dry after a long day of walking through the desert air. Needing to replenish my supply before I went on, I handed him my empty water bottles, which he graciously accepted. I was somewhat embarrassed to ask him for water instead of buying some from his store. Thus, I explained to him that I had no money, or I would have otherwise bought a couple of bottles.

When he handed me the full bottles, he dug in his pocket, pulled out a $5 bill, and gave it to me. I did not know what to say. 7-11 employees do not make a lot of money. Five dollars was a lot to someone who worked hard for a living, probably earning minimum wage at one of these quick mart stores.

When I taught Fugitive Recovery, students would often ask me how dangerous it was. ***How dangerous was it to go after fugitives on the run?*** I told them that it was more dangerous to work at a 7-11, at night, than it was to hunt fugitives. At this 7-11, they knew it and did not allow the door to stay open after dark. And this young man, who had been mopping the floor, took time to serve my needs without any personal or expectation of a returned favor. He filled my water bottles, and then gave me a five-dollar bill. I stood in disbelief.

I said the only thing I could say. **Thank you.** He smiled, shut and re locked the door.

I walked back to the exit ramp and bedded down for the night, thanking the Lord for this boy's great kindness. Here I was, a nobody without any money. I had to have looked worse than anyone else who made this part of town their **hood.** I had been on the road for two days, as a traveling nobody. And this young man, who I did not know nor ask anything of, except to fill my water bottles, took his own money and gave it to me. It was one of the kindest acts anyone has ever done for me, and I will always be thankful for this individual, whom I do not even know.

In writing this book, I wanted to honor this young man who, in darkness of the night, unlocked a door for one who was thirsty. He lived, Christ.

> *For I will pour water upon him that is thirsty*
> *And floods upon the dry ground.*
> *Isaiah 44:3*

Do you also stand alone in the night, your throat parched?

Have you failed at everything? Lost everything? Are you homeless, walking the streets of life without purpose, an outcast of society? Is your breath a sigh of resignation over your loss, or empty moments? If so, come with me on a journey of life. For it is the evening of the dawn, and you are needed. It *is* about you. The Lord intended it to be about you. That is why He chose to die, nailed to a cross, so many years ago. It was all for you.

Or...are you a member of a secret Christian Sleeper Cell? Are you simply hanging out, sleepwalking your way through life?

Then take my hand on a journey to renew yourself in the riches of God's grace. Let us step out of the shadows of sleepy-eyed, glassy confusion.

With a few breathing lessons, our vision will become focused, and we can walk once more in hope. With proper breathing, we will learn how to walk in **The Light of God's Greatness.**

You stand at the gates of eternity. You are on the edge of God's greatness. Wouldn't you like to step off the edge? What have you got to lose?

A little lost sleep?

A T.V. Crime

Drama?

You are already at the edge...

So take the next step...off.

Stop!!!!!!!!
Take The Quiz!!!

Before you read this book, please take this quick short quiz!

There are no right or wrong answers!

QUIZ

Your answers do not need to be long. Keep them simple. Just write down the first thought that pops into your mind after each question?

1. Where do you live? _____

2. What are you full of? _____

3. Where do you walk? _____

4. What do you hear? _____

5. Who's in your area? _____

6. Do you have a blanket? _____

7. What are you singing about? _____

8. How does your light shine? _____

9. What is your heart established in? _____

10. What flight are you on? _____

11. Who's your Travel Agent? ____   _____

12. Can you count…to One? _____

1

A Burning Light
Breath of Faith

He was a burning and a shining light.
John 5:35

He was in flames, literally, and sitting right next to me.

I had not noticed.

An individual sitting a couple of rows in front of me turned around. He had noticed. "**He's smoking**," he stated, referring to my prisoner. I ignored the man in front of me.

How could he be smoking, I thought? **His hands were cuffed behind his back.** I placed his hands in those cuffs earlier in the morning when I found him hiding at a local motel. He was being pursued for failing to appear in court on a criminal case, for which I had posted a bond. When I originally bonded him out of jail, I became his bail bondsman. Thus, if I failed to produce the defendant in court, the court would have demanded payment in cash.

Now here we were, in Denver Drug Court. We were sitting in the back row, and while he was burning, I was daydreaming.

Denver Drug Court is a huge courtroom, where upwards of fifty people per day appear on current drug cases, or while on probation. They are trying (or pretending to try) to show the court that they do not need to be imprisoned, and are straightening out their crooked ways.

This is where I brought my fugitive. Normally, when making an arrest, I surrender the arrested directly to jail. This time, due to lack of proper paperwork, I needed to present him in open court. This could mean a four hour wait until all the other cases had been heard. So…I waited, and he smoked.

A man, in front and to my left, began running down the aisle towards us.

To my right, two Sheriff's Officers were approaching quickly. The man running down the aisle on my left yelled, **He's on FIRE!**

What, I thought. Somewhat irritated, I turned to look. My irritation was doused by the sight of my defendant, his shirt in flames, the fire crawling up his back. No longer driving through **Dream City,** I used a coat to smother the fire. We now had the attention of the entire courtroom. Heads turned, and all eyes focused in on our heated drama. The Judge immediately called our case, but ruled from the bench without us having to move from our smoky, dazed position.

The defendant is remanded into custody, ordered the Judge. I relinquished the smoldering defendant to the sheriff's officers.

How had a quiet day at court turned into Dante's Mini Inferno? With his hands cuffed, my defendant had slipped a lighter out of his back pocket. Then, with a flick of his **Bic,** he lit the back of his shirt on fire. I had searched him when I arrested him, but left him with his ID, lighter, and cigarettes; subtle kindnesses to allow the defendant a bit of possessive comfort. What harm could it do? Now I knew. After apologizing to the guards and getting my handcuffs returned, I walked out of the courtroom, stunned.

How could I sit next to someone in my custody, as flames climbed up the flesh of their back, and not notice it?

Why did he do it?

As it happens, he was suspected of giving information to the police as a C.I. (*a confidential informant*) and was scared of going to jail. He was afraid the other inmates would attack him and probably even kill him. He hoped that by lighting himself on fire, he would be placed into solitary lock up, or the Mental Ward. This is what he told me before the guards rushed him out of the courtroom.

When I arrested him, he was just another fugitive. He was a fugitive, who did not want to go to court. I was a bail bondsman that did not want to pay the court. Only one of us, however, could get what they wanted. That is the end game of hunting fugitives. One wants to remain free, while the hunter desires to end their freedom. It is this process of hunting fugitives, knowing they fear court and jail, which can turn an arrest into a deadly game of life and death. Nobody wants to go to jail…or almost nobody, but this man's fear was truly a consuming fire.

Many bail bondsmen hire Fugitive Recovery Agents **(Bounty Hunters)** to locate and arrest their defendants, but I have always found and arrested defendants, personally. From the first day on the job, after being given a pair of handcuffs, I was told I could make my own arrests. So, I have.

When a defendant goes on the run, they can often become the primary focus of one's attention. However, here, as I sat next to him, this defendant did not exist in the forefront of my mind. As my own thoughts paced back and forth, impatient for the wait, he was in panic mode. His thoughts screamed in terror. His thoughts reigned in fear and ruled his actions. Sitting next to him, I was oblivious to his desperation and fears. His silent flame of pain had to be noticed by others, before I could take it in.

He was in the flames, literally, and they stood about watching. They had thrown him into the fire, themselves.

In a distant, desert land, across the ocean, a young boy was sentenced to fire by those who administered justice by the name of Allah.

While held captive by a group of marauding Muslims, who had just finished murdering his parents, this boy was given a chance for freedom; to escape the fire his captors had set. To escape a campfire of death.

The fee for his freedom was his conversion. If he became a Muslim, he could go free. If he remained a Christian, it was the fire.

He was alone with these men, who stood in judgment, their eyes blinded by the darkness that ruled their hearts. He was all alone as his parents were murdered for believing in Jesus. He was alone, **and yet he was not.** His Surety, Jesus Christ, was with him. His bail bondsman did know the fears and terror the young boy felt, and stood with him, strengthening him in his soul.

In the day when I cried thou answeredst me, and strengthened me with strength in my soul. Psalms 138:3

This boy's bail bondsman had already given the boy something no one else could ever give him. He had freed this boy from death's jail and given him the gift of eternal life. Jesus had become his **Surety (Guarantor).**

By so much was Jesus made surety of a better testament... Wherefore he is able to save them to the uttermost who come to God by Him, seeing he ever liveth to make intersession for them. Hebrews 7: 22 & 25

The boy did not lose his faith under their flaming madness. *I cannot deny what I am. I am a Christian.*

The men cast their orphaned hostage into the fire and left. The little boy burned.

And did you notice?

A BURNING LIGHT...BREATH OF FAITH

Did anyone tell you that he was smoking? Did you believe them, or did the thoughts that rule your silence say, **this couldn't be happening?**

Was his burning only a story to read in Jesus Freaks that made you want to say, **Wow?** Or, in the revelation of a moment, did it fill you with the passion to reach out and act? Did you feel compelled to touch a life for Jesus? To touch a little boy's life? He was your brother or...did no one tell you that?

Did the person sitting in front of you, fail to turn and let you know that your little brother was thrown into a fire by hateful men, because he loved Jesus?

The young boy endured the pain of the fire as it curled back the layers of his skin, in the darkness of the night. But...his Jesus was with him. And Jesus decided that this young boy would walk out of those flames, and he did.

A wonderful, moving story. Now can we go home?

Wait a minute! What became of the newly orphaned and burned young boy? The boy who was thrown into the campfire of death, because he would not recant his faith?

In the cruel **aftermath of death and fire, three began...one** remained. It was the cruel mathematical rule of subtraction, formulated in the hearts of hatred. One boy, with severe second and blistering third degree burns, equaled one life of suffering and agony.

The rehabilitation of third degree burns is a long, painful, and costly battle. Few took notice.

As the Shadows of death fell over one young boy's family, no reporter appeared to ask, **why?** Perhaps the boy's burning would have provoked more sympathy if he had been tossed into a fire during an earthquake. If the shadows of darkness had only flashed in flames during a flood, maybe then the boy would have gained TV. News Acclaim, or a monumental outpouring of love. But there were no cameras. No police or paramedics responded. There was only a dark night, a burning boy, and two dead parents. American Christians like to talk about great revivals. In other countries, they live, revivals. They are revived continuously. As others try to burn and kill them, the Lord revives them.

Today, one young boy, who stood for Jesus in the face of unimaginable terror, bears the scars of the flame. The world still does not care, but Jesus cares. In the material world, the boy is a nobody. In Heaven, his name has a place of honor in the Sacred Halls of Grace.

And the terror Christians face in Sudan continue to stalk the faithful, like an evil hunter after its prey…day and night, in relentless pursuit.

Who will stand up for the Sudanese Christians? Whom do you stand for?

If you are not suffering, are you reaching out to those who do, or are you like me? Are you sitting in the back row, daydreaming, while right next to you, someone is in flames?

As you lay down to sleep, does the alarm that sounds, increase in volume, or have you already knocked it off the table and across the room? **Across the ocean**…where he falls onto the dessert sand, in a silent form of burning pain.

The young boy had faith, and was not willing to surrender it for reward of hate. Though taunted with fire and flickering flames of threatened death, he would not budge. For faith, he burned!

The prisoner waiting in the courtroom had no faith, and lit himself on fire! With fears of darkened cell, under shadows of death, he set his own fire for lack of faith.

How important is Faith?

There was a man named Enoch, who lived over 5,000 years ago. During his life, the Bible says that he walked with God. The bible also says he pleased God, and because of that, he never saw death.

He did not die. At the point when God determined that his life on Earth had been fulfilled, God simply transformed him and took him straight into Heaven!

By faith, Enoch was translated, that he should not see death; and was not found because God had translated him: For before translation he had this testimony, that he pleased God. Hebrews 11: 5

Pleasing God is not considered a minor achievement by God! **Enoch never saw death!** After walking in faith for 350 years, God took Enoch from the world while he was yet alive!

Think about how that must have felt. Enoch is walking around, minding his own business, when God speaks to him. God says, **Enoch, I'd enjoy your company in Heaven. So come on up!** And just like that, Enoch is in another world of pure bliss. Because he pleased God, Enoch was transformed in the blink of an eye into an eternal kingdom.

What pleases God's heart to such a degree that He is moved to give life and raise one up...in life? As always, the Bible answers our question.

But without faith it is impossible to please Him. (God) For he that cometh to God must believe that He is (Is God) and that He is a rewarder of them that seek Him diligently. Hebrews 11: 6

Enoch had faith and believed God, and God was pleased, granting Enoch eternal life.

God's gift of eternal life still stands. Jesus said, *I am the resurrection and the life: he that believeth in me, though he were dead, yet shall he live. And whosoever liveth and believeth in me shall never die. John 11: 25 & 26.*

Simply believing in Jesus our faith affords us the same opportunity Enoch was given, to live forever. Jesus also spoke the following. **Verily, verily,**

I say unto you, He that heareth my word, and believeth on Him that sent me, hath everlasting life, and shall not come into condemnation but is passed from death unto life.

By believing in Him, the One who sent Jesus, (that is God), you please God. God is not wowed by world leaders, towering cathedrals, or stained glass windows. Pleasing God is as simple as believing in Jesus, with a heart stained in His blood. If you have nothing, and have failed at everything, but believe in Jesus, through your faith, **you please God! You!**

Two people were torched by passion. One boy endured the flames of fire for reward, by faith in God. One man suffered in anguish and loss, without faith. In faith, we are assured life. Yet, without it, only death in desolation is possible.

If you have never walked in faith or received the promise of life in Jesus, **His gift of life,** there is a prayer for you towards the end of this book. You too, can live forever and not fear death. The only requirement is **Faith**. Faith allows you this gift of life. It does not cost anything, and you cannot earn it. It is a gift of God.

For by grace are ye saved through faith, and that not of yourselves. It is a gift of God, not of works lest any man should boast. Ephesians 2 : 8 & 9

If your life feels as though it has been tossed into a campfire of death, and you have lost everything, then there is hope. In the fires that burned **everything** you ever had, you have been set free. With no baggage remaining, you have nothing to lug around. You are free to...**roam about the country.**

If your life is a mundane circle of empty motions, prepare yourself to **live, LIVE,** in bright passions of love. Prepare yourself to **live, LIVE** in **Jesus** and **walk in the Light of His Greatness.** This is only the beginning! This is ... the evening of the dawn.

And the evening and the morning were the first day. Genesis 1: 5

But make no mistake, the alarm bells *are* sounding. The Lord's alarm sounded in the Sudan one night. One night, those who professed to be Muslims, tossed a young boy into a campfire of death because he chose to hold fast, to speak the *words of life*. The alarm bells of the Lord are sounding. Can you hear them?

The Sudanese boy, who was thrown into the fire was a nobody, but he was God's nobody, and that made all the difference. *On that solemn night, one boy walked in the Light of God's Greatness.*

He could have walked away from the flames that seared his flesh. He could have cried, "Allahu Akbar," and would have walked away with the killers of his parents.

But he would rather burn than deny Jesus.

He was living In Victory Eternal.

Where do you live?

1

Breath of Faith
Faith In Action

Who are you sitting next to?

Are they on fire? Do you notice?

Or are you alone?

Is your life a lonely walk of grief and sorrows?

Do you live in failures and discouragement?

Do you live in fear?

Or…can you see the fear and loneliness of those next to you?

Scriptures say that our lives are like grass, and our glory, like the flowers that decorate the grass, blooming for but a moment in time, then withering, dying… **and are blown away in the wind.** I Peter 1: 24

Is that like your life…*blowing away in the wind?*

In life, our focus can easily become cloudy, when we pant for things we are told will make us happy…that are good for us. We become lost in the flames of want, burning for the world, begging for its' approval, and for acceptance. We strive to have it all, yet end up with nothing but the charred remains of a wasted life.

*Hell and destruction are never full,
So the eyes of man are never satisfied. Proverbs 27: 20*

Do you walk in those charred remains? Is your breath only a gasp, gasping for air, something to fill your lungs…something to fill your life? Does the air around you taste stale and unclean?

Is your life abundant, or just redundant?

Have you lost your way? Have you lost your breath?

Or…are you a member of that vast network of **Secret Christian Sleeper Cells** scattered across the American landscape? Saved, but dulled to the walk you once walked. Your life is now a mere existence as a volunteer to the whims of each moment; your breathing is short and shallow, as you sit in the back row… while right next to you, someone is on fire… and you do not even notice.

Have your desires become no more than the sooty ashes of a campfire long doused by the pouring rain? One day the Lord will return, and then, everything will be fine…divine…*hopefully?*

There is one, who once walked a dusty road, that you could climb a mountain. You may know Him, or perhaps you once thought that you did, before your breath became *The Breath of Death in Waiting.*

Jesus said, I am come that they might have life, and that they might have it more abundantly. John 10:10

Then why isn't your life abundant?

*Let's ride the time machine of thought, into the past. Let's go back about two thousand years...*to a dusty road lined with people laughing and mocking a prisoner on His way to die. He stumbles along a dirty road on His way to a Cross where He will be nailed and lifted up for all to see. His life will seep out through the wounds in his hands and feet. The ***blood and waters of life*** will spill onto the barren soil beneath his battered and whipped body.

While we watch Him struggle forward, we see another carrying His Cross for Him. The guards had ordered it so. They thought Him too weak to carry the Cross. They looked and saw a tired, beaten, bloody man, stumbling along, who could not carry His own cross. Time was being wasted! An execution was waiting! They had yet to pound in the nails!

Watching Him, it was obvious to the soldiers that He lacked the strength to walk forward and bear His ***Tree of Death***. That is why they called to another man in the crowd.

Hey, you! You over there! Come here and carry this man's cross!

The stranger in the crowd had to obey the Roman Soldiers' request. For he knew that these soldiers would just as soon raise a sword to cut down the life of the one who dared to refuse them, as they would nail a man to a tree.

Many sideline spectators crowded the route as if attending a Thanksgiving Day Parade, but could only watch with the eyes of a dead world. They inhaled the breath of death. Their shouts spread across the path of the wounded man like confetti, decorating their lust for His blood. They could not see with the ***Spiritual Eyes of Life***.

If their eyes could see, would their breath have escaped in the awe and wonder at Him, who had walked by? Would they have marveled at all he carried down that dusty, dirty road? If they had seen, would they have ***then*** fallen on their faces, and cried out, ***Jesus, Lord and God!***

The man's friends also followed the procession of death, as Jesus struggled on, lifting first one leg, and then another. One step at a time, ever determined to complete the journey set before Him. They saw a man who clearly appeared unable to bear the weight of His cross…a man weakened by a night of beatings, whippings and scourging.

Those who once followed Him, saw a man too weak to carry anything. Each believer could only watch with the eyes of a defeated heart, a feint heart. The hope they had lived in, became hopelessness.

They watched with the eyes of heartbreak, tears obscuring their vision. What would **they** have thought, had they seen with **Spiritual Eyes?**

With keen spiritual eyesight, would they have been astounded at the strength of this one man. This person, who carried such a heavy weight before them all… a weight none could see.

For as this bleeding man moved ever forward, no one could see all that He, the Son of God, chose to carry that day. No one could see the mighty strength of this one man who, after a night of horrors and merciless beatings and whippings, carried so much upon His own shoulders to the place called Golgotha, the Skull. For He not only carried His torn and bloody body down that dirty, dusty street, along a route filled with gawking spectators, but He carried the grief and sorrows of a world in darkness.

Surely He hath born our grief and carried our sorrows, Yet we did esteem Him stricken, smitten of God, and afflicted.

> **But He was wounded for our transgressions,**
> **He was bruised for our iniquities;**
> **The chastisement of our peace was upon Him;**
> **And with His stripes we are healed. Isaiah 53: 4& 5**

After being brutalized during a night of frenzied hate his back ripped to shreds Jesus was not forcing his body down that street EMPTY HANDED. For He carried every single sorrow and grief you ever felt, had, or will have. That day, as your salty tears stung the wounds in his back, while wrapped in the chains of your fear, He dragged those chains to Calvary… for you.

Forasmuch then as the children are partakers of flesh and blood, He also himself likewise took part in the same; That through death, He might destroy him who had the power of death, that is the Devil And deliver them who through fear of death were all their lives subject to bondage. Hebrews 2: 14 & 15

He carried the chains of your bondage upon his own back, that you might be free. He carried them…so you would not have to.

Surely He hath borne our grief and carried our sorrows.

And he did… one day, two thousand years ago.

And if it was *not about you*…

Whose grief and sorrow was He carrying?

Everyone else's but yours?

Thus, if Jesus carried your burdens to the Cross, to be nailed with Him, do you feel overwhelmed, as you struggle, trying to carry them back up the street?

And if your load feels heavy, then surely you can see that the load Jesus carried was beyond human endurance. He not only carried your grief and sorrows, but everyone else's as well.

He bore your grief and carried your sorrows so you would not have to. It is time for you to leave them at the Cross. Do not try to drag them back along the street stained in His blood.

He freed you. Be Free.

<u>But this one thing I do, forgetting the things which are behind</u> **And** <u>reaching forth unto those things which are before</u>**,** I press toward the mark for the prize of the high calling of God in Christ Jesus.

Let us therefore as many as be perfect be thus minded: And if in anything ye be otherwise minded, God shall reveal even this unto you. Philippians 3: 13, 14, 15.

How will God reveal this to you? Amazingly, He just has! He has revealed your **otherwise-mind,** through the light his word shined upon your heart, when you read the verse. And now, it is time to begin anew…to leave the past…in the past.

First, you need to reposition your life into a position reflective of your standing in Christ Jesus. Furthermore, did we not read, only a moment ago, that God has a unique placement already set up on your behalf?

It is the…
High calling of God in Christ Jesus.

With a High Calling of God in Christ Jesus, I'm not sure how you could start out any better…or any higher!

If you are a nobody, who before could only wish to **Walk In The Light of God's Greatness**, this repositioning will be a beautiful turn in fortune for you.

If you have failed at everything, and are uncertain in how to attain your high calling, a partner who can encourage you would be an invaluable asset. Let me introduce you to yours…

His name is God.

For we are laborers together <u>with God</u>;
Ye are God's husbandry, ye are God's building.
1 Corinthians 3: 9

Since God created the Heavens and the Earth by merely uttering the words, I would say you have a pretty good partner.

If you are a nobody, and/or a failure, let me assure you that the first breath you take, provided that you walk with the Lord, will be a new beginning! With an eternal program and God as your partner, you cannot fail!

If you belong to a SECRET Christian Sleeper Cell, this is your **activation notice.** It is time to **activate!** It is time to step out of **Redundancy** and into **Abundancey.** You are invited to step into the life Jesus has chosen for you! You also cannot fail!

Why is failure not an option? Because God never fails, AND... He is your new partner!

So, enough of panting and running around in moody disarray. It is time to begin anew. In beginning anew, proper breathing will be essential.

In learning to breathe, we must first believe in God, in Jesus His Son, and the **gift of life** he has promised us. However, before our breath, it is important to cut that twine of regret and let your grief and sorrows drop into the dust bowl of the past. A sharp word with a razor, cutting edge will be needed. The word we will select for this delicate operation and twine cutting ceremony will be the one syllable word, **Thanks.**

When we give thanks to God, we acknowledge His grace and Lordship over our lives, and, in gratitude for salvation, humble ourselves before Him. In our humbleness, He exalts us and lifts us high.

Humble yourselves therefore under the mighty hand of God and He shall exalt you in due time. Casting all your cares upon Him, for He careth for you. I Peter 5: 6 & 7.

By giving **Thanks**, we accept our lives as a gift, acknowledge that we are forgiven, and trust in a walk Jesus made over two thousand years ago, to carry our past... into the past.

In everything give thanks: for this is the will of God in Christ Jesus concerning you. I Thessalonians 5:18.

Do you feel as if each day is no more than a punishment? Give thanks.

My son, despise not the chastening of the Lord; neither be weary of His correction. Whom the Lord loveth, He

WALKING IN THE LIGHT OF GOD'S GREATNESS

correcteth; Even as a Father the son in whom He delighteth. Proverbs 3: 11 & 12

Isn't it wonderful to know that when the Lord corrects you, it is because he delights in your presence and the marvel of your being? So Rejoice! His correction is the irrefutable evidence that you are His! And He does not correct in the manner that we do, in hatred and anger. He corrects in Love. He always loves you. So give thanks!

And we have known and believed the love that God hath to us. I John 4: 16

And now you can rejoice over a partner who has also called you His son, or daughter. **Even as a Father, the son in whom He delighteth.** (We are all one in Christ Jesus, whether female or male.)

There is neither Jew nor Greek, there is neither bond nor free, there is neither male nor female: for ye are all one in Christ Jesus. Galatians 3: 28

With a partner who delights in you as a son or a daughter, I believe the winds of change are about to blow through your hair. And don't worry about where you placed your comb, simply enjoy the soft breeze of His touch.

Even the wind and the sea obey Him.

If you are where you are because others have hurt you, or stole from you, or cheated you...or forgotten you, give thanks!

For this is thankworthy, if a man for conscious toward God endure grief, suffering wrongfully...when ye do well, and suffer for it, and take it patiently, this is acceptable with God.

Foe even here unto were ye called: because Christ also suffered for us, that ye should follow his steps:

Who did no sin, neither was guile (deceit) found in his mouth:

Who, when he was reviled, reviled not again; when he suffered, he threatened not; but committed himself to him that judgeth righteously:

Who his own self bare our sins in his own body on the tree, that we, being dead to sins, should live unto righteousness: by whose stripes ye were healed. Peter 2: 19 through 24

What an awesomely amazing thought! Not only did Jesus carry our grief's and sorrows down that dirty dusty road, but also bore all of our sins. Though he was not guilty of any, he bore the sins of all.

So let us give thanks!

And in our thanks, let us bathe in the reassurance that from now on, everything will turn out good. Whether or not it appears good may not always be clear. But once again, we have the assurance of our never-failing partner, God.

And we know that all things work together for good to them that love God and are called according to his purpose. Romans 8:2

After giving thanks, you are ready for your first breath with us. If you have never trusted in a God, who loved and died for you, isn't that because you have never known Him? For how could you not desire such sacrificial love as our Lord has provided…just for you.

Herein is love, not that we love God, but that he loved us, and sent his son to be the propiriation (sacrifice) *for our sins. 1 John 4:10.*

If you are unsure, please just remain with us for a bit and learn more about this new life and God's grace. Then, at any time you feel led, turn to the back of this book and read a prayer of salvation.

It may be that…*as a light that shineth in a dark place,* the day may dawn and a *day star arise in your heart.* From II Peter 1:19

So, once again, let us give thanks!

After giving thanks, you are ready for your first breath with us.

In our **Breath of Faith**, we are going to believe and trust in God, as our partner, accepting His word as...**His Word**. We are going to believe that Jesus bore our grief's and carried our sorrows to free us from worldly regret and fear. We are going to believe that He will do as He promised and give us an abundant life in Him. Thus, we can all enjoy an abundant life, a life rich...in ***living!*** We are going to believe that He desires us to walk in the **Light of His Greatness,** and in ***believing***...we will walk.

And now...A Breath of Faith...

Simply close your eyes for a brief moment and...breathe.

You have begun, and now, it is time for a **Faith in Action Moment**. We breathe a **Breath of Faith** because we believe. In our belief, we act. Our acts then become the decorations that adorn our life. Instead of grief and sorrow, we will now decorate our life with **love, joy, peace, longsuffering, gentleness, goodness and faith,** by our **Faith in Actions. Galatians 5: 22**

And what is our first **Faith In Action Moment**? With God as a Partner, we should remember not to limit His reach, but also not forget the one sitting next to us. With these thoughts in mind, our first **Faith in Action** will be to begin a **Global, Worldwide Missionary Ministry!** Hey, don't worry, you can do that. Remember, God is your partner! He is the **Power** behind us, within us, and the **Lord** over us.

Ask yourself, since Jesus carried the grief and sorrow of the world upon His own back, shouldn't we be willing to carry His cross for the world, on ours?

And so Hence, we will establish a **Global, Worldwide Missionary Ministry!**

BREATH OF FAITH...FAITH IN ACTION

To begin, simply find an empty glass or mug and set it in a special place. This is now your **Missionary Mug**. You have herein established your very own **Missionary Mug Ministry**. And know that it does not matter how much money you are able to put into your mug. Only put in it what you can afford. The Lord is pleased with a cheerful giver and does not judge the wealth of a bank, but that of a heart, giving in love.

If you are in a secret, **Christian Sleeper Cell**, this *is* your wake up call, your first act of activation!

If you are homeless, rejoice! Jesus was also homeless throughout his adult life! He is now King of Kings!

While living on the streets, when you are able, designate one pocket as God's treasury. Put a nickel, a dime, or a quarter in it. Now you have established a **Pocket Missionary Ministry**! *You,* being homeless, have just done what many with homes, cars and multiple bank accounts never do. You have begun a **Global, Worldwide Missionary project.** With this **Faith in Action** step, you have come one step closer to **Walking in the Light of God's Greatness.**

For anyone reading this book, doubts that your efforts will amount to anything could float amidst the clouds of your mind, obscuring your vision. That is why we have taken our **Breath of Faith**, in a promise to believe the **Word of God**, above the words of men.

And... what does the **Word of the Lord** say?

Therefore, my beloved brethren, be ye steadfast, unmovable, always abounding in the work of the Lord, forasmuch as ye know that your labor is NOT IN VAIN in the Lord. I Corinthians 15:58

On your first day of starting anew, and your partner has now assured you that none of your labor will be in vain! All of your labor in him is guaranteed before you even begin!

This could be better than a government job!

WALKING IN THE LIGHT OF GOD'S GREATNESS

Now that you have taken your first breath, and have your work guaranteed, please do not forget the one sitting next to you. As they sit in perfect pose, looking peaceful and serene, their heart is crying, flooded with tears. In silent comfort of reach, can you put their hand in yours, or hold them for a moment. In one space of time, can you lose yourself in the needs of the person, who is sitting next to you? While everyone else becomes occupied with self-anointed importance, could you give of yourself, and spare a kind word to a lost soul?

Let's pray to God that He will help us.

Dear, Heavenly Father,

Thank you for letting me work with you. Thank you for delighting in me as your child and for granting me forgiveness. Thank you for guaranteeing victory, although I have yet to do anything for you in this new breath I have taken.

Thank you for the offering of your only begotten son, and for His willingness to carry my grief and sorrows upon His back. Please allow me the strength to carry His cross for the world, one day at a time, in this, my time.

Please watch over the brave young orphaned boy in Sudan, who had his parents murdered and was thrown into a fire. Please help him heal within and without. Please look after others in Sudan, targeted and hated because they love Jesus. Please help heal those who are harmed and let them know, somehow, that we pray for them. Let them know that they are not forgotten.

Please bless this new Missionary Ministry I have started, and help it grow. And Lord, please encourage all the other nobodies and failures, who will be learning to breathe with me. Speak to us, as we learn to breathe, that we may please you and honor the name of Jesus, in this new abundant life you have promised us.

And Please Lord... do not let me forget the person sitting next to me. Help me to open my eyes, so that I may see the fire, before it is too late.

In Jesus name, Amen.

If you have taken your first breath, then you have begun to **walk in the Light of God's Greatness**! Your journey has begun. And even as you wonder at the significance of this first breath, your life is being shaped by a sovereign God.

If at any time, you are unable to complete ***A Faith in Action Moment***, do not give up or fall back into fear. Keep your Faith. The Lord knows your heart. Ask Him for your own personally tailored ***Faith in Action***. Your partner is a living God, not a paper book.

> *Ask, and it shall be given you;*
> *Seek, and ye shall find,*
> *Knock, and it shall be opened unto you.*
> *Matthew 7: 7*

On a darkened night of terror, a young boy braved the fires of hate, to live, LIVE in faith, trusting in God, in His love and deliverance. He was a burning and a shining light that walked out of a campfire of death, and **Lived In Victory Eternal.**

Where do you live?

2

Door of Death
Breath of love

*If we say we have no sin,
We deceive ourselves, and the truth is not in us.
If we confess our sins,
He is faithful and just to forgive us our sins
And cleanse us from all unrighteousness. John 1: 8 & 9*

When he opened the door, he was shot dead.

He had been staying at a cheap motel in Denver, where drugs and prostitution reigned.

After I received the call to post his bail, the people I first came into contact with were scared of him. **Why don't you let him sit in jail?** I asked.

They were afraid to let him sit in jail, fearing what he may do later, if they did not help him now. What kind of fear is that, where dread holds captive the thoughts of what may be? How do you define the dread of an enemy who may destroy the sanctity of your tomorrow, if you do not offer help today? That is fear!

The day I posted his bail, after his release, I drove him across town to where he would be living. On the drive, he requested a quick stop to make some purchases. I obliged and allowed him to go to the store. He returned from the store with a bottle of bear. That was his first choice after being freed: a beer. He had the creeps, and was withdrawing from his constant state of drunkenness. In jail, lacking the blood alcohol mixture that normally flowed through his veins, his system began the never-ending craving for more. He needed the beer like you, or I might need water, after wandering in the blazing heat of a desert sun; lost in time, tongue stuck to the roof of the mouth.

He told me he needed the beer to stop the shaking. This man who caused fear to flow through the veins of others, trembled at the prospect of living his life sober. Perhaps I should have left him in jail to contemplate his end. However, my position in life is not to judge or decide the fate of those I am contracted with to bail out of jail. I have no crystal ball that will open my eyes to another's fate, or reveal their impending tragic end.

When someone is arrested in the United States, they are presumed innocent until proven guilty; unless, of course, they appear on one of the popular crime shows airing on cable news. As innocent citizens, in most cases, they have the opportunity to remain out of jail until their criminal court case is resolved.

There are different ways that an individual charged with a crime can be freed from jail, pending the outcome of their case. One way is to make bail. A court will set a monetary amount that must be pledged to the court for the defendant to be free between court dates. If he fails to appear after a bond is posted, the court must be paid the amount pledged, or the defendant must be found, arrested, and surrendered.

That is my job. I am not set over people to **_Judge_** their character or intention. The court judges when it places a monetary value on their freedom. Bail can be set anywhere from $200.00 to $2 million. My job is to post that bail, if able.

Life and Death are close associates of the bail business. They find people where they live, on the **Streets of Mean**, in the homes of broken-down families. Drugs, crime, and poverty are frequently the arms that embrace them. Imprisonment, and or death, is often their reward. They live and die in the undercurrents of society.

These are the people I deal with. These are also the people Jesus loves; for He loves each and every one of us. When the preachers and church teachers of Jesus' day observed Him eating with the dregs of society, they scorned Him. What was His reply? *I came not to save the righteous but the sinners.* Jesus did not come to save those He did *NOT* love.

In reflection, that is what makes the memory of this ride from jail so sad and miserable. I may not have mentioned Jesus to this man, who I was driving home, a man who would be dead within the year.

And one night…when alone in his motel room, a visitor came calling. When he opened the door to see who was there…it was death.

I wonder what darkness fills a person's mind when they die suddenly without knowing Jesus. Do they have a horrible waking moment, as they pass from life into a permanent nightmare of hell? An everlasting nightmare, where you realize, there is no way out this time. No bondsman, no defense, and no freedom; only eternal hell. And… the frightening knowledge that it will always be so. You would finally know, and be fully aware, that all of your cute lines, wit, and cunning thoughts were no more than the whispering murmurs *of Hell.* Do screams echo through the evil silence, along the dark corridors of your new, everlasting nightmare? Are you alone in the awareness of one bad choice too many? In attempting to escape from a nightmare in life, have you created another nightmare, that of living death?

After death, does an unsaved person re-live his bad choices repeatedly, like teasing thoughts that will not go away? Does their every evil deed haunt their every waking moment, as their mind races for the *OUT* that can never be found?

There is no movie here, no bad person returning to Earth and saving a marriage, or making a lonely person happy. There is no Hollywood script where, **An Angel Gets Their Wings.** There are no great songs like Sinatra's **My Way.** On a second thought, maybe that will be the song that haunts forever the nightmare of your living death, in the flames of eternal wrath.

It is a fearful thing to fall into the hands of the living God. Hebrews 10: 31

However, there is a way to leave fear behind. Today, you must choose which door to open.

Jesus said, *Behold, I stand at the door and knock: if any man hear my voice, and open the door, I will come in to him, and will sup with him, and he with me. Rev. 3:29*

My defendant opened the door and was shot dead. Wrong door.

Another man was shot dead.

This man, who lived in North Korea, was on his way home in the company of a friend. While walking, he was confronted by the North Korean Police. **Are you a Christian**, they demanded, **do you believe in Jesus?** They were trying to ensure that North Korea was protected from this **'dangerous criminal'** with his faith and devotion his only crime.

Yes, he said. They shot him in the heart, and he fell.

In North Korea, this man **had been greatly feared**. Not because he was a bully, but because he loved Jesus. He was not afraid to tell others about Jesus, and speak of love that cannot be comprehended...but can be accepted.

The man the police shot did not fear his enemies; he forgave them, wearing a smile on a face of light. He wanted freedom for his enemies, and their freedom did not scare him.

In shock, swirling in confusion, a stunned young man bent down to hold the body of his dying friend. A smile parted the bleeding friend's lips. His glassy eyes gazed upwards at the police that shot him, the love of God glistening in the blood that seeped from his body.

His last breath of life carried a blessing for his murderers. ***I forgive you***, he whispered to their hardened faces of stone. His smile remained, as his life slipped away, lifted beyond the reach of man, leaving behind the stillness of a moment; the stillness of death.

The police left. The dead man's friend went home, the lack of belief evident in the moment, mixing and circulating with the name spoken by one, and feared by others; the name *Jesus*. He did not stop off for a beer.

At home, in shock, fear, and wonder, he asked his mother, ***who is Jesus?***

Did his mother's heart skip a beat as her son mentioned the name of her Savior, Jesus Christ? Did her breath escape her, as her son spoke the name she had held in the silent reaches of her heart for years? Did tears streak down her face, leaving dampened stains upon her cheeks?

She shared with her son, who Jesus was, and shared with him the gospel of salvation. At that moment, her son opened the door of his heart to Jesus, and obtained that salvation. A brother, who returned home later and was told the harrowing tale of terror, but given the bright and shinning gospel of salvation, also opened the door of his heart to life.

What did they do next? In this country of darkness and cruelty where shadows of hell lurk behind doors of death, the two brothers decided to push open the doors of light.

They decided to become outlaws. They decided to break the North Korean laws and begin a smuggling operation. The drug of love they wanted to import would lead to an automatic death sentence if they were caught. However, the bibles they craved to bring into North Korea would be brought in anyway.

Without so much as a doctrinal thesis in theology, they began to smuggle bibles into the darkest of lands. They hungered to know more of Jesus. They wanted others to know more.

Blessed are they that do hunger and thirst after righteousness: for they shall be filled. Matthew 5: 6.

How are the brothers doing? I do not know. Theirs is not the right story line for Reality TV. No, **this week on Brothers for Bibles in North Korea, we will watch the terrifying sequel to...**

Even today, many Christians believe it wrong to smuggle bibles if local laws forbid it. They may be related to those who were outraged on hearing that a man, William Tyndale, decided to ignore the laws forbidding regular people from reading God's word.

In 1534, Tyndale desired that even a boy behind a plow should have the blessing and opportunity to read about God's love. The religious leaders of his day did not like that idea, and forbade it. Of course, the religious leaders of Jesus' day did not like Jesus teaching the people either. I wonder what their contemporaries do not like.

William Tyndale was finally betrayed for the crime of wanting others to know and read about Jesus for themselves. When those who Lorded over God's heritage in 1536 decided to strangle and burn Tyndale at the stake, many who **called** themselves Christians, consented. They either had not read the verse about those, who hunger and thirst after righteousness, or they conveniently chose to ignore it. Lacking anything substantial to satisfy one's hunger, or quench another's thirst, they became envious. They grew ugly within and murderous without. In North Korea, the two brothers decided that others should be able to read the gospel of Jesus Christ and be fed from this source of eternal love. They chose to disregard the treacherous leaders, who fear the word *Jesus,* more than the combined power and armies of the world.

The two Korean Boys opened the doors of life, and desired to live in that life. They decided to *Live in Victory Eternal.*

Who was the friend who was executed by the North Korean police? A **Nobody,** who believed in Jesus and dined at the table of grace. After dining, he was granted the strength of a man well nourished.

Before his King, in the **Majesty of a Moment,** he shined as bright as the stars of Heaven.

For this cause, I bow my knees unto the Father of our Lord Jesus Christ. Of whom the whole family of heaven and earth is named. That He may grant you, according to the riches of His glory, to be strengthened with might by His Spirit in the inner man. That Christ may dwell in your hearts by faith: that ye, being rooted and grounded in love, may be able to comprehend with all saints what is the breadth and length, and depth and height; And to know the Love of Christ, which passeth knowledge, that ye might be filled with the fullness of God. Ephesians 3: 14 through 19

With his last breath, he offered them love through forgiveness.

Who offers you love? Have you placed your hope in the only one who ever loved you enough to die for your sins and overcome death? He overcame death for you, so that you too, could be filled with the fullness of God, and overcome death. In Jesus, there **IS** life!

Jesus said, *I am the way the truth and the life. He that cometh to me, though he were dead, yet shall he live. And whosoever liveth and believeth in me shall never die. John 14: 6*

If Jesus already dwells in your heart by faith, but you have become inactive in a **Christian Sleeper Cell,** it is time to wake up! You must rise from your sleepy-eyed Christian life, to serve and walk with the Living God! Let us do the works of the Lord while it is the day.

WALKING IN THE LIGHT OF GOD'S GREATNESS

Jesus said, *I must do the works of my Father while it is day. The night cometh when no man can work. John 9: 4&5*

The alarms are sounding! It is no longer daytime. **It is the evening… of the dawn!** The night is edging ever closer. Your suffering brothers and sisters are crying out for you to join them.

They are mercilessly **killed every day. They are counted as sheep for the slaughter.** And as God's scripture declares that they are **more than conquerors through Him that loves them**, their supply line is crucial. An enemy knows if he can cut off an armies' supply line, he can disrupt and demoralize the soldiers at the front.

Has the enemy successfully cut off your brothers and sisters' supply line? Have you been cut off from the battle, hiding out on 5th Ave. or Rodeo Drive, thinking that you might be safer there?

Have you allowed a brother or sister's supply line to be cut off by inaction? Has someone told you that there is no point, there is nothing you can do anyway? That is what spies do. Did you know that? Spies plant the seeds of misinformation and doubt, to disrupt, discourage, and disengage those who would join the battle.

Even as you read this line, the brothers and sisters of Jesus are being beaten, robbed, murdered, raped, imprisoned, and tortured throughout the world. As they are hated, hunted, and hurt, with their last breath, they offer their lives as our alarm. As evening descends upon the history of life and death within man's rule, the alarm is sounding. Do not fall back asleep!

The love of God glistens in the blood they shed for His glory.

One day, as you stand before God, what will you say? Will you simply offer hollow words of emptiness, as your tongue sticks to the roof of your mouth? Will your knees weaken? Will a wave of heavenly regret, rising up from within, flood your eyes with tears? Will you feel nauseous from what might have been?

*If any man's work shall be burned, he shall suffer loss:
but he himself shall be saved; yet so a by fire.*
I Corinthian's 3:15

**As you stand before God, will your knees
feel weak as you suffer loss?**

Or ...before you can speak, will you see people rushing forward, calling out your name, speaking up for you? **Hey Jesus, I told you about this person. When my parents were killed and my home burned down, they sent a gift of love. Lord, this is whom I was talking of. When I was alone and without hope, she reached out to touch me... and she did not even know me!**

Jesus, this is one of those I mentioned to you who helped us get Bibles. Because they did, we were able to learn about you!

Will the voices of your persecuted brothers and sisters speak up for you? What will you do? Will you stand in silence at that moment? Will your eyes and heart drop to your feet, as you listen to them talk and boast of others that loved them?

And then, when you feel compelled to raise your eyes, to glimpse your Savior, will His eyes lock with yours and ask why? As His eyes hold your gaze of aching desire, will His look of questioning truth cause you to lose your breath in a moment of soul-regretting despair? **Why did *you* not help my brothers and sisters? *Why*?**

It is certain that one day in North Korea, a young man who believed in Jesus, a nobody by the standards of the material world, yet a prince in the Kingdom of Heaven, offered his life as a testimony to the Love of God found in Christ Jesus.

He lived in the *Majesty of a Moment!*

A nobody in the world,
...a prince of Heaven.

On this day, because this young Korean
man was filled with the fullness of God,
when a bullet pierced his heart,
the blood that oozed from the wound
that brought him death,
glistened with the love of life.

Does your love glisten?

Then what are you filled with?

2

Breath of Love
Faith in Action

I forgive you.

These may be the three greatest words one can ever utter. Equally, they may be the greatest three words one can ever hear. They are spoken in **the Majesty of a Moment** filled with love.

Forgiveness washes away pain and hatred like a river carrying away the dirt of the past, the debris of our lives. This river of forgiveness carries the dirt downstream, away from our hearts and into an ocean of forgetfulness.

Who is a God like unto thee, that pardoneth iniquity...He retaineth not his anger forever, because He delighteth in mercy. He will turn again, He will have compassion upon us; He will subdue our iniquities (Our sin) And thou wilt cast all their sins into the sea. Micah 7: 18 & 19

True Forgiveness is offered from a heart of love.
It refreshes and allows a new start.

And that is what your new boss is preparing to give you. The fact that you may have previously under-performed or failed on numerous occasions is irrelevant. You are going to be given a new start. You know your partner is God, but now you will meet your boss.

There is a TV show called, **Undercover Boss**. A major CEO goes under-cover to the lowest rungs of the corporate ladder. Here, the ordinary employees work away without any appreciation or recognition. The show follows the CEO as he labors under-cover, appearing to realize the struggles of everyday people. At the end, the CEO is enlightened, handing out several bonuses to those he met. Tears flow and everyone has been enriched. It is a heart moving show.

This is all well and good, but it begs a question. What about all the employees who did not appear on the show? On one episode, a single mother was given a new job with less tension and stress. She was overjoyed, and rightly so. But what about all the other women, who worked for the company in cities across the nation, who were over-worked and under stress? They did not all get promotions, or less stressful jobs. Why? They were not on TV.

Two thousand years before this show aired, before remote controls allowed us to step into the lives of great CEOs who humble themselves before the cameras; in the times before CEOs went **LIVE** in an attempt to understand their work force, a greater show took place. The greatest undercover CEO show was making history: The story of how God became man, so that He could walk where we walk, see as we see, and feel as we feel.

Who is like the Lord our God, who dwelleth on high, Who humbleth Himself to behold the things that are in heaven, and in the Earth. Psalms 113: 5 & 6

Forasmuch then as the children are made partakers of flesh and blood, he also himself likewise took part of the same... Wherefore in all things it behooved him to be made like unto his brethren; that he might be a merciful and faithful High Priest in things pertaining to God, to make reconciliation for the sins of the people. For in that he himself hath suffered being tempted, he is able to help and deliver them that are tempted. Hebrews 2: 14 & 17 & 18.

Now all this was done, that it might be fulfilled which was spoken of the Lord by the prophet, saying, Behold, a virgin shall be with child, and shall bring forth a son, and shall call His name Emmanuel, which being interpreted is, God with us. Matthew 1: 22 & 23

And This God, known as Jesus Christ, walked among those to whom He had given life. And when He walked, He walked as one who served those He met, in humbleness and love. However, few ever knew who He was.

He was in the world, and the world was made by Him and the world knew Him not. Matthew 1: 10

Jesus Christ was the ultimate undercover CEO. He not only walked among us; touching our lives, healing the sick and sharing God's truth, He suffered for us as well. He was whipped, His back shredded, so that we might be healed. After being beat and mocked all night, He carried our grief and sorrows down a dirty, dusty street for us. Finally, as He arrived at His destination Calvary He wanted to be sure that we would all know that He would never forget any of us. For this purpose, He decided to have your name engraved into His hands.

He did not go to a local tattoo parlor for this engraving, but to a Roman Soldier. Instead of an ink gun, He had the soldier use a steel spike. Instead of black ink, He used His own blood. And as His brutalized body was laid on the wooden Cross that He chose for His door of death, this CEO had your name engraved into the flesh of his hands.

He came into the world as a humble child, and walking in grace, He lived to serve others. He refused the riches of the world, as He desired the riches of… **you even more.** Moreover, before He left the show, He wanted you to know that He would never forget you or forsake you, each of you. Even those who did not appear on the show with Him. That is why He used His own blood as the ink, a steel spike as the tool, and engraved your name into the palms of His hands.

> **Behold, I have graven thee upon the palms of my hands: Thy walls are continuously before me. Isaiah 49: 16**

Hanging on a cross that day so long ago, He wore your sins, so that **you could be forgiven with His last... Breath of Love.**

Father, forgive them for they know not what they do. Luke 23: 34

With His last **Breath of Love**, His door of death opened to give you life.

Your partner is God and now you know your boss...

Jesus Christ.

You may say, *Hey, I thought Jesus WAS God?*

He is! What a great working relationship you will have! *And whatsoever ye do, do it heartily, as unto the Lord and not unto men: Knowing that of the Lord ye shall receive the reward of the inheritance For ye serve the Lord Christ. Colossians 3: 23 & 24*

And what is the first thing your boss would like to say? *Son or Daughter, be of good cheer; Thy sins be forgiven thee. Matthew 9:2*

He also wanted to add one other instruction:

> *In the world you will have tribulation: But be of good cheer, I have overcome the world!* John 16: 33

You knew you had a wonderful partner, and now you know you have a wonderful boss! It seems that His first instruction for you is to simply, **Be of good cheer!**

Have you ever in your life started a new job, where the first greeting from your boss, when you walked in was. **Be of good cheer?**

Jesus also wants you to know your sins **ARE** forgiven. He **ALREADY PAID THE PRICE FOR YOUR SINS** before you ever started to work for Him. That is how much He loves you!

But God commendeth His love towards us, in that, while we were yet sinners, Christ died for us. Romans 5: 8

This is why a young man in North Korea was so happy. He knew this love of Jesus and died for it. He died **in it** and was full **of** it. Before he died, he forgave those who executed him! He lived in the **Majesty of a Moment**, and walked in the **Light of God's Greatness.**

Two doors were opened.
One led to death. One led to life.

Is there a door in front of you? Is it the right door?

Is your heart filled with the fullness of God? If not...
what is it full of ?

Isn't it great to have a boss, who has overcome the world and loves you, a boss who wants you to **Be of good cheer?**

His next desire is for you to obtain a company manual. That manual would be the bible. It is the **Living Word of God.**

Begin in the New Testament. Many like to begin with St. John, one of four gospels. Matthew is also a good place to start. It is at the beginning of the New Testament. To expand the joy in your heart, try the Psalms. They are gift-wrapped in encouragement and written for you by a king! They are in the Old Testament. Sometimes you can find a New Testament Bible that also contains the Psalms. This bible is sure to be a treasure of riches to inspire, lifting your spirit.

If you do not have a Bible, get one. If you are homeless and/or jobless and cannot afford one, go to a church and ask for one. If they will not give you one, find your way to a Christian bookstore and ask if you can work for a couple of hours in exchange for a Bible. Tell them that you have no money, but have a strong desire to read the Word of God.

If you have a hard time getting a bible, this will only help you to grasp what these North Korean brothers are going through. Although you will not be arrested or executed for trying to obtain a Bible, you might begin to understand its value. Cherish your Bible. You do not have to understand everything within at once. Keep it simple. Jesus did not complicate salvation. Men did through their interpretations.

> *For after that in the wisdom of God*
> *The world by wisdom knew not God,*
> *It pleased God by the foolishness of preaching*
> *To save them that believe. I Corinthians 1 : 21*

What is Jesus Christ capable of saving you from? Besides anything and everything, He can save you from death and the power of the grave! Do you think the ability to call someone forth from the grave, so that they may have life once more, is just a minor accomplishment?

If you work at a McDonalds, ask your manager if you drop dead while flipping a burger, would he be able to call you back to the land of the living. Request to know whether the health plan you signed up for includes a manager that can give the **Breath of Life,** or would they just **send in the clown**? Let your employer know that your other boss can raise the dead. When he asks who your other boss is, tell him, **Jesus,** and walk away.

Let the Power of a name linger in the **breath of a moment**. Let the silence you leave behind allow the name *Jesus* to echo repeatedly in their mind. It will! Say the name *Jesus,* and walk away.

Now, if you have some spare change, add it to your **Global, Worldwide Missionary Mug or Pocket Ministries.**

BREATH OF LOVE...FAITH IN ACTION

And in the spirit of **Thanksgiving,** let us offer a sacrifice acceptable to God, by Jesus, the gift of **Thanksgiving.**

Dear Heavenly Father,

Thank you for forgiveness, in the Breath of Love, and for forever etching my name upon the palms of your hands.

I pray for those in lands of darkness where the gospel has been outlawed. I humbly ask that you hear our prayers to carry your words of life into the lives of those who want truth and life.

Thank you for sharing with me, the lives of those, who stand in courage and love, declaring your truth. Please let their stories lift my heart in boldness, filling me with the desire to walk in the Light of your Greatness. Help me live in the Majesty of the Moment.

Thank you for your eternal grace and salvation. Please decorate my life in the same grace and mercy for others, as you have given me.

Allow me the capacity of forgiveness for anyone and everyone, who has or will ever harm me, so that I may reflect your majesty, and those who wronged me may taste the fullness of your love.

In Jesus' name, Amen.

Now it is time to take your next breath.

The Breath of Love.

Are you ready? Close your eyes for but a moment and...breathe. Even now, your boss, as King, is preparing you for a **Majestic Moment or** perhaps many moments, where you will represent the Majesty and love of royalty. The Lord is also preparing the moment. He leaves nothing undone.

If you live in a **Christian Sleeper Cell**, get activated! Learn to live in majesty: **The Majesty of the Moment.**

If there is a person in your life whom you need to forgive, today is a good day. If it is difficult for you to forgive, ask God for His grace in this matter. **After all, He forgave you!**

And now...What are you full of ?

For your **Faith in Action Moment**, check out **www.persecution.com**. This is the official website of VOM, a site that speaks out for your persecuted brothers and sisters. This site can help open your eyes. After establishing a **Global Worldwide Missionary Mug or Pocket Ministry**, it is advisable to gain a realistic understanding of the world your ministry will reach, and the needs your endeavors will help meet. Let your **Ministry** become part of a supply line.

To help you in this outreach, let us award you a promotion to elevate your positioning in **The High calling of God in Christ Jesus.** We are promoting you, from a **private** in a **royal army**, to a **supply sergeant!** It is only your second breath, and you have already received a promotion! You are now a **conqueror** with the **conquering!**

If you are homeless, go to a library and use a public computer to get on-line. When you see how your sisters and brothers suffer as nobodies in other countries, I pray that you would draw strength and courage for your own circumstance.

If you are discouraged and weary, cry to Him who gives courage and comfort. If you are lost, take heart, the Lord reaches for you.

He will keep the feet of His Saints
And the wicked shall be silent in darkness.
For by strength shall no man prevail.

Is your walk unsteady, as you stumble in weakness and fear? Allow Jesus to place each step. He will help you walk. Even when you stumble, He will not falter.

The bows of the mighty men are broken,
And they that stumble are girded with strength.
I Samuel 2: 4

Open the door to life
And allow Jesus to enter yours.
You can rest in His assurance.
He will hold you in Love...
In the Breath of Love.

3

Held For Ransom
Breath of Greatness

*For there is One God
And One Mediator between God and Man
The Man Christ Jesus
Who gave himself a Ransom for all
Timothy 2: 5 & 6*

The parents were frightened. Their son had been kidnapped by a North Side Gang for failing to pay a drug debt. If the parents did not pay the debt, their son would be killed. That was the call I received one day as a new bail bond agent in Denver, Colorado.

Having previously posted this man's bond, I was now considered by law as his jailor. He was in my custody.

The term **In my custody**, does not imply that a defendant is handcuffed to my feet. It means that I have the jurisdiction to enforce rules I wish to set, and or arrest my defendant at any time, day or night. The **Power to Arrest** is the power to protect the financial risk a bondsman takes when he or she posts a bond. It is a civil agreement the Defendant enters with his bail agent, when he signs the bond.

When a defendant makes bail, the defendant has not attained freedom. In Colorado, their release on bail is considered a continuation of their incarceration. They are simply transferred from the county, or city jail, to the bail agent's jail. However, the bail agent's jail is not a building, with bars and a cot in a corner. A bail agent's jail is normally anywhere in the city, or State of Colorado, that the defendant may wish to go.

If a defendant fails to go to court, or a bail agent believes a defendant is packing their bags for an extended vacation, the bail agent plays travel agent, rearranging the defendant's itinerary. Bail agents and Fugitive Recovery Agents (people hired to arrest fugitives) can receive a nasty reputation when a poorly planned arrest makes the news. Yet, in America, hundreds of arrests are made by Fugitive Recovery Agents weekly, quietly and safely. It is a dangerous profession, but one in which many honorable men and woman work, without pay, unless they capture the fugitive they chase.

When I was hired, I was given a pair of handcuffs and was told that I could arrest my own fugitives. So I have. However, now, I was a freshly licensed bail agent, and my defendant was not trying to flee. He was being detained. He was being held for ransom.

The office manager of the bail company I was employed with did not want to get involved. These were the days of extreme gang violence in Denver, and the manager did not harbor a death wish. Calling the police never rose to the level of a thought. The defendant was in my custody, and was my responsibility.

The call to save was in my court, and following the scriptural insight to, **Pray without ceasing**, I headed to the address provided by the defendant's parents. The location was an older apartment house off Colfax Ave., the main east west drag in Denver. Once there, constant in prayer, I entered the building, climbed the stairs, and tramped down the hall. I knocked, using the old, friendly knock technique claiming, *I was a friend!* I was not.

A gang banger opened the door. I could see my defendant sitting on the couch in his underwear, on the far side of the room. Ignoring everyone else in the room, I said,

Hey man, the court called and said that you didn't show up today. Even though no such hearing had been scheduled, it seemed like a good thing to say at the time.

What court, the defendant asked.

Arapahoe, I answered, feigning annoyance, **I didn't have you set for court, but I'm just telling you what they said when they called me this morning. Either you come with me now, and we get this straightened out, or I'll call the police, and they can straighten it out.** (I used my tough, **I'M the Bondsman**, approach. One of my problems has always been that I hate debating with people. I am not a debator.)

It was a ridiculous conversation, I at the door and my defendant in his underwear on a couch across the room, as three babysitting, hostage-takers silently hovered about, listening. With a veiled threat of police involvement, I was hoping no one would ask, **hey, how'd you know he was here? Who gave you this address?'** No one did.

Finally, I turned directly to the **Doorman** holding the door ajar and spoke to him. **This is really crazy. My records don't show any hearing today, but unless he appears in court this morning, the court claims it will order the bond forfeited. I'm not going to risk losing my money.**

You a bondsman, asked the **Guardian of the Door.**

Yea, I replied, producing a business card. **If you ever get in a jam, call me. I never let my friends sit in jail.** I assured him.

My defendant was given his pants, and was putting them on. **I'll bring you right back after this is over,** I told my guy. **But hurry up, let's go! I've got other things to do.** (Another area I continually struggle with is patience.)

Pants pulled up, my defendant walked out of the room, and we eased down the hall. We were shadowed by two of the **Kidnappers in Training.**

This is a pain, I stated out loud, for benefit of the nearest Shadow. **I've got too much to do today and this screws up everything.** He backed off, letting us walk out of the building, but trailed us the half a block to where my parked car waited. Once out of the building, my defendant breathed a sigh of relief, **Thank God**, he whispered.

You better thank God, I hissed back angrily.

Saying, **Thank God**, as casually as if he were saying, **Boy, I'm glad that's all over**, disturbed me. He was not saying **Thank you God, for saving me.** He was saying, **Thank God, I'm out of that mess**. His fate as a Metro Crime Statistic, a lifeless body dumped in an alley, had been thwarted, but God was only a secondary statement in passing.

During this summer stretch within Denver, gang killings seemed to be part of a daily menu. It was not really a big deal, except to the police...and those who were being killed. However, to this man, who had moments earlier, sat in the care and company of those, who were planning his execution, God was no more than a brief word, in a sigh of relief.

On that day, we walked by the grace of God, not because I was cunning or daring. I had walked in fear, hiding under hope that the Lord would be with me.

And I, brethren, when I came unto you, came not in excellency of speech, or of wisdom, declaring unto you the testimony of God. For I determined not to know anything among you, save Jesus Christ, and Him crucified. And I was with you in weakness, and in fear, and in much trembling.

The Lord gave me the words and allowed the confusion of the surprise visit to baffle those, who had dark plans for this man. They did not know what to do.

The Spirit of the Lord descended upon that room, and an air of peace settled amidst the danger of the moment. The air of peace kept us safe. The confusion kept them off balance... and we walked away.

After we left, I immediately drove this man to the Arapahoe District Court where his present criminal case was pending, and surrendered him in open court. It appeared to me that he would be safer locked up, than running the streets trying to dodge those that wanted him dead. His life had meant nothing to that Gang, except for the money they hoped to collect from his parents for not killing him.

What had bothered me beyond reasoning, however, was who this man was. This man, who I bonded out of jail on a drug case, who allowed himself to be kidnapped by a notorious gang for failing to pay his drug debt, was a graduate of a major Christian University! This man, who had as casually said, **Thank God,** as you might say, **Nice Day today**, as we walked out of the Den of his impending death, was a Graduate that had completed his studies as a Seminary Student.

He graduated from the same major Christian University, whose founder once stated that God had given him a deadline for death. Once upon a time, God had determined that the Christian University Founder should either raise one million dollars, or die. This was before Madoff taught America to reach for billions.

This public proclamation absolutely amazed me. The thought that a founder of a Christian University could actually state in Public, **God is going to strike me dead if I don't come up with some quick cash**, is like a stun gun zapping my brain. It electrifies my thoughts with insanity.

Was God short on cash? Was God conspiring with the same gang members, who kidnapped one of his past graduates because he did not pay a drug debt?

Perhaps the gang holding my defendant hostage could have profited more by opening their own Christian University. Since a man in Florida heeded the call of the university founder, producing the one million cold hard cash, this process of proclaiming Gods' demand for cash, appears a safe and productive way to riches. For Kidnappers in need of raising quick capital, a Christian University, and a few Godly threats, may just be the ticket they have been looking for.

Lacking such a threat from God in my own personal life, the concept is a little hard for me to grasp. Maybe one needs a Great

Christian University named after them, before receiving such Godly attention. I have never even had a minor, side street, tent revival named after me. Maybe that is the difference.

I have no diploma in theology. My degree is on the **Streets of Mean,** where I would have died in my horrible sins, had not the grace of God by Jesus Christ reached all the way down from Heaven to save, miserable me.

God did not threaten me; but instead He forgave me, and did so with grace. Though I disregarded all that was right, and I admit that I hurt many, Jesus spoke to my heart and opened it up to desire for Him. And although I often fail to remain on the right track, He never gives up on me. He will not give up on you either. He whispers to you… **I am here.**

Whatever voice this university founder was listening to, it was NOT the Spirit of the Lord. And that, my friend, is the Truth. It does not matter to me how many highly educated Christian Graduates of Theology claim that this man is a great man of God. I consider his public proclamation of God's threat for cash, the highest degree of shame!

Maybe Christians, who feel compelled to give this Christian University monetary gifts could ear-mark a portion for any graduates destined to be kidnapped by criminals. An Appeasement account should also be set up to pay any financial ransom demands their God may decree in the future. This would be a good way to insure the safety of future Deans, prior to any Godly threat, if more cash is required.

Make no mistake; I do know the verse that asks us to, endeavor to keep the unity of the Spirit in the bond of peace. I have simply failed to find the one that proclaims that we should **endeavor to keep the unity of the spirit in the bond of a lie.**

God is NOT a man that He should lie. Numbers 23: 19

And Thus, I state with all that is in my heart that God never held the life of any Christian University Founder under ransom, at fear of death, if he failed to come up with one million dollars, cold hard cash.

That is a lie. I deal in lies daily, I know.

In Asia, in the Golden Triangle, where drugs are harvested for profit and sale, eventually ending up in the hands of America's Gangs; (**the same Gangs that kidnap Graduates of Great Christian Universities for failing to pay their drug debts**) a young teen is being beaten. He is hit in the mouth and the stomach. He passes out; his face bruised and bleeding. He is NOT the founder of a Great Christian University, and God did not tell him to come up with a million dollars or die.

He is a 16-year-old boy from the tribe of Dao in Southeast Asia. His name is Minh. He tells others about the love of Jesus. He sold a Buffalo he owned. It was all he had. He sold it so he would have the money to go get bibles, that others in his village could read about Jesus, and about how Jesus loves them. He also wanted to learn more about Jesus himself.

On his way home, he was stopped by the police and dragged off to the police station. When asked if he would stop trying to bring bibles to his village, his honesty shined in God's Light. He said, **If the officers confiscate all our books, when I have money, I will go again.**

Why don't you obey your government? demanded the interrogators. They must have thought that beating up a teenager that loved Jesus, was more important than finding drug smugglers and thieves.

I trust my Lord, said Minh. **I will never reject Him. I need the books, so I can understand Him.**

Minh leads a church in a mountain village of North Vietnam. He is not a graduate of a Great Christian University, just a 16-yearold who loves Jesus.

His church is a mini Christian University that educates his fellow villagers about the Gospel, and Grace of God found in Jesus.

This young boy has dedicated his life to setting free those held in bondage. This teen is determined to free those held hostage by dead spirits and village ghosts. He has dedicated his life to freeing the hostages of death. He walks the prison jungles of a darkened night, to share the freedom and joy of Light.

Minh tells people that they are Free. He tells people that Jesus has ransomed them from the power of the grave.

In America, Mega-churches with Mega-Budgets and colorful leaders with the gift to orate, inspire the masses and lead others… to salvation.

In Minh's village, salvation comes in the form of one young teen, who believes in Jesus Christ and spreads his good news, even after being beaten.

In America, no expense is spared. With glitz and glamour, and sparkling sermons by the beautiful and elite, in sacred halls of ornate churches, all are combined like a dynamic sales presentation, to provoke and move…a heart.

In Minh's village, he knows that it takes faith in the Cross and the Savior, who died on that cross, to pay the ransom for all who believe. Minh knows that, **the preparation of the heart in man, and the answer of the tongue are of the Lord.**

And I brethren, when I came unto you, came not with Excellency of speech, Proclaiming unto you the testimony of God. For I determined to know nothing among you save Jesus Christ and Him crucified. And I was with you in fear, and in weakness and in much trembling. And my speech and my preaching was NOT with enticing words of man's wisdom, but in demonstration of the Spirit, and of power.

That your faith should not stand in the wisdom of men But in the Power of God. I Corinthians 2: 1 through 5

What does your faith stand in?

Minh's faith stands in the power of God. He and others like him dare to tread through jungled prisons, leading others to freedom in Jesus. They are the Lord's Bondsmen. They offer bail to those imprisoned in sin. Their companies are established by God and their services are free.

What is their link to the outside world? One would be VOM, Voice of the Martyrs. VOM is a Christian organization dedicated to the care and assistance of persecuted Christians around the world. For the families of imprisoned pastors, for children whose parents are killed, for the wives, who are left alone after their husbands have been murdered, VOM offers the outstretched arms of Jesus Christ. One at a time, as each has need, VOM gives. In **Truth and Deed**, in love and understanding, to comfort and strengthen. They brazenly walk into the fires of hell on Earth, to reach and touch their suffering brethren. A network reaching the front lines, where the slaughter of the Lord's family continues daily, they are there with them, sharing and caring in the grace of God.

When the blanket of despair falls upon those who struggle to walk in the Light, VOM pulls back the covers and with outstretched hands of love, lifts up the fallen and feeds the weak. This is the sole purpose of Voice of the Martyrs. It is a voice of our brothers and sisters, fathers and mothers, as well as little children. It speaks for them as a witness to their sufferings, and touches them with the blessings of God, caring for their needs.

VOM was founded by one who spent over 14 years, tortured and beaten, locked in a communist prison for telling people about the love of Jesus.

The founder of VOM and his family were persecuted by those that hate the name of Jesus, suffering torture at the hands of human demons that walked as men.

He knew torture and…he knew love.

His response? To reach out to those Jesus haters with love, while caring for those who are now persecuted.

How much time did you spend in prison because you told someone about **Jesus?**

I *have* spent time in jail, but shamefully, NOT because I loved Jesus or told someone about Him.

No... we were not imprisoned. He was imprisoned.

And now V.O.M. reaches out to others, to the imprisoned, brutalized, or those abandoned by the world and society. They reach out to the faithful in Jesus, who suffer for love.

In the jungles of Asia, a 16-year-old believes that *it is about him.* That is why he chooses to follow Jesus in spite of the persecution, the beatings and loss. He sees his loss as a gain. He believes that the **Good news of Salvation** should be spread out and allowed to reach all. He believes that he was called to share this news with those in the uttermost villages, in the jungles of the Golden Triangle. Others also believe.

The bondsmen of the Lord, who live in the uttermost regions, within the densest jungles of Asia and remote mountainside villages, believe that even there, the Lord's hand is able to save.

***Wherefore He is able to save them to the uttermost that come to God by Him Seeing He ever liveth to maketh intercession for them.* Hebrews 7: 25**

And in jungles deep, and up obscure mountainsides, to reach the remote, they travel. They cross jungle paths by motor bike or on foot; traveling for days, to carry the good news that He who saves, can save even the uttermost. The Love of God burns bright in their hearts. Their feet, though weary, are beautiful feet.

How beautiful upon the Mountains are the feet of him
That bringeth good tidings, that publisheth peace;
That bringeth good tidings of good,
That publisheth salvation;
That saith to Zion,
Thy God reigneth! Isaiah 52: 7

And in the jungles of Asia, they do! They tell all about the God who reigns. They tell about His love and Salvation. And within that jungle maze of life, one 16-year-old boy was crowned with the courage of a mighty warrior. His weaponry is Truth. His armor is the Lord, and his heart's desire is for others to know the truth. He did not beg for a million dollars because he was threatened by God.

Instead, he sold his only item of value, a buffalo, because he was touched by the love of God. He wanted to buy bibles to learn and to teach others.

Minh, the 16-year-old, was beaten because of his faith. He is **Living in Victory Eternal**. He knows it **IS about him**. He knows he is... **more** than a conqueror through Jesus, who loves him.

If it is **NOT** about you... why did Jesus allow himself to be struck, spat on, beaten, whipped, and mocked...with your name engraved into the palms of His hands, as he was nailed to a tree?

> *I create the fruit of the lips;*
> *Peace, peace to him that is far off, and to him that is near,*
> *And I will heal him. Isaiah 57:19*

If it is **NOT** about you... *Who is Jesus going to heal?*

> *Minh knows that Jesus paid deaths ransom.*
> *Minh knows that Jesus paid the ransom for everyone.*
> *Minh is telling everyone.*
> *Minh is More than a Conqueror!*
> *He walks in the Light of God's Greatness.*
>
> *Where do you walk?*

3

Breath of Greatness
Faith in Action

The tomb was dark and silent,
Its entrance sealed by a huge boulder.

In front, soldiers were on guard.

Their job?

To guard a dead body, the body
of one who had been crucified.

No one was to enter the tomb.

And...no one was to leave it.

This was the third day after the body had been placed in the tomb. This was the day religious leaders feared. This was the day on which, *He might show up again. They had forced the certainty of His death, consenting in approval, as He was nailed to a tree. But He had said that He would not stay dead.*

In town, a man lay atop his bed in fitful spurts of unrest. His body could not stay still, jerking and convulsing in uncontrolled spasms. A Chief High Priest vainly wandered the chambers of his mind, leafing through the religious relics he stored in his memory, hoping for an answer. There were none. It had been like this all night. Vivid pictures of the dead, rising from their graves, marched through the corridors of his thoughts. The ground would open and out they would come, one by one, smiling, their eyes twinkling, like stars of light piercing the night.

The Chief Priest turned over, squeezing his head between two hands, as if the pressure exerted could squeeze out the attacking sights and sounds erupting within. *This is foolishness*, he thought. ***This man had deserved to die. No...maybe He wasn't a horribly bad man, but He had said that He was the Son of God! He deserved death! God was not a man with kids. He had no son! I should know***, he thought, ***I am a Chief Priest!***

The Priest, weary and ragged from the long day and restless night, fell back into the misty haze of his chilling nightmare.

Within the recesses of his tormented sleep, a grave stone slowly pushed its way up through the Earth, breaking the ground. Darkness darted about in shades of gray, through a forest of howling laughter, eerie gifts from the void of endless time. The gravestone continued to rise, into the Heavens, to tower majestically as a throne of gold.

The Chief High Priest gasped, as a hand emerged from the stone, reaching out in motion of want. It reached for him. His breath escaped, as the hand grasped his wrist, pulling him up. The Priest, trembling uncontrollably, tried vainly to resist, but was forced to stumble forwards. As he neared the Rock, his eyes began to adjust their focus. They zeroed in on a series of words that were etched in the stone, in blood-lit colors that glimmered in the night. From deep within the confines of his soul, a scream exploded. Shards of sanity splattered against the walls, inside his head.

> ***Who hath ascended up into heaven, or descended?***
> ***Who hath gathered the wind in His fists?***
> ***Who hath bounded the waters in a garment?***

Who hath established all the ends of the earth?
What is His name,
And what is His Son's name, if thou canst tell.
Proverbs 30: 4

The Priest bolted upright in his bed. ***No***! he screamed. **He wasn't God's Son!** Sweat dripped down his forehead, his sleeping robe was drenched. **He is Dead!** yelled the Priest to the horror of his solitude. His voice reverberated, bouncing against the walls of his darkened room. Shadows with wicked smiles, seemed to laugh and play in frenzied movements of nighttime haunts.

He lay back down and closed his eyes, trembling with fear. Then... as the weary Priest finally began to feel the desired waves of sleep caress his mind, his body was hurled out of bed and thrown hard against the wall of his hollow room. As the earth beneath him shook violently, the Priest's last hope for sleep shattered. Terror filled the priest like a satanic possession. He could not stop shaking.

At the tomb, as dawn began to rise in the east, a violent earth quake took hold of the land. The Soldiers guarding the tomb staggered atop the ground that would not stay still. Then, they froze in fear, as one whose **countenance was like lightening** wearing **raiment as white as snow, descended from Heaven and** touched Earth. The angel of God rolled away the huge boulder as if it had been a play toy. The soldiers became as dead men, frozen in **breath of death.**

The angel had not rolled away the huge boulder so a dead man could walk out of the tomb. There was no dead man in the Tomb. He had already risen and left. The angel had been told to roll away the huge boulder, so that others might see, and that seeing, they might believe.

For the man, who had been beaten, whipped, and nailed to a tree, seemingly destined to die a savage death in front of crowds eager for the blood lust of a moment, could not stay dead. As the early morning sun began to rise in the East, on the first day of the week, some two thousand years ago, the **Early Morning Star** had already risen. From a night of death, *Jesus* rose as the **Early Morning Star of Life**, in the light of a new day. **In rising, He became the Light** of a new day.

Others also rose that day. It was a part of His desire that others should rise. If Jesus alone had risen, people might believe but wonder. *Yes, He rose. He was the Son of God. But what about me? Will He raise me up too? I'm just a nobody, a sinner. I'm a failure. How do I know that He will also raise me up?*

Jesus had said, *I am the resurrection and the life, he that believeth on me, though he were dead, yet shall he live. And whosoever liveth and believeth in me, shall never die.*

After Jesus rose from the dead, He desired to highlight the power of His words. And so, by His power, others too, rose from *their* graves. Except, this was not the *Dawn of the Dead. Not* another Sci Fi Zombie movie. This was *The Day of the Living. A Day of Greatness.* A day when the world would see the power of God to raise the Dead.

...and the earth did quake, and the rocks rent; And the graves were opened; and many bodies of the Saints which slept arose... and came out of the graves after His resurrection... and went into the holy city...and appeared unto many. Matthew 27: 51, 52, 53

They rose from their graves to bear witness of the Majesty of the Lord, and His power over death. They had been given the Breath of Greatness, and they rose from the slumber of their rest, to walk, once more, among their brethren. They were to bear witness to the very *Words* of Jesus Christ. They witnessed His power to raise the dead, who are not dead at all, but as the scripture says -, *are only sleeping.*

These witnesses could tell everyone, *Do not fear death. For death has no hold on anyone who believes in Jesus! We slept, but could not die. Jesus IS life!*

These Saints, who rose from the Dead, had been given the **Breath of Greatness.** Jesus gives the **Breath of Greatness** to all who trust in Him and His words. He alone has the Power to give this breath.

Jesus paid the ransom for Death by defeating Satan and Death openly, overcoming both in Victory. In His Victory, rising from the tomb, He became our Bail Agent. He became our Surety. He paid the price of our bail, in blood, His own. As His, we who believe are free from the prison of sin; we can leave the grave and our empty lives. Freed from the worlds' slavery, we are free to live life abundantly, in Him.

> *For there is one God*
> *<u>And one mediator between God and Man.</u>*
> *The man Christ Jesus,*
> *Who gave Himself a ransom for all.*
> *Timothy 2: 5 & 6*

Today, are you still held in the ransom of a lie, in a **breath of death?** Are you held captive by fear? Are you a slave to the world? Has no one told you that Jesus led "**Captivity Captive?**" **Jesus unlocked the prison doors. So, why have you locked yourself up again?**

After Jesus paid for your freedom with His own blood, have you walked back to the prison cell block, a set of jailor keys jangling from your belt, to the place of your previous confinement... and locked yourself up once more?

Why are you so afraid of Freedom?

Do you prefer the slavery of the World, to the Freedom in Jesus? Do you really prefer sleeping? Do you enjoy your bed of death, and stale breath? Is your darkened room really worth keeping? The alarm *IS* ringing!

> *Wherefore He saith,*
> *Awake thou that sleepest,*
> *And arise from the dead*
> *And Christ shall give thee light.*
> *Ephesians 5: 14*

The alarms are ringing. It is time to turn on the Light and rise. It is time for life.

> *And this is the record, that God hath given us eternal life*
> *And this life is in His Son.*
> *He that hath the Son hath life;*
> *And he that hath not the Son of God,*
> *Hath not life.*
> *I John 5: 11 & 12*

In this, your third breathing lesson, after getting a new job **The high Calling of God in Christ Jesus,** with God as your partner, and **Jesus as your Boss** you are now herein guaranteed Eternal Life in the **Breath of Greatness.** Here it is recorded before the Courts of Heaven, that you have made bail! You are free, no more a criminal refugee!

Within your freedom, Jesus has also guaranteed your Greatness! Unless of course, rising from the dead is no great thing to accomplish. **What do you think?**

Besides rising from the dead, Jesus intends that you become as Great as the Greatest Prophet, who ever lived!

He has what? Your Boss, Jesus Christ, has proclaimed that you, who are reading this page, in this book, this very minute, will be as Great as the Greatest Prophet that ever lived! What a guarantee! Is your Boss the best ever, or what?

Oh... you have doubts? Then listen to your boss for yourself

> *Verily I say unto you,*
> *Among them that are born of women*
> *There hath not risen a greater then John the Baptist:*
> *Notwithstanding he that is least in the Kingdom of Heaven Is greater than he.*
> *Matthew 11: 11*

It seems that, if Jesus dwells in your heart by faith, your position in Heaven is already set. You will be as **Great** as John the Baptist! As a new employee, you're starting out in pretty good company, I'd say. Is your head swimming in amazement, or are you simply treading in an ocean of wonder?

What a fantastic guarantee of greatness! And this is only your third breath.

So let's wait a minute while you catch your breath. While you catch your **Breath of Greatness**...

The Breath of Greatness

And in the joy of the Lord and His promise of Eternal Life... and His guarantee of Greatness...let us accept the gift of God by Jesus Christ...the Breath of Greatness...*Breathe!*

Before we move on, however, we must take care in our new walk of greatness. Just because you are now a **Child of God**, a member of a **Royal Family** with **a High Calling,** and all your work in Jesus guaranteed successful... don't go strutting around like a peacock on steroids!

Jesus, to show the world the grace of God's Royalty, first walked Himself, as a humble servant of love.

Let this mind be in you, which was also in Christ Jesus. **Who, being in the form of God, thought it not robbery to be equal with God, But made himself of no reputation and took upon himself the form of a servant, and was made in the likeness of man.*

And being found in fashion as a man, He humbled Himself, and became obedient unto death, even the death of the cross. Philippians 2: 5, 6, 7, & 8.

Since He freed us from the bondage and slavery of the world, He does not desire us to walk in the ways of that bondage, enslaving others to our own needs and wants. Let us listen to our boss, as He guides us in our **Breath of Greatness.**

The Kings of the Gentiles exercise lordship over them; And they that exercise lordship over them are called benefactors. But ye shall not be so. But he that is greatest among you, let him be as the younger; And he that is chief, as he that doeth serve. Luke 22: 25 & 26

Because we have been given and guaranteed so many wonderful gifts and promises, none of which we earned, Jesus wants us to walk in the same **Greatness as He** walked. He desires us to walk in **humbleness** of heart and mind, touching others.

To touch the life of another in the name of Jesus is the Greatest act one can ever hope to achieve in the **Breath of Greatness.** In the Light of God's Greatness, *there is more wealth in the touching of one life*, than all the wealth hidden in the diamond fields of Africa; The Greatness of your walk holds a deeper value than all crude oil buried in the Oil Fields of the Middle East. The tenderness of a touch shines brighter than the glittering wealth on display in the self-glorified stories of Hollywood. To touch, just one life, is Greatness in the eyes of God.

For this purpose, in our High calling of God in Christ Jesus, we will endeavor to touch one, within one, within our Breath of Greatness.

<u>Faith in Action</u>. In this ***breath***, our ***Faith in Action*** will be… **to begin a Great Christian University.** This University will be established in a Jungle or remote mountainside village in Asia, Indonesia, Africa, or South America. We will then pray that our established university will touch one, within one. One person, within one village.

This will be a marvelous act of activation for Christian Sleeper Cells! Waking up to strap on the love of the Lord, and finance a Christian University, will allow you to share grace with a beating heart, in a hungry soul.

If you are a failure, or Homeless, and have little or no money, do not faint. Pray to God, your Father. Tell Him that you would like to finance a Christian University in a jungle or mountainside village. Ask Him to help you achieve this ***Faith in Action. That is what partners are for, to help. In everything, Prayer. By everything, Prayer.***

Now set up **Mug 2.** The first Mug is for the persecuted brothers and sisters who are beaten, tortured, and imprisoned and their families. This second Mug will be your Christian University Money.

BREATH OF GREATNESS...FAITH IN ACTION

What will this cost? No worries. During the Christmas season, VOM creates village packs priced at $75.00 each. These **Village Packs** hold everything needed to teach others about the love of Jesus and Salvation. One village pack supplies all the instructional information required to begin a Christian University. You will not be required to appoint a Dean, who can be threatened occasionally by God, when additional cash is needed. You will not need a planning board, or an investment bank, just $75.00.

The villagers will take all the risks. They may build their campus with mud, straw and bamboo, but they will build it. They may be attacked, beaten, imprisoned, or killed, but they are willing. *Are you?*

There is a news bulletin that is worthy of publication. Can you assist with the distribution?

Extra.! Extra! Read all about it!
Freedom is here! Your ransom has been paid!
Jesus has paid the ransom for death!
Extra! Extra! Read all about it!

And when you start a **Great New, Christian University** in a remote jungle or mountainside village... **they will.**

If you are homeless, before you start collecting for the Christian University, you will need one envelope and one blank sheet of paper. You will address the envelope to VOM, because they are the ones who put together and send out these village packages.

V.O.M. P.O. Box 443, Bartlesville, Oklahoma, 74005-0443

Before you send the money, please take a blank sheet of paper and write:

Dear Sir or Madam,

I have enclosed $75.00 for a Christian University (VOM's Christmas Village Package Program.)
Please see that it goes to a good village. I, myself, am homeless,

but I know that I have a mansion waiting for me in Heaven and I would like these villagers to have mansions there as well. It would be nice to have such great neighbors!

Then sign your name.

Do you want to see people praise God in celebration and wonder?!! You want to hear angels rejoice?!! You want to **walk in the Light of God's Greatness?** Fulfill this one **Act.** Be the first Homeless person to start a Great Christian University!

If you are homeless, but sincere in your desire to raise money for a Christian University, here is a suggestion. Go from one church to another and tell them you are trying to raise money to start a Great Christian University, and you were wondering if they have any odd jobs you could do. If churches fail, start visiting Christian Bookstores.

Try it and blow their minds!

By saving a little change each day, your University fund will grow faster than your utility bill! If you are homeless, it takes only one quarter a day. Begin saving in January and by October, your goal will be achieved!

If you have friends that may like to join you in this University fund, start a **Christian University Club.** Let your friends join in the **Majesty of a Moment in the breath of greatness,** and the joy of the **Act.**

When your University goal is achieved, do not wait for a rainy day. Mail the gift to VOM. Tell them that the money is for their **Christmas Village Pack** program. Even if they receive the $75.00 long before Christmas, they will make sure the money is earmarked for the program you request.

Dear Heavenly Father,

Thank you for your love. Thank you for your kindnesses to me. Thank you for freedom. Thank you for paying my ransom with your own blood. Help me walk in the Light of the Early Morning Star,

Jesus Christ, that I may also help another walk in the Light. Help me touch…another.

Please help Minh receive the bibles and materials he desires. Strengthen him and guide him as he shares your grace with others. Crown him with courage and strength as he spreads the word of Freedom and love.

Please bless this Christian University fund I am starting. Please help me save the money to establish this Great Christian University, in your name. And please prepare the hearts of those who will hear about Jesus Christ, and your Great plan of Salvation. In Jesus name, Amen.

> In the Golden Triangle,
> where Drug Lords reap billions in the **Trade of Death,**
> A 16-year-old trades in Love,
> preaching freedom and life,
> **Freely.**
>
> He teaches others how to Breathe,
> how to breathe the **Breath of Greatness.**
> Minh walks in the Light of God's Greatness.
>
> And Where…**do you walk?**

4

The Run
Deep Breath

And the Light shined in darkness And the darkness comprehended it not. John 1:5

He was running...and I was chasing him.

Across the streets and down the alleys of Downtown Denver, he was determined *NOT* to get caught. He did not want to go to jail!

We arrested the defendant earlier that morning as he walked out of a Denver Court Room. Because the man I needed to arrest was big and mean, I decided to ask my partner, ***a big and mean, 14 Year Jefferson County Sheriff's Deputy Crime Scene Investigator***, if he would come along and assist. He did.

We arrested the defendant when he left a Denver Court Room without an incident. With his hands cuffed behind his back, we took him out of the building, across the street and towards the City Jail. The Denver Courthouse was just kitty-corner from the Jail. Once across the street, I entrusted the care of my defendant to the capable hands of my partner. I needed to go to my car for the paperwork required to admit the defendant into the jail. Reaching my car, a voice hit me from behind.

Hey, STOP, the voice screamed. I pivoted around in time to see my defendant flying across the street.

My defendant was no longer in the capable hands of my **big mean, Jefferson County Sheriff's Deputy Crime Scene Investigator.** Nope, he was not. With hands cuffed behind his back, my defendant was racing across the street. My partner had not moved from his spot of stunned confusion. And so began a mad dash. The Defendant had long legs and could run fast, even **with** his arms pinned behind his back by my Smith and Wesson, stainless steel handcuffs.

When someone fears going to jail, their determination is displayed through the effort they use to escape. My defendant's motivation was clearly not in question. I, however, having little breath, had stopped running Marathons after high school. When I lost sight of him, I actually caught a **breath of relief.** I had an excuse to walk.

Then he popped up like a jack in the box. Having ducked behind a garbage bin, he was as safe from jail as the trash within. Once he was in full view again, as he separated himself from the safety of the trash, the race was on.

He took an alley and was easily out-distancing the rubbery legs on which I ran. I called 911 and began a literal, running dialogue as to who I was, where I was, who I was chasing, and where, **huff... huff...puff...puff...** he was going. I prayed for strength.

At the time of the chase, I was a very heavy smoker. I loved smoking. Even though my chest had recently started to hurt on each drag, smoking was my fix. I had smoked since I was sixteen. I was a little older now.

Two weeks previously, my son had come up to me and asked a serious question. He was 10. He said, **Dad, you know that one verse where**

THE RUN...DEEP BREATH

Jesus said if two of you ask for anything in my name, I will grant it?

A little apprehensive, I answered, **Yes.**

Could we pray that you would quit smoking?

What could I say? Maybe have a long discussion on the theology of what Jesus really meant? Alternatively, just respond with a, **No, I'm going to smoke and that's that!** Humbly, I said, **Okay.** And right then and there, we knelt down bedside and prayed. Now, two weeks later, here I was, unable to catch my breath, with legs that felt like gummy bears, talking on the phone to 911, talking to the Lord on **Heaven 1 1.** My mind forced my legs to carry me ever forward, **as they** continually threatened to stop.

Across the streets and down the alleys we raced, closing in fast on Denver's Green Belt Walkway. Running along the western boundary of downtown Denver was a Green Belt set like an inlay, next to a river. It runs for miles and is a favorite of joggers and dog walkers, hikers and bikers, and on this day my defendant. Normally, one descends a stairway down to the walkway. My defendant did not look for the stairway. He jumped. I jumped after him.

Across the river, splashing in splendor, and along the scenic trail, I trailed him. Each time he stopped, catching his breath, I also stopped, in a moment of thankfulness, in panting pause of relief. And there we would stand, unable to move, as our lungs gasped for life from the air that floated by.

You misewell...*huff, puff*... give up...*huff, puff*... I won't quit, I'd yell to him as our sagging bodies rested. Then, as if regenerated, off he'd run. I was not regenerated, but I went anyway.

Down the Green Belt we stumbled, back and forth across the river, **splash and splash and on and on.**

Then it ended. It ended as he attempted to climb out of the Green Belt. Tiring of the run, the defendant had turned to the wall that lined the Belt

WALKING IN THE LIGHT OF GOD'S GREATNESS

Way and prepared to jump up. That is when his mind must have switched on, like a light bulb. He could not jump up and out. The wall that lined the green belt was over seven feet tall. A person would need their hands and arms to reach up and grab the top ledge to pull themselves up. He did not have that luxury, with his hands being clasped behind his back by my designer bracelets.

My defendant sagged with the resignation of capture, and I sagged from exhaustion, coughing nonstop.

Then, in a scene reminiscent of many a movie, the Calvary showed up. In the middle of downtown Denver, after a ragged chase, the police finally made it to the party. I'll never doubt those 30 minute, extended, foot-chase movie scenes again. There is a road for emergency and park vehicles that leads down to the Green Belt, and as I got my defendant's arm and began to escort him back the way we had come, two police cars rolled down into view. They took my defendant from me, and I walked back to my car alone, my tennis shoes sloshing with each step. For two weeks afterwards, I coughed non-stop. However...I quit smoking!

One hard running chase through downtown Denver; **One** Smoke Away Program I discovered in Florida; and **One** prayer with a 10 year-old, equaled the ability to quit smoking. I would still like to smoke; I enjoyed it and miss it. Yet, since I firmly believe the Lord heard and answered a prayer offered one day at bedside, I don't think I should allow His gift of freedom to go up in smoke.

The race through downtown Denver was not a race for the gold, but as my ragged body pursued this prisoner athlete, it was a race of determination. The prize a pair of soaking wet tennis shoes and one prisoner safe and secured.

She was running...and the words of a little girl were chasing her. She was running back to prison as fast as she could go!

THE RUN...DEEP BREATH

She had previously been arrested for believing in Jesus and sharing His love with others. When she was arrested, the Chinese authorities arrested her five year old with her. They were making sure, no doubt, that this very dangerous little girl was not able to roam the country side at will.

The Chinese authorities wanted the woman to give up being a Christian. Communists hate those who love someone more than them. This woman loved Jesus more.

When she would not give up Christianity, she was treated with disdain by the other inmates, who wondered why she made her little girl suffer too.

The other inmates must have thought that this woman had arrested herself, and then placed herself and her little girl in prison.

The authorities also ridiculed the woman. **Don't you have pity on your daughter? It is sufficient for you to declare that you give up being a Christian and will not go to church anymore. Then you and your child will be free.** They told the mother that she was to blame for her five year old being in prison.

The authorities must have forgotten that they were the ones who had arrested her, and that they were the ones who had thrown the little girl into prison with her.

THE CHILD CRIED. What little girl wouldn't cry after being thrown into a dungeon of darkness? Her tender life of sunshine and laughter torn from her world by communist authorities, who wished to ban the name of Jesus from under Heaven.

And her mother despaired at her little girl's tears. What mother wouldn't, with the looks of hate that other prisoners accosted her with? The trauma of prison for having love in a heart, can paint the colors of doubt and uncertainty across the canvas of one's thoughts.

John the Baptist, whom Jesus said was one of the greatest prophets of all time, once doubted. He feared neither man nor king. He saw the Spirit of

God descend as a dove upon Jesus, allowing him absolute assurance that Jesus **WAS** the Savior of the World, the promised Messiah. Yet, when John the Baptist was thrown in prison, into the dark chambers of hatred under King Herod, he told his disciples to go inquire of Jesus if, in fact, he really **WAS the Messiah** all were waiting for. He had known once, and was sure. Now however, alone in the dank, filthy darkness of Herod's dungeon, doubts toyed with the certainty he had once possessed.

Prison can distort a man or woman's perception and feelings. Things minor on the outside are enlarged beyond all measure on the inside. It is a mean trick of confinement that can torture a soul without a blow being struck. Even John the Baptist once had doubts.

And what of a woman arrested and cast into prison, with her child in tears? The lies of madness began to play with her faith and rewrite the script. She began to doubt herself. The child's tears broke her heart. The child's tears watered her doubts until they grew into a weed that choked the truth. She told the authorities that she would no longer be a Christian. She promised she would not go to church anymore.

She and her child were released.

Soon after, the authorities wanted a little more propaganda for their anti-Christian hatred. Thus, they made the woman stand up in front of 10,000 and publicly claim she was no longer a Christian. The woman complied.

I am no longer a Christian, she stated in front of the huge crowd. Her little girl stood near, listening to her mother's every word.

Returning home from the crowd pleasing event, in the stillness of a moment, the woman's daughter looked up at her mother **with the eyes of a babe, and stated,**

Mummy, today Jesus is not satisfied with you.

> *In that hour, Jesus rejoiced in spirit and said,*
> *I thank thee O Father,*
> *Lord of heaven and earth, That*

> *Thou hast hid these things From*
> *the wise and prudent*
> *And hast revealed them unto Babes,*
> *Even so Father,*
> *For so it seemed good in thy sight.*
> *Luke 10:21*

The mother tried to explain her actions. **You wept in prison. I had** to say this out of love for you.

The five-year-old little girl, Siao-Mei, answered her mother's statement of love. *I promise that if we go to jail again for Jesus, I will not weep.*

And so, the mother was running. She ran all the way back to the Prison Director and stated. *You convinced me I should say wrong things for my daughter's sake, but she has more courage than I.*

Both went back to prison. And Siao-Mei? She kept the promise she made as a five-year-old, and never cried again.

Jesus gave Siao Mei the courage of King David. Jesus crowned her with courage so that she could **Live In Victory Eternal** and walk in the **Light of God's Greatness.**

In Almanach St. Peter Clavier, a little girl stood against the powerful forces of darkness and secured victory. That is why the communists fear the name of Jesus. They know the power of **The Word**. Deep in their hearts, they know. They know their time may be short, and the Light of God is ever growing. They fear the Light.

> *And this is the condemnation.*
> *That Light has come into world*
> *And men loved darkness rather than light*
> *Because their deeds were evil.*
> *John 3: 19*

WALKING IN THE LIGHT OF GOD'S GREATNESS

This is why those who live in the darkened halls of sin, cannot stand those who walk in the Light of Christ Jesus. This is why, if they cannot darken the brightness in the hearts of true Christians, they will try to bury the Light in the deepest, darkest prison cell. They think that if they bury the light, no one else will see it.

They are wrong. God sees it. God bears witness.

If I say surely the darkness shall cover me; Even the night shall be light about me. Yea, the darkness hideth not from thee; but the night shineth as the day: The darkness and the light are both alike to thee. Psalms 139: 11 & 12

**And God has others keep watch for him.
Others witness the Light imprisoned in darkness,
And they tell the world!**

In China, where the governments desperate struggle to darken the Light is pierced by over 80 million who shine, confessing Jesus as Lord, the communist agenda and promises of utopia are no more than mud pies in the dirt. The Communist Agenda, which is also Satan's agenda, is to turn off the Light, to extinguish each bright spot. They use brute power, prison and torture, intimidation and threats. The hatred in their hearts, mirror the acts of violence they mete out to anyone who dares call Jesus, Lord and King.

However, soon their reign will end. As Satan's days are numbered, so is their feeble attempt to darken hearts and crush hope. They are limited in time... to the days allotted men to choose life or death. They walk in Death and temporarily cast their shadow of Death upon the living. The Chinese authorities belong to the world of Death and wish to rule the Dead. They do.

Those who believe that Jesus is the son of God have life in Jesus and have overcome death and the world. They walk in the Light of Eternal Victory.

> *Who is he that overcometh the world,*
> *But he that believeth that Jesus is the Son of God.*
> *I John 5:1*

A little girl in China overcame the world and sounded an alarm. She wanted her mother to know, *It is the evening...of the dawn. Her mother* heard the alarms and awoke.

> **Lift up your eyes to the heavens**
> **And look upon the earth beneath.**
> **The heavens shall vanish away like smoke**
> **And the earth shall wax old like a garment**
> **And they that dwell therein shall die in like manner.**
> **But My salvation is Forever**
> **And My righteousness shall not be abolished.**
> **Isaiah 51: 6**

The young girl in China chose Heaven over the material world, and rejoiced. She knew her salvation from the Lord was forever. A **PRINCESS** in God's Royal family, this little girl chose to magnify Jesus, and embrace the *Majesty of a Moment!*

She walked in the Light of God's Greatness. She wanted her light to shine.

> *Let your light so shine before men...*
> *Matthew 5: 16*

> *It did...*
> *She shined!*

In China, the rulers walk under a darkened shroud of unbelief, boldly proclaiming their stand.

In America, it is the promises of riches and ease of worship that easily lull too many Christians into a sleepy, second hand faith. In America, the shroud falls in the quiet stillness of a fading day, like a drifting cloud, carried about on the winds of want. The clouds of pleasure drift through one's thoughts like sedatives. Faith becomes a fading illusion... a mirage. As they approach, it disappears, lost amidst the vibrant hues and neon signs that flash out, in desires sure to please.

In these clouds of smoke and mirrors, have we lost sight of our Christian brothers and sisters who suffer? Is their tale no more than a horror show not to be watched, less we become sad or fearful? Do we hold precious the desires of the Lord, the desires of men, or the empty desires of self?

> *Precious in the sight of the Lord is the death of His saints.*
> *Psalm 116: 15*

American Christians and the American News Media had a debate over the movie, **The Passion of Christ**. Was it too violent? The debate was not about the blood and gore. That was only the cover story. The unseen debate, was about guilt. The world did not want the guilt. The world does not want to admit that Jesus was whipped, beaten, spat on, and crucified because of a world in wanton wreckage of sin.

Jesus was mocked as he hung on a tree, His life's blood dripping to the dirt beneath His bruised and battered body, bearing our reproach and our sins! That is what the world does not wish to witness. To witness the brutality of His suffering, is to witness the results of one's sin. **I didn't do it,** is easier than falling to our knees in humbleness of heart, begging for forgiveness.

The world did not mind the violence and the blood in the movie, they just didn't want the guilt. The world wishes the Light to stay off.

> *And this is the condemnation,*
> *That light is come into the world,*
> *And men loved darkness rather than light,*
> *Because their deeds were evil.*
> *St. John 3: 19*

In darkness, the violent suffering and savage cruelty against our brothers and sisters in Jesus cannot be seen. With the Light off, we can sanitize their deaths. With the Light off, we can sanitize the Death of He who bore our sins on a cross. With the Light off... there is no guilt.

THE RUN...DEEP BREATH

Do you think the evil they suffer from, will never reach our shores?

Do you think the evil they suffer from, will never reach you... or your family... your children?

Do you not hear the alarms? Does the Spirit of God not whisper to you?

> A Little girl in China had a heart that heard the Spirit of
> the Lord.
> She desired happiness in the Lord
> And so
> When the alarm sounded
> She woke.
> When the alarm sounded,
> She woke up her mother as well.
>
> Once awake... the little girl's mother began running.
> The little girl's mother was running in a race for the Lord.
> She was racing back to prison and Freedom,
> The little girl's mother was racing back to the Light.
>
> With the eyes of a babe, And a heart of love,
> When the Spirit of the Lord spoke...
> *A little girl, Siao-Mei, listened... She heard.*
>
> *What do you hear?*

4

Deep Breath
Faith in Action

On your mark...

Get ready...

Get set...

Go!!!

And here in the announcer's booth, as we watch this great race unfold, we are thrilled to...*I'm sorry... what's wrong...? Oh, you didn't know anything about the race? Sorry...but your boss just contacted us and informed us that he had entered you in this great race.*

No... not *The Amazing Race.* This is not a T.V. show. He has entered you into *The Amazing Grace. This is a Heavenly Race.*

This will be a Heavenly Show and your Boss, Jesus Christ, has registered you as one of the racers!

Now wait a minute...hold on just a second.

Don't Panic! Everything's going to turn out okay.

This race requires no experience. It is not important if the last race you entered was in high school. It is not even relevant that you lost that race. It doesn't matter that you never made the varsity team.

It's alright if you are a little out of shape, because your boss has contracted with a Top of the Line Coach! This Coach has a 100% success record! With God as your partner, Jesus as your Boss, and your New Coach, you are sure to do well. You have the ideal racing *Dream Team!*

They planned the course carefully. They have outlined and constructed the track on which you will run. They have defined the road blocks, the individual tasks and the layovers. And remember, they are on your side! How can you lose?

Who is your Coach? Why, He is the Holy Ghost, the very Spirit of God Himself. And this Coach will dwell within you. In fact, if you are a member of the Royal Family of God, having accepted Jesus into your heart by faith, this Coach is already within. He now desires to guide you without, along the course, through the race, and on to victory in the winners' circle!

Yes, this will be a Great Race! *The Amazing Grace... Race!*

Hey, hold on a minute! Don't get *All Frantic* on me! Just because you are in a race doesn't mean you need to run around like a hyena with its tail on fire. We did not say this was going to be a *Mad Dash*! First, you just need to take a *Deep Breath, a deep breath and a moment of pause.*

As of early last night, we have not even been informed as to the length of your race. Only the Lord knows. That is why we should have a *Deep Breath* before we begin.

DEEP BREATH...FAITH IN ACTION

When running a marathon, starting at a sprint could leave you gasping for breath before you reach the midway point. If you crawl forward, you have no hope of winning. (*Your Coach does not coach losers.*) Well, He does, but He coaches them to win! So just don't *Go Frantic.*

Instead of freaking out, before you begin, let me share the story of another race, two thousand years ago. Let me share with you about two contestants who both had their own idea of how to start a race. Jesus had been their coach, so His training techniques could be very useful to you.

The story begins on a day that Jesus was visiting a friend's home. There were two women getting ready to begin their race. One sat at the feet of Jesus, listening. One was running all around getting everything ready for Him. She was frantic, trying to gather all the equipment she felt was required. She was trying to do it all.

After a while, Martha, the one running all around, complained. She said, **Jesus, tell Mary to help me. I have to do all of this work by myself. Don't you see I'm getting everything ready for you?**

What was Jesus' answer? Did Jesus ask Mary why she was so lazy? Did Jesus scold her for her lack of effort in preparations?

No, Jesus did not scold Mary. He spoke calmly, inquiring why Martha was so frantic.

Martha, you're always so busy about everything. Mary has chosen the best part. She has chosen to sit here and listen to me.

"Be still and know that I am God."

And that is what we should do first. We need to take a moment, in peaceful stillness, of prayerful thought. We need a quiet moment to listen to our Coach, The Holy Spirit. We need to be still and listen.

That is what our *Deep Breath is for*. To help us listen. To help us *Be Silent and Listen*.

Then, we move to step two. Racers in training, prepare for a race before the first step is ever taken. In their training, breathing becomes one of the most important elements.

These racers always incorporate breathing practice into their regimen. They use mini breathing exercises throughout each day to help condition their lungs. You have already begun these exercises with your first few breaths. The Breath of Faith, the Breath of Love, and The Breath of Greatness will help condition your spiritual lungs.

Then, the Ultimate Training Exercise follows. This exercise is ***High Altitude*** breathing. Since your race is a Heavenly Race, the ***Amazing Grace…Race, High Altitude*** breathing is excellent training!

Practicing ***High Altitude*** breathing a week or two before a race increases the strength of the lungs. Oxygen clears our body's cells of impurities, just as our spiritual breaths are to help cleanse us from spiritual impurities. This will allow us more energy and flexibility, increasing our discernment. Flexibility is vital. You never know when you will hit a Road Block, or find a sealed envelope at a Course Site with an unusual task needing to be completed.

High Altitude breathing helps our body learn to gain the utmost from each breath, increasing our faith. And for our race, in our Deep Breath, we must learn to walk in Faith, not make a mad dash for the border!

The race before you is a Walk of Faith, ***not a Mad dash***. One of the Lord's first race instructors explained the race this way.

…let us lay aside every weight, and the sin which doth so easily beset us, and let us run with patience the race that is set before us. Looking unto Jesus the author and finisher of our faith; who for the joy that was set before Him, endured the cross, despising the shame, and is set down at the right hand of the throne of God. **Hebrews 12: 1 & 2**

Clearly, this instruction explains that our race is one of patience. We are to run with patience. We are not to scramble off in a **Mad Dash**. I have never read a verse that says, *Behold Brethren! The course is set before us! Let us take off quickly because Christianity is a Real Rat Race!*

Our race is one of patience and persistence, continuing in the faith and listening to our Coach, the Holy Spirit of God. God alone knows the length of our race and, thus, *only He can set the pace.*

Instead of taking off at an unsustainable clip, panting all the while, we need to take a Deep Breath and listen to the Lord. We need our race instructions, and continuous spiritual guidance.

OFTEN, in this Amazing Grace…Race, well-meaning Christians choose to be, *Side Street Coaches.* They know exactly what type of race *you should have run*, what *you should have done*, where *you should have gone* and can quickly tell you what *you need to do now,* where *you need to go next.* When you listen to others on the side lines, instead of your Coach, your race can turn into an insane and irritable stumble of confusion.

Although the Lord has supplied a wonderful support team…

And He gave some, apostles; and some, prophets; and some, evangelists; and some pastors and teachers; For the perfecting of the saints, for the work of the ministry, For the edifying of the body of Christ:
Ephesians 4: 11 & 12

…these are given for your edification, to help nourish you on your race. They will have water bottles at the ready, as you race by. They may share words of encouragement from your coach. **They are there for support and fellowship, but they cannot determine your course** or the pace of your race. They cannot set up your *Road Blocks,* or *Stopovers,* or *Tasks* along the way. Your own personal race was designed by God Himself. That is why only His Spirit*, the Spirit of Christ*, can lead you. He will direct and strengthen you in this race if you allow Him.

He may direct you to stop, (on a layover) and...*be still and know that He is God...*while everyone else is screaming, *Go baby, go!*

He may move you to sing, while others tell you, *Be quiet!*

He may lead you to a rest area, so he can refresh you, while others complain **you are not doing enough, time's being wasted!**

He may have a **Road Block** where you will be instructed to separate yourself from your route and perform a special feat in a **Moment of Majesty.**

For this race of yours is a *Divine Race* and needs a *Divine Coach.*

That is why God sent His own spirit to dwell within you.

For what man knoweth the things of a man, save the spirit of man which is in him. Even so the things of God knoweth no man, but the Spirit of God. Now we have received not the spirit of the world, But the Spirit which is of God; That we might know the things that are freely given to us of God. I Corinthians 2: 11 & 12

<u>RACE DISCLOSURE</u> # *In this race,* it *is* likely that *you will be* injured, hurt, and/or trip and fall from time to time. You may even lose your way occasionally, becoming lost and sad. You may feel that you are all alone and off track. Injuries suffered during your race may overcome you, but do not lose heart. They cannot overcome God. That is why He wants you to have His Spirit within you. For He is there to comfort and guide you.

When Jesus walked the Earth, His presence was a comfort to everyone around Him. He was their Light of Grace. When they had questions or concerns, hurt or pain, Jesus was there for them. Jesus never turned His back on a friend. Even in death, He cared for those He would leave behind. Before He left, He promised that His Father would send another comforter after He was gone. He knew that a hurting racer would need comfort.

DEEP BREATH...FAITH IN ACTION

And I will pray the Father,
And he shall give you another Comforter
That He may abide with you forever;
Even the Spirit of Truth; whom the world cannot receive,
Because it seeth Him not, neither knoweth Him;
But ye know Him; for He dwelleth with you,
And shall be in you.
I will not leave you comfortless:
I will come to you.
John 14: 16, 17, 18

And He has...
And He is here to help us.

And He is here to comfort us and to pray for us.
Likewise the Spirit also helpeth us with our infirmities;
For we know not what we should pray as we ought:
But the Spirit maketh intercession for us with groanings
Which cannot be uttered.
And He that searcheth the hearts
knoweth what is the mind of the Spirit
Because He maketh intercession for the Saints
according to the will of God.
Romans 8: 26 & 27

With comfort and guidance assured,
you are almost ready to begin.

Preparing yourself through His teaching, the Bible, will help you with another area of importance in this race. Because your race is a mystery track, you will need divine wisdom to run. Your race may take you through valleys, atop mountains, through darkest forests and dessert plains or across oceans. Your own, personal track was laid out, planned, and ordained before the world was ever created. Your course is a deep mystery hidden in God but known... to your Coach.

*But we speak the wisdom of God in a mystery,
Even the hidden wisdom,
Which God ordained before the world unto our glory:*

Woe...*"unto your glory."* Looks like your Boss and Coach already expects you to place high in this race. Guess we'll be seeing you in the winners circle after all!

So, are you ready?

I mean, now that you know that you will be running for the Dream Team, *I ask you...are you ready?*

Well...ready or not...hold on to your hat, because here we go... Deep Breath

Allowing for His divine will in your life, and His guidance and direction through His Spirit, with His Lordship over you, let us take our Deep Breath..................................Breathe.

<u>**FAITH IN ACTION**</u> Today, begin High Altitude Breathing (H. A. B.) exercises.

H.A.B. 1.

Pray in Spirit, in moments of solitude. Take a moment alone in your car, before you open the door, before you walk into a store, pause in stillness and say a prayer. Before you walk into your office, at lunch, before returning home, gather yourself with a deep breath of silence, and say a prayer. Pray as He leads. In any moment where an opportunity, though brief, may visit you, accent the moment in prayer.

H.A.B. 2

You have taken a Deep Breath, so I will not write out a prayer for you. You write a prayer...then pray it. Write out your prayer and save it. Put it somewhere special and hold onto it to remind you of your moment before **His Throne of Grace.**

H.A.B. 3

Select a short and simple bible verse to memorize. Use this verse during the day as part of your High Altitude breathing regimen. Tomorrow you can choose another! *It pleased God by the foolishness of preaching, to save them that believe.* Enjoy yourself in the foolishness of God, by memorizing a simple verse each day. *For the foolishness of God is wiser than men.*

If you become discouraged, take a Deep Breath and re-read your first three **Faith in Actions.** *Be renewed daily.*

Add some change to your **Missionary Mug**, and if you have it, to your **Pocket Ministry.**

Do not forget your **Great Christian University** in prayer.

Your Faith in Action, Deep Breath

Call V.O.M. and request a free subscription. Their monthly magazine will help open your eyes and your heart. (918) 337-8015

If you are homeless and have no address, do what I did when I lived in a car. Use the address of a Post Office as your mailing address. Use one that allows for **General Delivery**. Then ask V.O.M. to send your magazine as **General Delivery.**

If you do this, ask V.O.M. when the magazine will be mailed, so that you know when to go to the Post Office. Many Post Offices will not hold General Delivery Mail for over ten days, and you may not want to go down every day. Thus, if you know when the magazine is coming, you can time it right.

In the previous story you read, there were two runners. One was running away from jail, for fear of punishment. One was running to jail, for joy of reward. **Are you running somewhere? Where?**

A little girl in China heard the Spirit of Christ. She took a deep breath and obeyed. Her action **Magnified Jesus** in the **Majesty of a Moment.** One day, she will be standing in the winners' circle in Heaven. **She won her race**! When the medals are handed out, **she'll be wearing gold!**

Pray for Siao-Mei that she might know that in her race she has circled the world in victory. Let her story encourage and embolden you to walk in His Light, as it did a five-year-old's very own mother!

Say a prayer for a mother, who regained the courage of Grace, in the halls of communist hate.

*After hearing the Spirit of the Lord,
A 5 year old took a Deep Breath and obeyed.*

*She was led by the Spirit of God,
And entered the Amazing Grace...Race.
She won.*

*Because she heard the Spirit of God...
She chose a Prison of Hope, over the freedom of the dead.*

What do you hear?

SECTION TWO

For a short period...burned out on bail and jail,
Financially ruined...
I spent a short time homeless.
Reasons do not matter.
There are always reasons...

Oh Lord,
I know that the way of man is not in himself:
It is not in man that walketh to direct his steps.

O Lord, Correct me,
But with Judgment;
not in Thine anger,
Less thou bring me to nothing.
Jeremiah 10: 23 & 24

5

Homeward Bound
Breath of a Moment

But my God shall supply all your need According to His riches in glory by Christ Jesus. Philippians 4:19

There I was, homeless, standing uncomfortably in a church office. I was not asking for money. I was not asking for a place to stay. I was asking about a place to shower and shave, so I could begin job hunting.

There I stood…homeless.

A lady sat at a desk in front of me working studiously. I interrupted her with my request. She informed me that before I could receive any help, I would need to be processed at their homeless program center, located away from the church. This would need to be done in order to see if I was in their area.

In their area? I'm homeless, standing in front of her, but I need to be processed to see if I am in her area. Where else could I have been? Perhaps, more importantly, where was I? Maybe, I was not really there. Possibly, I did not even exist. Was I was merely a figment of my own imagination? **What an imagination!**

On the other hand, maybe it was this large Christian Church that was no more than a city mirage?

I asked, politely, if I could speak to the pastor. Needless to say, I was informed that I could not. Without an appointment, speaking to the pastor was impossible. This was a good lesson in homeless planning. It is important to set up a pastoral appointment prior to losing your home.

I quoted the famous Sunday sermon verse many Pastors enjoy preaching.

But whoso hath this world's good, and seeth his brother have need, and shutteth up his bowels of compassion from him, how dwelleth the love of God in him?

My little children, let us not love in word and tongue, but in deed and truth. 1rst John 3: 16, 17, 18

The lady sitting at the desk quoted the last part of the verse with me, in unison, like we were a duet. But alas, they would still need to be sure that I was in their area.

Perhaps this church was like **The Floating Castle.**

The Floating Castle, was a movie about a group of people on a quest. They had to find a particular castle, but there was one slight problem. The Castle kept moving. Every so often, the castle would rise into the air, and move off to another location. **Maybe this was T he Floating Church.**

That morning, after waking up, I had not drawn a church name out of a hat, and then driven over to waltz inside and demand care. After having a cup of steaming coffee, and driving all night from Colorado, I had contacted the city to discover any possible outreach programs where I could get cleaned up.

I wanted to go out and find a job. The problem was with the way I looked. After driving all day and night to get to San Diego, I needed a shower and a shave, or the odds of finding a job were as plausible as starting the next NFL franchise in Nome, Alaska.

The first call of the day was to the City Government, asking if there was a place that would allow me to shower and shave. After they inquired where I was, they supplied the number of this Christian Church. This church had volunteered as a beacon of refuge for those in need. I called the church number given by the city. A lady at the church, who first answered the phone, told me that before I could get a shower and a shave, I would need to be screened to see if I was in their area. *I'm homeless,* I stated, *I do not have an area.*

She persisted that, all things considered, I would still need to be screened. That was the reason for driving out to this church. If a Christian brother stood in front of her, being homeless, she would have to admit that yes, I **WAS** in her area. She did not admit anything.

I left wondering how a Christian Church could define their area.

Sorry Lord, he wasn't in our area. You should have led him to another church, you know.

I wonder if I had been a multimillionaire looking for a church to attend, and walked into their office in a three-piece suit, with manicured nails, asking about their ministries, what would they have said. *Sorry, you'll need to be processed to see if you are in our area.*

I wonder if they have a colorful banner over the entrance of their worship hall. *Please, only those who are in our area may attend! To be screened, please go around the back and...*

I decided a dedicated church, skilled in determining a homeless person's area, was indeed, a skilled church. My only error was leaving the church before they could process me. They may have been helpful in explaining to me, the *Area* I was actually in, or should have been in.

WALKING IN THE LIGHT OF GOD'S GREATNESS

Why was a nobody like me in Southern California, homeless and looking for a job? I had an appointment set for 3:30 in the morning. The Lord had previously set up a brief meeting He wished me to attend. Even though here, in the church office, I knew nothing of the meeting, location, day or time, that would not hinder, or alter the plans set by God.

There he was, homeless, with no family or means of support, wandering the streets. This had been a practice of his now for more than a month.

On this day, as he walked down an empty street, a couple of men walked passed. Vassant, the name of the homeless man, thought he recognized one of the men.

He did. Vassant had met this man once before. On their first meeting, Vassant had beat and ridiculed this man. This passing man was a Christian.

In Vassant's previous life, he took great joy in beating up Christians.

Not just a slap in the face and ridicule. Vassant relished in beating up Christians until their blood glistened from their Christian wounds. Back then, Vassant had no idea that the blood they shed at their beatings glistened with the love of God. At the time, Vassant had been studying to be a Hindu Priest. While studying the Hindu Priesthood, Vassant's recess consisted of seeking out and beating Christians. In those days, he held the love, adoration and respect of his family and friends. He enjoyed beating Christians until they bled. They always had to bleed.

Vassant's Grandfather was a renowned Hindu Priest, his older brother a Swami. A Swami is an honorific title for one who has become a master of… one's self. A Swami is normally a regular Yoga practitioner who has a devotion to the Gods. The Gods a Swami may be devoted to include a variety of entities. India and the Hindu religion have a smorgasbord of Gods for the choosing.

One day, though, Vassant came into possession of a Bible. Reading and comparing bible verses with his Hindu text, the Truth of Life began to open Vassant's deadened heart. Vassant quit his studies as a Hindu Priest and was transformed. The blood he had made others shed in the hatred of the moment became the love that Jesus used to lay the foundation of Life.

Vassant became a Christian.

After becoming a Christian, the love of his family and friends evaporated. Vassant was rejected and ostracized. He became homeless, disowned by everyone he once knew.

Now, months later, wandering the streets alone and abandoned, he encountered the man Vassant had once beaten. The man was an evangelist who handed out tracts about Jesus and his love. What did that man do when he recognized Vassant?

He did not wonder if Vassant **was in his area**. There he was, right in front of him. He **knew** Vassant was in his area! This evangelist did not live in **The Floating Castle**.

This man Vassant had beaten, an evangelist named Banoli Annayya, chose to care for this homeless brother. This evangelist gave Vassant a bible. He also gave him money to stay with a Christian worker in a nearby town. **Deed and Truth.**

Since then...since that day the beaten helped the beater, Vassant has himself become an evangelist, handing out more than 50,000 gospel tracts about Jesus and salvation.

Vassant has now been beaten himself. He was once tied to a pole, turned upside down and set on fire. The flames that charred his clothing and skin only seared the love of Christ into a heart of devotion.

Even on fire, hanging upside down, Vassant's faith was **Right Side Up**. In the flames of hate, Vassant's Lord and Savior provided his rescue. A neighbor cut the rope that held the swaying body and Vassant was rushed to a hospital.

They had tried to kill Vassant. In their torturous zeal of madness, they had tried to light the fires of death. The fires of passion in Vassant's heart burned hotter.

Vassant is now considered a danger by all Hindus because of his successful witness for Jesus. The love of Jesus threatens those who desire the divinity of choice and selection from among their vast assortment of selfcreated Deities.

One evangelist, who was once beaten, did not wonder or ask, **is Vassant in my area**? When the man who had ripped up his bible and caused him pain appeared before him, homeless and in need of a friend, Banoli Annayya became one. His act of kindness to Vassant laid the foundation for many others that have now heard of God's gift of Salvation and Love in Jesus Christ.

These days, Vassant oversees nine churches, and runs a Bible Camp for young Indians. He lives in the Greatness of God, and walks in the **Light of that Greatness.**

Vassant was a nobody, who walked the streets of Challakere, India for months. He was homeless and without a friend in the world. However, He did have **ONE in Heaven**. His name was Jesus. And Vassant was God's Nobody. Just the type of Nobody God likes to use.

Are you a nobody too? Do you wander the streets of life alone, afraid and unsure? If you belong to Jesus Christ, then you are **His** nobody. If you are **His** nobody, look out… for you too, are on the edge of Greatness, **God's Greatness!**

Lift your eyes up to the heavens and behold! Who hath created these things, that bringeth out their host by number and calleth them all by names by the strength of His might. For in that He is strong in Power, not one faileth. Isaiah 40:26

And His purpose for you cannot fail either!

As a Nobody, simply continue to prepare yourself by staying in prayer and reading your bible. He will unveil your moment for you. Perhaps He has many moments in waiting. He will prepare your debut. Just stay in the Word and in prayer.

Wherein ye greatly rejoice, though now for a season, (if need be,) ye are in heaviness through manifold temptations:

That the trial of your faith, being much more precious than of gold that perisheth, though it be tried with fire, might be found unto praise, and honor, and glory, at the appearing of Jesus Christ. 1rst Peter 1: 6& 7

The evangelist, Banoli Annayya
was Living in Victory Eternal.
He walked in the Light of God's Greatness.
He walked the *Streets of Mean* for Jesus
He walked those streets with love in his heart,
And lived in the *Majesty of the Moment.*
One day He was beaten bloody by Vassant.
Another day, he helped Vassant.
Why?
Because Vassant was in his area....

Who's in your area?

5

Breath of a Moment
Faith In Action

Moment by Moment,
As we dance in visions undefined,
Moment by Moment,
As we fool ourselves within our minds,
Moment by Moment,
All is saved or all forever lost,
Moment by Moment,
Do we see enough to know the cost?
Moment by Moment,

As ocean waves crash on the shore,
Moment by Moment,
As storms relentless, ravage sore,
Moment by Moment,
With clouds of darkness over head,
Moment by Moment,
just a vapor rising out of bed.

Scripture says, *your life is but a vapor.*

You are here for but a moment...

Perhaps two or three moments,

Then you will be gone.

When you are...

Where will you go?

And what will you take with you?

The Breath of Life was a gift of God, allowed you at birth. Eternal life is the gift He offers now, in the Majesty of a Moment.

Each moment, the Kingdom of God is being ordained and shaped by a Divine God whose love flows from a **Throne of Grace.** Within these moments, eternal destinies are being created. These designs will become the paintings of each life, and adorn the Royal Halls of Heaven, or be rejected, and burned in the trash heap of useless scrap.

Every man's work shall be made manifest: For the day shall declare it, Because it shall be revealed by fire; And the fire shall try every man's work of what sort it is. If any man's work abides which he hath built there upon, he shall receive a reward. If any man's work shall be burnt, he shall suffer loss.
I Corinthians 3:13, 14, 15

When the artwork of your life is on display, what will be revealed? Will others be awed by a masterpiece an oil painting in bright and vivid colors? Or...will their eyes behold a bland work of nothingness?

Since beginning your breathing lessons, you have learned about many wonderful gifts and promises of Greatness, Love and treasures of the heart! You have received guarantees and bonuses. You have been promoted.

You have even been entered in the **Great, Amazing Grace...Race**. If you are not flying on cloud nine, it can only be because you are soaring on cloud ten...or...you have yet to realize that your life is only a vapor preparing to rise, or dissipate into emptiness.

You have only a moment in space to walk in the Light, or stumble in the dark, only a moment. Then you will walk here no more.

Within each moment, you have a choice. You can decide to live in the **Majesty of a Moment,** and rise in the Light of God's Greatness, or... you can choose the Death of the World, and rise from the mud, like the tower of Babel... only to return to the dust of delusions, when the winds of time blow over your grave.

    What will you choose?

    What will your artwork reflect?

Will your life rise as a sweet vapor, reaching Heaven, a Masterpiece of Grace, or...will it dissipate into the emptiness of space?

When you accepted Jesus into your heart, you were adopted into a Royal Family. As Royalty, you became a Prince or a Princess in that Royal Family, a family of God. You are now heir to all the riches and wonders owned by God the Father. He willed it all, according to His own pleasure. It pleased Him to adopt you into the Royal Family.

According as he hath chosen us in Him before the foundation of the world, That we should be holy and without blame Before Him in love;

Having predestinated us unto the adoption of children by Jesus Christ to Himself according to the good pleasure of His own will. Ephesians 1: 4 & 5

After choosing to adopt you, God the Father, determined that you would become a Royal Priest and represent a Kingdom of Love, Joy and Mercy.

But ye are a chosen generation, a royal priesthood, a holy nation, a peculiar people; that you should show forth the praises of Him who hath called you out of darkness into His marvelous Light. I Peter 2: 9

He also has designs on your future, to make you a King!

And they sang a new song, saying, Thou art worthy to take the book, and to open the seals thereof: for thou wast slain, and hast redeemed us to God by thy blood out of every kindred, and tongue, and people, and nation;

And hast made us unto our God, kings and priests: and we shall reign on the earth. Revelations 5: 9 & 10.

You will be a King and Reign...
But for the moment, you are in training...
To learn how to reign in love, with peace and kindness.
To learn how to reign... moment by moment. To learn how to live,
in the *Majesty of a Moment*.

One day my friend, Star, was driving down a side street a few blocks from home. She observed a lady walking down the road, carrying a heavy load, talking to herself. Having never before stopped to offer a stranger a ride, on this occasion, she did. She said she could not explain why, but felt that it was what the Lord wanted her to do.

She asked the lady if she wanted a lift. The lady got in the car, extremely grateful for this act of kindness. She told Star that she was so tired and had been praying constantly that the Lord would have someone give her a ride. She was weary and exhausted. In her exhaustion, she had cried out to the Lord. The Lord said, **No problem, I have someone on the way.** That is when Star drove up.

In the Majesty of a Moment, Star was asked by God to offer a ride to a tired and weary lady, walking down the street. She did. On that day, in that moment, she lived in the Majesty of A Moment

and reflected the Royalty of God. Was her act an earth shaking event, televised on each Cable network simultaneously? No, but *it was* painted on the canvass of her life, and will hang in the Royal Halls of Heaven. One day, all eyes will light up when they behold a *Moment in Majesty.*

One day they will...*by your good works which they shall behold, glorify God in the day of visitation. I Peter 2: 12*

Walking and weary, a lady had appeared in Star's **Area**. The Spirit of God moved Star to offer her the comfort of a ride. Star obeyed.

How does a person know where their **Area** is located? The boundaries of each Area a person lives in, are the boundaries of God.

> *Thus saith the Lord,*
> *The heaven is my throne, and the earth is my footstool:*
> *Where is the house that ye build unto me?*
> *And where is the place of my rest?*
> *For all those things hath mine hand made, And all those things have been. Isaiah 66: 1*

Many Christians allow their **Area** of concern to be defined by the location of their church building. They go to their **Area** church on Sunday. There, they pay a Godly Sin Tax, and leave, rest assured God is content once more. God is happy, and will patiently wait for them to return next week. Their **Area** cared for they can thus, resume their normal day to day activities of this and of that. Isn't God happy we visit him on Sunday? Each week, everyone gets together to say, *Hi,* to God. Hope He doesn't get too lonely while we are away.

Knock...Knock...*Hello God, are you home? Were back! Bet you're glad to see us, aren't you?*

Question? In a Kingdom, the King sits on a throne. A footstool is used for his feet to rest on. Are a throne and a footstool all there is, then? Or... does the throne sit in A Sacred Royal Hall, within a palace or castle, within a city... within a country...within a Kingdom... within the Universe?

Then...if that is so...and if Heaven is God's Throne, and the Earth His footstool, are the Heavens, His Sacred Royal Hall... the Universe, His city... beyond the Universe... His Kingdom?

And, as part of His Royal family that will inherit the Kingdom, would *our area then...well, encompass the entire Universe and beyond?*

Before you answer that question, (or start wondering how to purchase a space suit.) take a Deep Breath. Scheduling a trip to Mars can be postponed. I do not think God has called us to touch a Martian for Christ.

However, within any Moment that you **ARE** in, *where ever you are*, does that area become *your Area,* by your very presence?

The lady Star saw walking was in Star's **Area.** The Lord wanted the lady to have a ride, and Star was happy to oblige. Star lived in the *Majesty of a Moment* and walked in the *Light of God's Greatness.*

As a Royal Family Member, her Moment was lived in the *High calling of God in Jesus Christ.*

Obeying Jesus **is** of **Higher** value than the building and completion of the Burj Khalifaset of Dubai, raised upon the dessert sands of the Middle East. The Burj Khalifaset is currently the highest skyscraper in the world. *Historical Note:* The term Skyscraper originally belonged to a small triangular sail set above the Sky Sail on a sailing ship. On a ship that would sail across the oceans.

Contrast Note: The Burj Khalifaset Tower of Dubai can not even sail across the street.

Star was able to help a tired and weary woman *down the street.* Who did the sailing?

Please draw a big circle below.
Any weird shaped circle will do just fine.

After you have drawn your circle, practice holding a pen or pencil up in the air. Then, with one swift, graceful move,

bring it down onto the page and into your circle.
With your eyes open, can you hit the center?

Okay, it's time to close the eyes. Close your eyes and lift your pencil high in the air. Without looking, bring your pencil down until it lands on something and make a dot where it lands.

Do not cheat! Keep your eyes closed until you have made a dot to mark where you landed.

After you have made your dot, open your eyes. You are the dot, and all around you, within your circle, is your Area.

Why did you close your eyes? Because when you walk in the Light of God's Greatness, you are asked to trust in His Sight, not your own.

O Lord, the way of man is not in himself,
It is not in man to direct his steps.

What if your pencil failed to land in the center of the page? Do not let this wandering act dishearten you. As Nobodies, we are seldom at the center of anything. Why should our dot be at the center? When we are led by the Spirit of God, our wandering becomes the route He has selected for us. What may seem off course to everyone around you, may be right on course for the Lord. He has you exactly where He desires you to be!

And we know that all things work together for good
To them that love God
To them that are called according to His purpose
Romans 8: 28

Did your pencil miss the paper entirely? That's okay too. Often, Nobodies like us are way out in left field to begin with.

(or right depending on where your pencil landed.)

But the purpose of left field can be crucial.

It is the World Series, the bottom of the ninth, with bases loaded, two strikes and two outs. The batter hits a high fly into left field. The ball soars over the heads of the pitcher and the infield. The ball reaches the edge of the stadium. It appears that the game may be over! Even so, the left fielder reacts with a dedicated purpose. He does not give up. He leaps into the air, arm stretched to the Heavens, every effort expended as he reaches for victory.

If the ball reaches the bleachers, the Grand Slam will allow the opposing team a win by one. If it is caught, the left fielder will secure the win, and his team will be titled, **World Champions**!

Tell me, how important is Left Field now?

It may be that left field is exactly where the Lord has placed you for the last crucial play of the game. So, if your **Area** is **Left Field,** get ready for the play of a lifetime!

The Lord is preparing you. He is preparing your area. He is preparing the play.

The preparation of the heart in man
And the answer of the tongue, is from the Lord.
Proverbs 16:1

He is preparing your heart for that moment.

There may not be many more…

There may not be *ANY* more…
How will you live in it?

In Majesty…?

Or in the frantic pant of confusion.

In the blindness of a dead world?

If you belong to a **Super Secret Christian Sleeper Cell**, God would like to electrify your desire. He wants you to Breathe in the Moment with a **panoramic vision**. He wants your breathing enlightened, so you can live in the **Majesty of a Moment** given by God. To touch a life with tenderness. To touch a life with hope.

Remember, you are in a race, **The Amazing Grace...Race**. Races are not stationary. They cover a lot of ground. And all the ground you cover in your race... **is your area**. Your Coach, the Spirit of God, leads you through this race, while the Light of Christ shines upon your racetrack. As it shines, and as you walk in the Spirit, you will begin to see the **Stopovers**, the **Tasks**, and the **Detours**. As you do, and each time you do, you will have the beautiful opportunity of living, in **The Majesty of a Moment**.

Your Faith In Action?

Today it is my pleasure to inform you that 50% of the Royalties received from the purchase of this book, goes to VOM's general fund, to help your brothers and sisters who suffer for Jesus overseas. The act of purchasing this book sailed the ocean! **The Burj Khalifaset...it remains put, atop the dessert sand.**

Your desire to read this book has already touched another life in Majesty. Without you doing any more than having a desire, and purchasing this book, before you even opened its pages, 50% of the royalties were pledged to V.O.M. Your desire alone gave the breath of life into a **Moment of Hope** for another. Your desire to seek the Light of God's Greatness sailed to a distant shore to touch another life for Jesus. If this book was given to you, celebrate the vitality of joy as a member of a Royal Family, the body of Christ. You are part of a living, breathing ocean, whose depths cannot be measured. Who will feel the majestic, Heavenly touch of grace today? Whose life will you touch?

Dear Heavenly Father,

Thank you for the beautiful design of a day. Thank you for the newness of life each day. As I walk through the day in the newness of spirit, and mind, do not allow me to miss the Majesty of the Moment you prepare for me.

Activate my heart, teach me from your Word, and shine your Light into my Area, so that I do not miss the one you send me to touch. Thank you for the love you have, that cannot be measured, or confined. Strengthen me in your *glorious might,* and fill me with the desires of your heart, that I may delight in the living God. Help me love you.

And please, as your hand holds those in far away lands, that suffer for believing in your love, strengthen and comfort them. Thank you for enriching a desire to walk in your light, with a gift that has sailed the ocean.

In Jesus' name, Amen.

The Breath of a Moment

And now, close your eyes. You are about to take your Breath
The Breath Of A Moment...breathe.

In India, Banoli Annayya was beaten, bleeding, mocked, and scorned. His Christian leaf lets were ripped from his hands and burned.

Several months later, he saw one of the men who beat him.
He saw Vassant.
And, in *The Breath of a Moment*
Banoli, lived in the *Majesty of Grace.*

Vassant was homeless.
But he was in Banoli's area.

Tell me, Who's in your Area?

6

An Appointment
Breath of Warmth

*Give to him that asketh thee,
And from him that would borrow of thee,
Turn thou not away.
Matthew 5: 42*

It was the Lord's appointment, not mine.

It was 3:30 A.M. on the streets of downtown San Diego. It was not the pretty section, where the upscale spend their evenings until late, drinking and playing. Neither was it the extreme seedy side of downtown, where the homeless bed down in every other store front and sleep on the sidewalks. It was in between.

I had just finished my shift delivering pizzas to San Diego's finest hotels. Now, my pockets were full of cash, and I was tired. My plan was to drive 35 miles north, to a rest stop where I was currently living. I would sleep there in my car for the night, and get up early to shower at a Mission the next day. Then I would drive back into town, to do it all over again.

My Honda was resting on a side street, in the semi-darkness. On the sidewalk in front of me, a figure sat, cross-legged. I began to take a short cut through a parking lot, when I heard his voice.

Do you have a blanket? A blanket? ***Did it look like I had a blanket?*** Of course not! ***No***, I said firmly and walked on, quickening my pace.

Who carries around a blanket at 3:30 in the morning, in downtown San Diego? Unless of course, he's homeless, and living on the streets, and sleeping in a doorway. Crazier yet, who asks a stranger if he has a blanket on him, while sitting cross-legged in the middle of a city sidewalk.

They beg for spare change, a drink, or a beer. But a blanket? That is insane! Like people strolling along the city streets carry spare blankets.

Hey, brother, can you spare a blanket?

No. And that's what I said.

Then ***He*** spoke. ***Give to him that asks, and to him that would borrow, turn not away.***

That was when His Spirit rose up and filled me, and I knew... I did have a blanket.

I went to my car and opened the trunk. I retrieved a blanket my wife and son gave me one Christmas, and walked back to the man, still sitting cross-legged on the sidewalk. Approaching him from behind, I draped the blanket over his shoulders.

His heart percolated with joy. He had been shivering in the dark of the early morning, but he was now warm. He did not turn around to look at me, but I heard him say, ***Thank you!*** He said, ***Thank you***, to the night air hanging in front of him.

I walked back to my car, ashamed of the hardness of my heart, but ever so thankful for the Spirit of Christ, that whispered to me... ever so gently...

ever so quietly... *Give to him that asketh of thee and to him that would borrow, turn not thou away.*

This one act the Lord moved me to complete, gave me happiness for days. In fact, it filled me with such joy, that I became embarrassed. I was not jumping with glee when first asked for a blanket. I was hard and cold like the night. And giving away one silly blanket was not really THAT big of a deal, was it? My act was no more earth-shaking, than throwing a dime to a sidestreet beggar, right?

But this had been an appointment the Lord had set for me; thankfully, He was gracious enough to help me keep it.

What leads me to believe the Lord called me all the way to San Diego, California, so that I, after losing everything, could give a man a blanket at 3:30 A.M.? Because there I was, and there he was, and I had a blanket he needed. Because after I refused, the Spirit of the Lord chastised me, and insisted that I give this man a blanket.

Had this man prayed, *Lord, I am so cold! If you love me, please give me a blanket. Give it to me right here and now!* And Jesus answered, *No problem, I've sent for one from Colorado. It should be here presently.* Had this man only been thinking about Jesus in the early morning chill? Watching him, did Jesus decide that one lone soul should feel the warmth of love, and desired the man be covered?

At first, I must have believed that this man, who sat in the early morning dark, **was not in my area.** Jesus, **the Early Morning Star, said he was.**

I was hard, Jesus was soft, and one man was cold.

I thank God, my Father, by the name of Jesus, for His Spirit and His love. With his desire for a blanket, God made this man's want, a wonderful treasure for me. Even though I did not deserve it, this man was a gift from the Father of Lights.

Isn't this often how the Lord loves to move? Not always with great Christian organizations, set up with multi-million dollar contributions, needing a steady flow of thousands, simply to keep afloat and pay the mortgage on their newest headquarters. It often appears the Lord loves to use Nobodies, like you and I. Why?

How can **we** glory in the Lords' preparations, when we find ourselves in the **Light** of **His Greatness**? We cannot! We can only catch our breath in awe, at the Majesty and Power of our Lord. We can only marvel how He has not overlooked the smallest, tiniest detail of our life.

The very hairs of your head are numbered

As a Nobody, our opportunities to get Lost in the Greatness of God are numerous! We may fail to understand, but we can believe and Trust. Therein, is the Lord delighted with us, when we trust in Him instead of ourselves, when we look up to him in faith.

Christian organizations can serve wonderful purposes, but do not allow them to enslave you. Do not worship Christian leaders. Walk in the fresh glow of your Savior. Stroll in the freedom that Jesus allows. You serve He, who sits on the right hand of majesty, in the Heavens. The creation and running of an institution, no matter how noble, is as nothing, if you are not trusting and following the Lord!

Be FREE in Jesus, as He is the one that called you. He is the one who died for you. It is in **His Will** you will find joy, excitement, and fulfillment. When you are a Nobody walking in the **Light of God's Greatness**, you are **free to Be…His.**

They sit in the cool of the night and shiver. They were not killed today.

They were not chased today by the Muslims, who do not like them.

They were not cut into pieces by machetes, swung by those who hate the name of Jesus.

They were not blown up by bombs dropped from government planes.

It was a good day.

Now they are just a bit cold. These are the Christians, and the children, of Southern Sudan.

One day, a TV Journalist visited Sudan, looking for the next great **Headliner.** He decided to interview some children. He chose to interview some Sudanese children from a local Sunday School. Many of these children's family members and friends had been murdered by roving fanatical Muslims, aflame with the fires of hate. They were killed because these Muslims wanted to extinguish the love of Jesus, throughout their domain.

The journalist asked the children, **Would you turn to Islam, or would you prefer to die for Christ? If so, why?**

The children did not recite a hundred verses, or explain the fundamental differences between Islam and Christianity. The Children had not taken extended courses in Apologetics, so they could show the foolishness of not believing. The children simply stated, **We would remain Christians, because this is the Truth.**

That is what they answered. Because, **This is the Truth!**

As nobodies in the **Light of God's Greatness**, these children kept it simple. They lived in the **Majesty of the Moment**, a moment of Truth. They believed the Truth.

What do you think went through the reporter's mind? Do you think he knew the interview he thought **he had set up** was actually **an appointment set by God?** Do you think he heard? Do you think others heard?

The Truth is always... the Truth.

The children of Sudan were courageous. Their families were butchered and murdered **before** they answered their interviewer, yet they were not fazed. The question was not complicated. The answer, **easy to be entreated.**

> *But the wisdom that is from above is first pure,*
> *Then peaceable, gentle, and easy to be entreated,*
> *Full of mercy and good fruits,*
> *Without partiality, and without hypocrisy.*
> *James 3: 17*

What they spoke with beauty and grace must have caused joy to overflow from Heavenly fountains. **We would remain Christians, because this is the Truth.** They lived in daily danger. Their homes burned, families murdered, food gone. But they will remain Christians...**because this is the Truth.** I wonder if you walked by any of them at three in the morning, would they ask, **Do you have a blanket?**

Darkness hangs over the early morning, like a covering in the cool of a moment. Your feet carry you over a dirt path. Death stirs in the air. A pang of danger tweaks your heart, as shadows in vague, undistinguishable forms stalk your movement. You do not dare to stop... even for a quick breath.

Involuntarily, you cry out a whispered prayer for protection, **Lord, help me.** A voice of terror urges you on, quickening your pace. Your brain screams, **Move faster! Hurry up!" Then...**You hear the voice of a child, whose parents are dead, burned earlier in the day, in the fires of madness. The child's voice reaches into your heart, pleading. You stop, frozen in time. **I'm cold. Do you have a blanket?** begs the child. What do you do now?

Or, is it the voice of a weathered and pained old man, whose family had been murdered? He sits alone in the cold, the wind whistling through the hole in his heart that his family once filled.

Perhaps a female voice would shake in fearful, whispering words. The voice is afraid you might be the one, who raped her earlier that day... after you killed her husband...after you sold her children into slavery. Perhaps it would be her voice you would hear, as her chilled body forces out a whisper of need, slowly rising from the desert floor. **Do you have a blanket?**

What if members of your own family, a mother, sister, or a brother were bare, and freezing in the night? What would you do if a daughter or a son sat alone on the desert floor, shivering and cold?

For whosoever shall do the will of my Father which is in Heaven, The same is my brother, and sister, and mother.
Matthew 12: 50

They are Christians because that is the Truth. They would rather die in the Truth, than live in a lie. They are the children and people of southern Sudan. They are nobodies, but they are God's nobodies, walking in the Light of His Greatness.

They are cold.

Do you have a blanket?

6

Breath of Warmth
Faith in Action

First, a slight tingle of pain...then numbness.

As the temperature drops, the heat escapes...*into the night.*

Winter sets in

You shiver, becoming mildly confused. You try to preserve your heat, but the cold refuses to hold the warmth you desire.

The Freeze has begun.

You begin to stumble; your every move a slow, laborious attempt to retain the heat that continues to...*slip away.* You glance in the mirror. You appear alert...but there is something wrong. You seem pale...your fingers and toes are blue... *Slowly you begin to lose the feeling of touch.*

Your confusion rises, as sleet begins to fall.

You try to speak...to sound strong...to sound like you care... Your words are sluggish, and you begin to forget.

Your mind cannot remember... those you loved...those you once knew. Who are they? Where are they now?

Your coordination is poor, and walking seems impossible.

Wasn't it just yesterday...

Or when... when you first believed.

Believed what?

Oh yea...believed in...

What am I talking about? It's so cold!

Does anyone else feel how cold it is?

Your behavior becomes irrational and nonsensical. Your heart begins to shut down. You become clinically dead...but the freezing fear of isolation and confusion...**It does not die.**

In winter's night, they told you that this would happen if you left the cabin. They told you that if you walked away from the fireplace, you would grow cold. But the snow flakes gently falling looked so beautiful... and you just had to dance in the fluffy lightness and merry pleasantries of the moment.

To taste the cool, the upbeat...out of the heat, a bit more fun.

You didn't look back though.

You failed to strip the veil off the pretty face, to see the howling winds, the freezing rain. *You thought it playtime, a gay time.*

BREATH OF WARMTH...FAITH IN ACTION

And now where are you? You cannot remember. Your brain is caught in a blizzard, a chaotic snow fall.

Then your skin flushes hot, flaming, burning.

Enough! Enough already!...man is it hot.

You disrobe.

You rip off your shirt...then your pants...your shoes and socks. Now you stand naked, but still the hated heat flares from every pore. Your soul smokes, crackling under fired flames. As your scream departs, in charred words you do not understand, the heat leaves, as suddenly as it arrived.

The cold resumes in sleeting attack, of icy death.

You drop to the ground, crawling over the frozen tundra. Your thoughts are no more than silent images, impulses that reign over you, and force you on.

Your teeth chatter, as you drag your body over the bitter arctic wasteland. That is when your eyes glimpse a haven of beckoning warmth. You creep forward, into the space of your hope. Your body curls up in a fetal position... back to the womb.

*An explorer of the finest magnitude, you have discovered a safe place to curl up! And you do. You curl up...*and you die.

Someone stumbles upon your naked, lifeless corpse the next day. They find your body crammed into a small cabinet, left out for the trash. The clothes you discarded the night before, strewn across the snowy ground, like a trail to death...yours.

Jesus said that in the last days, **because iniquity shall increase, the love of many shall wax cold.**

The lives of those who freeze to death, follow a pattern of numbness and life escaping warmth. In 20% of freezing cases, a syndrome known as **Paradoxical Undressing** occurs. This act occurs in the latter stages of freezing. A person's mind, devoid of reason, perhaps fooled by body cells making one last stand at life, feels the sensation of heat. The intensity of the heat causes this person to undress. They could be standing in -10 weather, but they suffer under the burning feel of fire.

After undressing, some begin a crawl of death. For reasons unexplainable, after their **Paradoxical Undressing**, these now naked individuals fall on all fours, or flat on their stomachs, and crawl. In their delusional state, they crawl toward, and into, any enclosed space they can find. In their chosen coffin, whether under a bed, in a cupboard, or any small cave-like structure, they die. They freeze to death. This is known as **Terminal Burrowing**, an animal burrowing their own grave, seeking comfort from fear and the freezing cold, but finding... **death.**

How many American Christians are now in the cold state of freezing? How many Christians are becoming numb? How many Christians have left the warmth of the fireplace, the burning embers of love for Jesus that once glowed within, and have begun to play in the fluffy snowflakes of the world? In the snow, have they become numb, their life a mere collection of frozen desires. Have their minds fallen into a blizzard of confusion... forgetting the words of life?

> *And let us not be weary in well doing:*
> *For in due season we shall reap if we faint not.*
> *As we have therefore opportunity,*
> *Let us do good unto all men,*
> *Especially unto them who are of the household of faith.*
> *Galatians 6: 9 & 10*

As many American Christians slowly begin to freeze, are they also undressing? Are Christians removing their royal robes of righteousness, hand-tailored, woven by Jesus Christ? Do Christians prefer to crawl over the icy wasteland of the world, naked and exposed, welcomed by others that boast how winter is not that bad?

How many Christians are becoming spotted with the world, as their fingers and toes turn blue, the Words of Life becoming no more than faded sights and sounds?

> *Do not worry about the cold! What you should actually worry about is Global Warming!*

The globe is overheating! The lost sheep are bleating. Turn down the thermometer quickly! Mother Earth is really getting steamed! Rise up, and turn your thermometers down. Quit mainlining quarts of oil, junkie! This is no time for minor religious beliefs like, *Truth*, like *Jesus, or God.* The Earth is melting right before our very eyes. What are we going to say when *He* returns?

> *Sorry, God, we really blew it. Sorry we melted the Earth. What did I just say? Oh yea, it is so hot, so terribly, brrrr. What was that? So cold...It is so terribly cold! What happened?'*

Global Cooling happened, as hearts and minds become cold and numb, selfish in their lust for self-preservation. Minds and thoughts turned away from their Heavenly Father, to proclaim a mound of dirt, their mother. What is left? The crawl of death and terminal burrowing await. For Christians, who do not come out of the cold, the crawl is left.

In frozen breath of death, they will seek a dark womb to hide within, and curl up... to die for sin.

> *Out of the heat and into the cold... their bodies found... dead, stuffed in a cupboard, naked and alone.*

> *Will you crawl on, in frozen-wealth of death?*

> *Or live in fires-warmth of Life?*

It is time for us, for those who believe in Jesus as our savior, to begin a *Fast*. Not a *Fast* of not eating, but one the Lord has chosen. It is the evening...of the dawn. Before the dawn arises, we must begin a *Fast* of the heart, in *Deed and Truth*.

My little children, let us not love in word, neither in tongue; But in Deed and Truth.
And hereby we know that we are of the Truth, And shall assure our hearts before Him.
<u>*For if our heart condemns us,*</u>
<u>*God is greater than our heart, and knoweth all things.*</u>
I John 3: 18, 19, 20

In silent moment...alone and cold
A hand reached out, to touch and hold
A kindled flame, of love unfold
To earn itself, a crown of Gold.

Today we are going to begin a *Fast* the Lord has chosen.

Is not this the Fast I have chosen
To loose the bands of wickedness
To undue heavy burdens
To let the oppressed go free
And that ye break every yoke.

Is it not to deal thy bread
To the hungry

And that thou shall bring the poor
That are cast out,
To thy house

When thou seest the naked,
That thou cover him:
And that thou hide not thyself from thy own flesh?

Then shall thy Light break forth as the morning.
Isaiah 58: 6, 7, 8

Have you ever Fasted, a Fast the Lord has chosen?

One family did. They recently made a movie about the woman, who reached out to touch the life of a homeless youth. In a beautiful display of one person walking in the **Light of God's Greatness,** and **Living in the Majesty of a Moment**, a lady saw the poor outcast, and brought him home. There, he became part of her family and then...*a* **Football Great!**

Love is not a word, or a promise of imagined impossibilities that can never be delivered. Love is an act, based on **Deeds and Truth**. The mother who saw a homeless boy walking the streets, had the love of the Lord, and knew His truth. She acted in **Deed and Truth, because she desired to be In the Truth, not just talk about it.**

> Before the deep freeze sets in...
> we need to begin a *Fast* the Lord has chosen.

If you are currently cold and distant, movement is crucial to warming up the heart. You need to get the blood circulating again. You must move, even when the move is not felt within. That is why your *Faith in Action is important.* By your *Faith in Action*, by *doing the works of love, in Jesus' name*, God promises to perfect the love within you. Are you cold within? Doing nothing will assure you a terminal death by freezing. Doing something, by faith in God's word, will produce the warmth needed for life. *If you are freezing, now is the time to act.*

> *But whoso keepeth His word,*
> *In him verily is the love of God perfected:*
> *Hereby know we that we are in Him*
> *I John 2:5*

The **word** of Jesus to keep, is to, *love thy neighbor as thyself.* Jesus desires you to love and not be weary in well doing, not to faint. As a King of Kings, Jesus has set a royal standard for the laws of Heaven.

> *If ye fulfill the Royal Law according to scripture,*
> *Thou shalt love thy neighbor as thyself, ye do well.*
> *James 2: 8*

> *For all the law is fulfilled in one Word,*
> *Even in this,*
> *Thou shalt love thy neighbor as thy self.*
> *Galatians 5:14*

If you feel cold and isolated, begin your walk in love, by acting in small ways, by offering a kind word to someone who is having a bad day. Offer a smile to one who is sad. Try to touch a person, who is lonely. Buy a gift card, or a coffee, and a rose...and give it to a homeless woman walking the streets, without hope. A small gift of hope to one who is without can teach a heart to live in heated passion of Jesus' love. Try just one, each day, and see if God is not faithful! See if God does not return your gift, with a new heart of love.

Just act for a few days, and feel God begin to restore the embers of love within you.

Act on behalf of one near...and one afar.

These are not **Random Acts of Kindness**. You have not been called to **randomness. These** are acts of faith, performed unto the Lord Jesus Christ, **in faith**. You serve a living God, not randomness, or select TV personalities.

> *For we are His workmanship, Created in Christ Jesus unto*
> *Good works Which God hath before ordained*
> *That we should walk in them.*
> *Ephesians 2: 10*

Before the world began, God planned a series of good works for you to accomplish deeds of warmth that would melt the frost that covers a heart needing love.

Today you must move, tomorrow could be too late. Do not continue to freeze in the wastelands of a frozen tundra. Do not allow yourself to reach the state of **Paradoxical Undressing and Terminal Burrowing.**

Faith in Action Today in your **Amazing Grace...Race,** in your new position in, **The High Calling of God in Jesus Christ,** you are going to have a **Stop Over** in Sudan. However, you won't need an airline ticket or Passport, just a blanket and $2.00. You are going to open a **Warm the World Ministry**.

We are going to mail V.O.M. one blanket and $2.00. Our gift will jet around the world to Sudan, to wrap itself around a cold and shivering body. We will live in the **Majesty of a Moment, by warming a ravaged soul.**

This will be our **Faith In Action.**

You may already have a large and colorful, warm and snuggly blanket stashed away in a closet! Now is the time to get it out! If it is in nice condition, and currently unused, send it to one who will use it.

If you do not have a used blanket, purchase a new one. The mailing address for sending the blanket and $2.00 is,

V.O.M. 1815 Southeast Bison Rd., Bartlesville, OK. 74006

When V.O.M. receives your blanket and $2.00, they will add the gospel of Jesus, and mail your package of warmth overseas for you. Your blanket will travel the globe, and land around the shoulders of one who asks...

Do you have a blanket?

Remember, we are now on a **Fast** that the Lord has chosen. So do not allow "**Fast**" to mean the left lane in traffic, as you race along the highway of life. In the confusion and mayhem of your race, you will fail to notice the warning signs.

WARNING!!! WARNING!!! WARNING!!!

Extreme drops in temperature could induce slow freezing, leading to Paradoxical Undressing and Terminal Burrowing, followed closely... by certain death. Do not be ruled by the icy mayhem of the Moment.

One early morning in San Diego, I only saw the mayhem. Jesus knew the Majesty, and insisted I live in it. Wouldn't you love to live in The Majesty of the Moment and have a joy that exceeds your wildest wonders?

By mailing a blanket and two dollars, you have begun your own **Warm the World Out-reach Ministry**! That's **walking in the Light of God's Greatness!**

If you are homeless, short on cash, but want to mail a blanket, ask a thrift store if you can work in exchange for a blanket. Explain why you want the blanket. You may ignite a flame. For a homeless person to get and mail a blanket to a Nobody in Sudan…well, I could not begin to describe the joy that will erupt in your heart, once the package is mailed! Mail a blanket and *find out!*

If you belong to a Christian Sleeper Cell, I challenge you with this **Faith in Action,** as a new call for activation. Take part in a **Fast** the Lord has chosen. Touch one in need in **His name.** Touch just one!

Then one day, while you are preparing for a feast, at the table of the Lord, a person right next to you may say. **Hey, I know you! You're the one who gave me a blanket, one night when I was cold.**

How will you feel then?

Even though the action may take a few days, after you firmly commit to this blanket mission in your heart (**One blanket and $2.00**) you are ready for our next breath.

Breath of Warmth

With a prayer for their warmth, and your heart fired up, close your eyes and …breathe.

God has a Kingdom prepared for you, can you prepare one blanket for Him?

BREATH OF WARMTH...FAITH IN ACTION

Dear Heavenly Father,

Thank you for your tender kindness and deep love. Please help us use that kindness and love for others, in this Breath of Warmth. Please guide us in, from out of the cold. Dress us in warmth, under your royal robe of righteousness.

Please help us warm one who is near, and one who is afar.

Please watch over and comfort those in Sudan, who suffer in the night. Prepare the way for my blanket to warm the body of one who is cold and weary. Help me to Fast in the Light of your Greatness that I may learn to live in the Majesty of the Moment.

Help me step out of winter's icy mayhem. Help me learn to be still...and know that you are God. Help me remember that you have not forgotten me and that you have already worked everything out. Help me to be still and know these things.

And Lord, help me walk in the good works that you have set before me... before the foundation of the world.

In Jesus' name, Amen. They are cold...they ask...

Do you have a blanket?

7

Sing a Song
Breath of Song

*The Lord is my strength and song
And is become my salvation. Psalm 118:14*

The most beautiful sound of singing I ever heard was when I was homeless.

As I walked along the waters edge, on the western bay of San Diego, their voices ascended up into the evening air, mingling pleasantly with the calm of the night. A serenade under the stars of Heaven, sharing grace with the listeners.

Ten of them sat around a camp fire, their voices soft and warm, candles flickering in the harmony of love. Their hearts held this love for their savior, Jesus Christ.

My heart was flooded. Tears filled my eyes.

Their gathering was casual, friends together in company and song. And their songs were songs of praise. They wanted joy in companionship with the Spirit of Christ, and sang with **grace in their hearts unto the Lord.**

On this night, my Pakistani boss had demanded that I take a night off. My recent grumpy attitude and irritability had spoken up on my behalf, and my boss's hearing was very good.

It was a night off from racing around San Diego, delivering pizzas to the visiting tourists, hotel to hotel. This strip of land I now strolled down, a peaceful setting lined with Palm Trees, was a perfect location for the nighttime viewing of the downtown skyline. The lights of the city glistened and sparkled across the waters of the bay. This site had also become a wonderful place to rest and sleep, after all night shifts with Broadway Pizza. This site was much closer than driving up to my normal rest-area bedroom, 35 miles north. If my Honda Condo was pulled in next to the other parked cars, I could spend the night here without being bothered by anyone. I could slumber peacefully, in relative comfort.

And here I was, tears in my eyes, listening to this group of young people, who thought it good to get together and sing songs to magnify their love for Jesus Christ.

After a few minutes, when they paused, I rudely inserted myself into their tranquil night. I fell to my knees, before their fire, and set out 10 one-dollar bills before me.

I wonder if I could ask a favor. My voice surely reflected the unsteady lack of control I had at that moment. **My son is currently in a Youth Detention Center in Colorado. I have asked other Christian Organizations and members if they would write him a letter of encouragement, to encourage him in faith, but they have not responded.**

Except for the crackling of the wood in the campfire, silence held the night in hand. I searched for words. **He needs to hear from other Christians that he is not forgotten. That others care.**

Could I ask each of you to write my son a letter?

Please, I asked them, *if you each could just write him one letter. There is a dollar here for each of you, to pay for the stamp and the envelope. If my son could just see and know that other Christians do care about him, I think it would mean so much to him. It would be a start.*

They prayed with me, and graciously accepted the request. They wanted to refuse the money, but I did not feel I could allow the refusal. The one-dollar bills were my tokens of faith. They were my own, *Faith in Action* before God.

Deep in my heart, I wished my son had been there, that he had been one of these young people, sitting on this beach around a campfire with friends. In the midst of God's love, to feel the joy and peace of God. If only he could know true friendship and pure love in Jesus Christ, and in knowing, let his restless heart feel peace.

> *And let the peace of God rule in your hearts,*
> *To the which ye are also called in one body*
> *And be ye thankful.*
> *Colossians 3: 15*

His current Colorado friends could be named in a who's who in the world of auto thefts within the state. They had chosen the fast lane of thievery and inflated adrenalin, as their ride through life. His friends did not care about him. They did not know how to care about him. He did not know how to care about them either.

Here in San Diego, a group of young people had chosen the walk of faith, and the thrill of Salvation that leads to eternal life. While my son's friends were on a collision course, ending in wreckage and destruction, these men and women were on a walk of grace. Their walk would lead them to adventure and riches beyond their wildest dreams. I had never encountered a group of young people as likeminded as these, on this shoreline, secure in their faith, open in their love, and vocal with their praise.

By Him therefore, (By Jesus) let us offer the sacrifice of praise to God continually, that is, the fruit of our lips giving thanks to His name. Hebrews 13: 15

Getting up to leave, one individual came up and offered **me** ten dollars. He told me this was to aid me in finding, meeting, and asking ten others to pray for my son. Humbled at his kindness, I thanked him, but could not accept his offer. The Lord had specifically set these young people before me, as a gift. I wanted His gift preserved, as he had given it.

A few weeks later, calling my son on a pre-arranged, pre-approved phone call, an excited voice told me he had received a number of letters. He was surprised and I was thankful.

Was this the great turning point? Was this the miracle that changed our lives? Is that what freed us from troubles and trials? No, but it was one moment where I was allowed to watch, see, and listen to those who **Live In Victory Eternal... in sincerity of faith.**

After that day, the desire of my heart continued to be, that my son would come to know this **Victory** and **Sincerity**. That one day, my son might have friends just like these, and sit on a shoreline singing praises to the Lord, because *that* was what was in his heart.

Often, as I think of these faithful servants of the Lord and their songs in the night, I am moved to give thanks for them, for that moment, and their prayers. And I believe this is how the Body of Christ lives and breathes. In Him, By Him, and through Him, in an ocean of life, that Jesus is magnified.

Jesus was the melody within their hearts...the song of their life.

I will sing unto the Lord as long as I live:
I will sing praise to my God while I have my being.
My meditation of Him shall be sweet:
I will be glad in the Lord.

SING A SONG...BREATH OF SONG

Their churches are burned, the authorities kill them, and they are beaten. But deep in the jungles of Southeast Asia and Indonesia, their voices can be heard, singing with grace in their hearts...

Their voices rise up to the heavens,
To ascend before God and His Throne,
And flow like a river through the beauty of His sanctuary.
ANON

These Christians, *love to hear the Christian radio at six in the morning. They also learn many songs from the radio. When they have worship service, they many times sing by their heart; there is no book.* This insert is taken from the May 2008 issue of V.O.M. Magazine, Editorial.

Speaking to yourselves in psalms and hymns and spiritual songs, singing and making melody in your heart to the Lord. Ephesians 5: 19

I read a book about a preacher in Europe, who decided he would not allow singing in his church for a number of weeks. He was determined to teach the people in his church other ways to worship God. He must have thought singing was over-rated.

After his allotted weeks of non-singing had passed, everyone was allowed to sing again. And what did one member of His congregation do to commemorate the weeks the singing mouths were silenced? *He wrote a song! Amazing!*

His song is now famous, and everyone sings it, as if to commemorate not singing by...*singing.*

Jesus is quoted by Paul as saying; *In the midst of the church will I sing praise unto thee. Hebrews 2: 12.*

I wonder if Jesus had been sitting in that preacher's pew in Europe, if the preacher would have told Jesus, *Excuse me, Lord, but we are not*

135

singing this week. I want you to learn another way to worship your Heavenly Father.

One Christian book implies that feeling joy within ourselves, when we sing praises to the Lord, is irrelevant. The purpose of singing worship songs, according to the book, is to praise the Lord, not to feel good. Searching diligently for a verse that admonishes us not to feel happy when we sing, or that feeling joy in song is not relevant to the song, I have failed miserably. What verse allows men to decide, **we sing about Jesus too much?** What verse states that feeling joy in song is irrelevant? Where do the scriptures explain that singing should be an un-moving, experience of duty, to God?

I am constantly amazed at what I hear being stated, as if on authority from God, and yet can find no scripture to underline the bold statements proclaimed. Why does scripture clearly inspire us to, *Let the word of Christ dwell in you richly in all wisdom; teaching and admonishing one another in psalms, and hymns and spiritual songs, singing with grace in your hearts to the Lord. Colossians 3: 16*

Apparently, if the word of Christ dwells in us richly, we are to teach and admonish one another in...*60 minute sermons?* Perhaps, Paul got somewhat confused when he commanded us to teach and admonish *with psalms, hymns, and spiritual songs.* And...we should do this, with grace in our hearts? Can one have grace in their heart without being moved?

Jesus, himself, declared that He will sing praise unto the Lord *IN THE CHURCH!* I hope He is not happy or feeling good when He sings. I also suppose the verse that states Jesus will sing in the church, would depend on which church Jesus chose to sing in... and whether or not that church would allow it, on that particular week.

HISTORICAL NOTE # When Saul had failed as a King and disobeyed God, God removed His Spirit from Saul and sent him an evil spirit to cause him discomfort. What was the only thing that could calm this evil spirit within him? You have three choices.

A. *A highly paid professional, Exorcist Hit Team from the Vatican?*

B. *Three Charismatic, Mega Church Preachers to "Preach Quite The Spirit!"*

C. *A young Shepherd boy who could play a harp really well?*

Times up. What's your answer?

Do you remember the Shepherd boy, David, and his music before the Lord? When David played the harp, the evil spirit within Saul was quieted. Later, David, himself became King, chosen of God and called by God, "A man after His own heart."

It was a nobody, the Shepherd boy, who pleased God
In music and song.

What a gracious Lord, who created so joyous, enriching, and heartfelt ways to share **His Truths in song. Psalms, hymns and spiritual songs** are, the soft touch of Jesus delivered through musical melody.

Softly and tenderly Jesus is calling,
Calling for you and for me..
Come home... Come home...

Ye who are weary, come home..

This song was written in 1880
by a man named, Will L. Thompson.

How great was this song, is this song?

On his death bed, breathing his last breaths of life, a man named Dwight stated that of all he had ever done, he would have traded everything to have been able to write this one song. Of all his books, ministries, and preaching, he would have given it all over to another, for the joy of having written this one **melody. A melody that has graced the hearts of so many, over so many years.**

How great a statement was this, as made by Dwight L. Moody, owner of his own Publishing House, and founder of Moody Bible College? Moody Bible College is considered one of the most famous Christian Colleges ever established. (**God never needed to threaten Moody with death, if he didn't come up with enough cash to get the job done.**)

This college has faithfully educated and commissioned thousands of missionaries to preach around the world. Many of these missionaries have given their lives, and had spilled their own blood, so that others could hear the gospel of salvation.

Yet, in his last reflection of life, Dwight L. Moody showed an enlightened depth of grace, in understanding the power of the Lord to move a heart in a song of grace.

And how many people have committed their lives to the Lord after listening to the lyrics of, **Softly and Tenderly.** How often has the Spirit of God softened hard hearts with this tender song? What is the current, ever rising count of broken hearts turning to Jesus, as these sweet words float through congregations, across the cities and towns throughout America?

And of all of his works... all of his sermons...and all of his books and published pieces...Dwight L. Moody would have traded everything to another, for the treasured gift of writing this one song.

Softly and Tenderly, Jesus is calling
Calling for you and for me.
See on the Portals, He's waiting and watching
Watching for you and for me.

Come home, come home
Ye who are weary, come home
Earnestly, tenderly
Jesus is calling
Calling O sinner, come home

SING A SONG...BREATH OF SONG

Why should we tarry when Jesus is pleading
Pleading for you and for me.
Why should we linger and heed not His mercies
Mercies for you and for me.

Written by Will L. Thompson, this song has been used by the Spirit of God to open the hardest of hearts.

In the jungles of Viet Nam and Indonesia, where villagers with little or no money, live in huts of clay, straw, and bamboo, hearts of praise are raised to the Lord, in the voice of song.

By Him let us offer the sacrifice of praise to God continually, that is the fruit of our lips giving praise to His name. In Vietnam, Laos, and Cambodia and on the Isles of Indonesia, they do offer the sacrifice of praise. *And they do it with ...psalms and hymns and spiritual songs, singing and making melody in their hearts unto the Lord.*

And soon, perhaps, the long, unfruitful meetings attended by rulers of the world, each proclaiming their own greatness, will forever be changed in song. Instead of long, meaningless speeches, they may be singing.

Psalms 138 states; *All the Kings of the Earth shall praise Thee,*

O Lord, when they hear the words of thy mouth.
<u>Yea, they shall SING in the ways of the Lord</u>
For great is the Glory of the Lord.

In the jungles of Asia and Indonesia, they already do.

In the jungles of Asia and Indonesia, they are beaten and murdered...
and they sing.

They are chased from their homes, tortured and imprisoned...
and they sing.

While they are constantly attacked, their churches burned to the ground, living under constant threat of terror from those, who hate the name of Jesus...*they sing.*

In these jungles, often running red with their blood, The nobodies of Jesus live in Victory Eternal. And they sing about it!

What are you singing about?

7

Breath of Song
Faith in Action

Sing...sing a song
Make it simple
To last your whole life long!
Don't worry that's it not good enough
For anyone else to hear,
Just sing...sing a song.
By Joe Raposo

God gave us the capacity to sing, and enjoy singing for a reason. Music can bring joy to a heart. Music can express the deepest sadness. Many times, we even judge and remember our lives by music.

How often does a song come on, and we think,

Oh, I remember...

When walking in the **Light of God's Greatness**, it is good to hold a song in heart. A melody in a heart *is* pleasing to the Lord.

But before we travel forward, let me take a moment for anyone who may feel discouraged. Have things in your life grown worse since you began reading this book? Does the voice that paces within each thought, rage on, **Man, I don't get it...I've done everything, and... you just don't understand? Everything keeps getting worse.**

Are dark clouds swirling overhead, crackling with thunder? Has your heart been pierced by a strike of lightening? If fear is on the attack, now is when your faith is so important. Before you give up, just take a heart-break, and listen to a little story on fear.

They had been slaves. For hundreds of years, they had been slaves, forced to work at the feet of their oppressors. Then one day a man came forward and proclaimed, **The Great, I Am, has sent me to free His people**! The man was Moses. The people were the Israelites. They were first happy that Moses appeared promising freedom but life quickly took a downward spiral. Instead of immediate freedom, they were granted additional suffering, as Pharaoh, the supreme ruler of Egypt, rebelled against God. Finally, after God sent horrible plagues upon Egypt, and its people, the Pharaoh let the Israelites go, and they were freed.

They were not only freemen and woman; they were wealthy. Before they left Egypt, the Egyptians had lavished upon them, silver and gold, the wealth of their country. **What could have been greater or more thrilling than the day the Israelites walked out of Egypt? They were over half a million strong, wealthy and free, with dreams and hopes of joy and life, in a land of milk and honey, promised by God.**

However, soon life took a dramatic turn in appearances. Reaching the Red Sea, their path of promise dropped into a watery roadblock. Then, a ferocious army of Egyptian warriors appeared from behind. Mounted on horses, riding chariots of war, Pharaohs' army had raced after the departing Israelites. The Pharaoh had changed his mind concerning his decision to allow their departure. As the Israelites carried off the spoils of Egypt, the

Pharaoh's new strategy was a simple plan of obliteration and destruction. Blood would flow!

The terrified Israelites stood frozen in fear. Their precious hopes began sinking beneath the waters that had them trapped. Their voices cried out with begging pleas for deliverance. Moses cried out to the Lord for salvation. And just when the story of Israel was to end in the wholesale slaughter of an entire race of people, the Lord accepted the prayer of His faithful servant. God rewrote the last chapter, changing the storyline. The Lord lowered a cloud from Heaven, to bury the enemies in blindness. He brought a powerful wind from the treasured storehouses of His wealth, to part the sea, creating a highway of life for His children. And the watery roadblock, that had sealed their fate, opened before them, allowing their safe passage.

And thousands of years ago, the chosen people of God, the Israelites, escaped Pharaoh's plan of death, under a cloud of fog, through a sea of hope. On that day, the wind of God blew ***fiercely kind*** for the Israelites.

Seeing their prey escaping, Pharaoh's army made a mad dash for victory. They charged into the path opened by the winds of God, the Pharaoh tasting the blood his soldiers would soon spill.

That was when God re-***gathered the winds in His fist***, returning them to His storehouse. Once the winds were re-gathered, the walls of water collapsed, carrying away an Egyptian army, swept away by the raging waters of God.

Safely, on the opposite side, the Israelites praised God. They did not first learn the forty approved methods for offering praise. They just let loose and worshiped loudly in song and dance! ***Furthermore,*** they probably felt joy and excitement while praising Him!

> *I will sing unto the Lord,*
> *For He hath triumphed gloriously:*
> *The horse and his rider hath he thrown into the sea.*
> *The Lord is my strength and my SONG,*
> *And He is become my salvation.*
> *Exodus 15: 1 & 2*

If you are also weak and weary, tired and exhausted, cry out to God. If you are trapped between Pharaoh's army, and the Red Sea, take heart. The Lord has a cloud with your name on it, and He hasn't forgotten how to part a sea. The waters of life are not too difficult for God to part. Place your hope in He, who can do anything.

> *Be strong and of a good courage*
> *Fear not, nor be afraid of them*
> *For the Lord thy God, He it is that doth go with thee.*
> *He will not fail thee nor forsake thee.*
> *Deuteronomy 31: 6*

Historical Note# During the American Revolution, his army on the verge of annihilation, with the British secure in their upcoming victory, history took a detour. As evening fell upon the weary and worn soldiers of the American Revolution, fear began to roam their hearts, with visions of a slaughter awaiting them at break of dawn.

On this Eve of certain defeat, camping on the edge of death, in rain and night's mist, a mysterious fog descended. This thick fog separated the armies of George Washington and the British, limiting their vision. And it was under this mist, a nighttime cloud, that George Washington safely guided his troops across the watery barrier to escape the morning bloodbath.

Using rowboats and stealth, Washington led his entire army quietly out of harm's way and wholesale defeat. While the British slept on, in sweet dreams of victory, the Americans escaped. The American Revolution, covered in the safety of a majestic mist, lived to fight another day.

In the early morning gray of dawn, one group of soldiers guarding the rear, still remained. While they appeared forgotten and abandoned, God continued to remember. The cloud of fog obscured their escape, and did not disperse until late in the morning, after every soldier reached safety, on the opposite bank.

BREATH OF SONG...FAITH IN ACTION

This miracle allowed George Washington to lead his men out of the battlefield and beyond the reach of the British.

The following day, the British, ready to make short work of the Americans, were left with an empty battlefield and no one to kill.

And now, as it is the evening...of the Dawn, we are arriving at the edge of eternity, and your Savior is preparing to help *you* slip away. So do not lose hope yet.

> *Be ye also patient; stablish your hearts:*
> *for the coming of the Lord draweth nigh. James 5: 8*

For this reason, do not let your hope dissolve into a cloud of depression. Trust your Lord to send you a cloud of hope, to cover you in your time of fear and uncertainty. And when it is done raining, ask Him to set a *Rainbow of Grace* across the Heavens of your heart. He will.

> *For I am persuaded, that neither death, nor life, nor angels, nor principalities, nor powers, nor things present, nor things to come, nor height, nor depth, nor any other creature, shall be able to separate us from the love of God Which is in Christ Jesus.*
> *Romans 8: 38 & 39*

Although God may give *you more than you can handle,* **He will never give you more than He can handle!**

So...sing!

To help you sing, here is your **<u>Faith in Action</u>**. You are to write a song of praise. **Wait a minute**, before you flip the page. No one is demanding of you to write a song to rock the halls of grace. No one is going to put your performance on stage. Just compose a song of praise to sing alone, when you have a moment to yourself.

Writing a song is much easier than you think.

The song the Israelites sang just outlined what had happened. But instead of writing a story to read, they sang the story! Instead of listening to a sermon, they sang one. They sang a story about **God's Strength** and **Salvation!**

And now you can write your own short, musical story. Your composition will be a song of worship and praise, which you can sing whenever you are so moved.

There will be no Simon, sitting behind a desk, mocking your musical talents. Only God will be in attendance. So let the voice of your heart float up to Heaven, in pleasing notes of love.

Next, as you run the **Amazing Grace…Race** throughout the day, listen to music that praises the Lord. Find a Christian channel on your radio. Play a CD with Christian music you enjoy and sing along.

Stay in Song, in the Spirit!

**If you do, you will be obeying
scripture that commands us to:**

***Be not drunk with wine, wherein is excess;
But be filled with the Spirit;
Speaking to yourselves in psalms and hymns
And spiritual songs,
Singing and making melody in your heart
Unto the Lord;
Ephesians 5: 18***

Celebrate the entire day in song.

Try this…….

Whenever you have a spiritual thought, or a message to the Lord, don't say it, sing it! Are you smiling now? You will then!

And now let us take our next breath, the breath of song, in praise and worship of a King!

The Breath of Song
Close your eyes just for a moment,
and with a melody of the heart, just...breathe.

Don't forget about your **Mug and Pocket Ministries**.

...or your **Great Christian University** plans!

Remember your **Warm the World Ministry**. In fact, singing your song while locating, buying, and mailing the blanket, may brighten your day. Wrap *IT* in song!

Dear Heavenly Father

Thank you for the most beautiful gift of music and song. Thank you for desiring our praise in song and worship, to you, O Lord. Thank you for allowing us such a magnificent way to praise you, with joy in our hearts.

Because you are the God of Heaven and Earth, and everything within, you are also the God of Song. Your precious gifts are more than can be counted, and your love and mercy, eternal. Fill our hearts with the rejoicing of your Holy presence and the desires of your will.

Please help us remember our brothers and sisters in jungles of death, and all those that walk in newness of life. Encourage and strengthen them and accept our humble prayers for their well being and salvation.

Please bless our ministries for their help, to aid and comfort them.

In Jesus' name, Amen

And tell me...

What are you singing about?

8

Vanished
Breath of prayer

*If I take the wings of the morning
And dwell in the utter most parts of the sea;
Even there shall thy hand lead me
And Thy right hand shall hold me.
Psalms 139: 9 & 10*

Pulling off the highway, onto the exit ramp, there he stood, a man with joy overflowing in his heart! He had a bible in his hand, and words of thanks on his lips. A sign, held in his second hand, asked for spare change from the passing motorists.

It is not my practice to give, merely because I see someone on a corner with a sign. Most signs are simple with a, **Homeless, anything will help**! A few try creativity to earn a buck. **Why lie, I need a beer!** Or, **I bet you a dollar you will read this sign.** I like the creative signs, they allow for a quick, easy decision **NOT** to give.

Then you have the regulars, who hit the same corner day in and day out. It has become their job, their way of making a living. While many people consider it lazy, I certainly would not want their job. The verbal abuse they take daily must be on par with what 7-11 workers experience, or worse.

During the space in time when I resided in my Honda Condo, I once drove through an **In And Out Burger.** There, a sign holder's sign proclaimed, **I'm Hungry**. This was a slick tactic, and worked on me. I purchased a burger, fries and a coke, handing him the goods as I passed. This man with the **Hungry** sign did not eat and leave. As I parked to eat my own food, I watched him. He put the food I had given him into a backpack and once more raised the sign. He must have been in the catering business, because while I sat eating, he did quite well. He was still claiming hunger when I left.

Another time, while finishing an early morning pizza delivery, I noticed a well-dressed man holding a sign. Actually, the sign should have been my first **Sign,** that he wasn't what he said, *a man out of gas.*

He stood in downtown San Diego, late at night, in a three-piece suit. Because I had to stop and get gas myself, I gave him $5 or $10. Back at work, I heard other pizza delivery drivers talking about his nightly act. This man is often in need of gas, late at night, at the exact same spot where I made contact with him. Sorting through the sincerity of sign holders can be a constant hit or miss game, where one is never sure.

And now here I was, pulling off an exit ramp near Carlsbad, California, and there was this man praising God, and kissing his bible. It was the afternoon. Afternoon off-ramps in Carlsbad are crowded with cars waiting for their turn to get off the ramp, and off to home.

That is why I was able to observe this man for a few minutes, before I pulled parallel of his position. I was immediately reminded of the woman who washed Jesus' feet.

Jesus had gone to a religious man's home for dinner. The custom, at the time, was to wash the honored guest's feet, or provide water for washing. Walking on dusty streets, in bare feet or sandals, left one's feet caked in a dirty frosting of earth. The religious man, who invited Jesus over for dinner, provided no such service, or water. Then **SHE** showed up.

Shamelessly, this woman fell to the feet of Jesus and, with her own tears, washed his feet, using her hair as the towel. She then kissed His feet, in humble adoration and worship.

The religious man, a Pharisee, was amazed within himself and thought, *if this man Jesus were a prophet, he would know who was washing His feet and what type of woman this was that touched His feet, for she is a sinner.*

By these thoughts, the Pharisee must have been implying that he, himself, was not a sinner, as well as that Jesus was also a **Fraud**.

Jesus asked the Pharisee a simple question. *Who will be more grateful for forgiveness, and who will love the forgiver more? One who has sinned a little and been forgiven, or one who has sinned a lot?*

At this, the Pharisee got it right with his answer, even though his heart was still wrong.

Jesus said, *Seest thou this woman? I entered into thine house, thou gavest me no water for my feet: but she hath washed my feet with tears and wiped them with the hairs of her head. Thou gavest me no kiss: but this woman, since the time I came in, hath not ceased to kiss my feet. My head with oil thou didst not anoint: but this woman hath anointed my feet with ointment.*

Wherefore I say unto thee, her sins which are many are forgiven; for she loved much: but to whom little is forgiven, the same loveth little.

And He said unto her, *Thy sins are forgiven.* Luke 7: 40 through 48

WALKING IN THE LIGHT OF GOD'S GREATNESS

Too often, herein also lies American Christianity. Many American Christians appear to feel as if they have, somehow, attained their righteousness through their own, well, righteous ways. They forget their sinful nature and look down, with disdain, on others still caught in the deception of sin and death. This is an unseen Christian thought that, unintentionally, sets up shop within hearts not attuned to God's righteousness.

How many, who call themselves Christians, are like the Pharisee, who invited Jesus into his home for dinner, but not into his heart as Lord? How many, who call themselves Christians, are like this Pharisee, who clearly believed it was **he,** who should have been honored by Jesus? He must have felt that after he had been so inclined to invite Jesus to dinner, it was **Jesus**, who needed to be thankful for being allowed in his home.

I read a sign on a church recently that read, **Believe in Jesus, because He believes in you!** What? Are we now the saviors, and Jesus the sinner? There is even a song where a lady sings, **But if you (Jesus) believe in me, that changes everything.**

Here is a **late breaking News Flash**. Jesus did not suffer, being nailed to a tree and die, after being mocked and scourged, because He believed in you, **OR** me. He did it, because He loves you and me. He, being God, clearly knows better than to believe in us! He believes in Himself, and in His own power to save, and heal, and change lives. Jesus doesn't **believe in us,** as though He needed to believe in anything but Himself! Or, that He sat around looking, watching everyone, thinking, **You Know, I trust that Girl. I think I really believe in her!**

Jesus offered Himself as a sacrifice for our sins. He alone, paid the ransom of death, that we might be free and have life,

> *When He had, by Himself, purged our sins, sat down on the right hand of the majesty on high.*
> *Hebrews 1:3*

And because He offered Himself in our place, to suffer and die in our place, we can trust and believe in Him.

We were the corrupt, under sentence of death. Jesus stepped into the courtroom and declared, **Your Honor, I accept the guilt, and will accept the sentence of the court for the guilty.**

Because He did, we can trust and believe in *Him*.

> *Be afflicted and mourn, and weep:*
> *Let your laughter be turned to mourning,*
> *And your joy to heaviness.*
> *Humble yourselves in the sight of the Lord,*
> *And He shall lift you up.*
> *James 4: 8, 9, 10*

This woman, who washed Jesus' feet, was not thanking Him for believing in *her. **She was worshiping Him, and desiring His love, and His forgiveness. She was humbling herself, and believing in Him.***

Believe in Jesus because *He believes in you? No!*

Believe in Jesus, because there is no other way to life! Jesus said,

I am the resurrection and the life. He that believeth in me, though he were dead, yet shall he live. And whosoever liveth and believeth in me, shall never die. Believeth thou this? **John 11:25 & 26**

Believe in Jesus, because **No other name** can save!

> *Look unto me and be ye saved all the ends of the earth*
> *For I alone am God,*
> *And there is none else.*

> *Neither is there salvation in any other. For there is no other name under heaven Given among men,*
> *Whereby we must be saved.*
> *Acts 4: 12*

> *For there is ONE God*
> *And ONE mediator between God and man,*
> *The man Christ Jesus*
> *Who gave Himself a ransom for all*
> *To be testified of in due time.*
> *Timothy2: 5 & 6*

If you understand nothing else, **do not get this one fact of Truth wrong.** You **DO NOT** believe in Jesus, because you think, **He believes in you!**

Jesus loves you beyond all imagination, and human comprehension. He proved His love, by offering Himself as your ransom on a cross, bearing your sins! That is why you should believe in Him. Believe in Jesus for your own salvation and forgiveness of sins.

Believe in Jesus, because **there is NO other name under Heaven, given among men, whereby we must be saved.**

Do NOT, however, walk in the elation of your own self-worth, as the Pharisee did when he invited Jesus into his home. He had hoped his invitation would end with Jesus believing in him. The Pharisee wanted Jesus to see how wonderful and righteous the Pharisee was. However, the Pharisee was neither righteous nor wonderful. The Pharisee wore the robe of Self Pride, part of Satan's wardrobe.

Who, in this story, received forgiveness for sins, **for many sins?** It was the sinful woman, who fell at the feet of Jesus. The Pharisee, who glowed in the flickering neon lights of sin, was left to his hopeless intentions and empty self-worth.

The woman was seeking God's love and mercy. The Pharisee was seeking God's approval and worship.

Because she fell at His feet, wanting mercy, Jesus gave one woman mercy and love.

And now let us flip back to the present, w**here we were sharing a moment of the past!**

On an exit ramp, he stood, homeless, in worn clothes, asking for help, praising God and kissing a bible! The Lord moved my heart. When it was my turn, I handed him a couple of dollars.

Then, as I turned and pulled away from the exit, and onto a city street, the hand of the Lord would not let me go. I pulled over and got out a twenty.

I walked back to the man on the ramp, handing him the twenty. He was overwhelmed with gratitude, brimming with the love of Jesus.

I became embarrassed, as I bathed in the richness of his joy.

He told me his story of homelessness, about his life on the streets. Then the Lord intervened, and brought an old friend by. The friend had a home, and was willing to share it with him. The man would no longer wander the side streets of despair, but with hope refreshed, would celebrate the grace of God, in the daylight of a new beginning.

And is not this the Fast that I have chosen...
That when you see the poor cast out
That you bring them to your home?

When the exit ramp man saw the twenty he was handed, his joy exploded in a burst of laughter. He said that was all he needed. He had only been short twenty for a bus ticket north, and a waiting friend, with a home the friend was willing to share.

Praise Jesus, he said, kissing the bible. If Jesus had been there, no doubt, that as his tears fell, he would have been on the ground, kissing even the hem of Jesus' robe.

What revelry of heart! Jesus had given this man, a deeper and purer excitement, established in grace, than many Christians will feel in their lifetime. Especially those, who accept Jesus into their lives because they think, **He believes in them.** Or those, who belong to un-activated, **Christian Sleeper Cells.**

This man knew he was a sinner, but rejoiced in Jesus. Because he **believed in Jesus, he was over-flowing with a heart of grateful thanks to his Savoir.** And…he was not ashamed for the whole wide world to see his tears of joy and public display of unabashed worship.

Walking back to my car, I felt as if I too had caught this man's strange, deeply held reverence and awe for a Savior, who hears the humble, and loves the poor.

I drove my Hondo Condo past the exit ramp as I left and glanced over, but no one was there. I looked to my right and to my left. My eyes searched up the street and down. The man I had met was nowhere to be seen! It had only taken a couple of minutes after I left the man to reach my vehicle and drive by. However, in that short time, the man had disappeared!

The man at **In And Out Burger**, had packed his bag with burger upon burger and fries galore, wanting more…ever more. He had an unending hunger that no one could satisfy. The exit ramp man, receiving what he needed, had departed. With praise in his heart, flowing forth in joy, he had been given enough, was satisfied, and headed out on his journey.

And as I drove by where he had once stood, only a moment before, the exit ramp man, receiving what he needed… **had vanished!** Maybe he was really a…no, couldn't be.

One night, a worried little girl offered a prayer of want to the Lord. A difficult test was waiting for her at school the next day, and she simply never did well on tests.

Test day arrived, and the child studiously focused on each question, with a determined effort to get it right. When the test was over and graded, she exceeded the teacher's expectations by far. Her teacher, familiar with the small child's sub-par test history, inquired how the girl could score so highly. The young child had no hesitation in revealing for the teacher the secret of her success. **By the Grace of God,** she replied.

The little girl...and her family, were never seen again.

This is the fear that hangs in the air, which North Korean's breathe daily. A nightmarish dream, ready to swallow them up for uttering one wrong word.

North Korea could be called a kingdom of darkness. It devours its own citizens, imprisoning and starving the innocents. It is a country that mandates a religion they refer to as ***Juche*** (***Self Reliance***) upon its helpless citizens.

That alone could produce great roars of laughter, if it were not so terribly and deathly tragic. North Korea has failed to be self sufficient for years. That is why they play the game of death. Their game is to use fear, extorting other countries into supplying the food and the necessities needed for life. It is unable to supply its' own. And so, when the dinner bell rings, they threaten a nuclear holocaust, if they are not fed.

In North Korea, the citizens walk in the shadow of a leader, who proclaims himself, ***Divine.*** Every family dutifully hangs a photograph (***in a place of prominence***) of the ***Divine Leader*** in their home.

The current leader's father was also ***Divine***. At least he was ***Divine,*** until he died. After his death, his son, apparently, inherited his dead father's divinity. I assume that this means that their divinity lasts only until death. They have not yet developed the power to rise from the grave.

One evening, I watched a TV. Special where an American eye surgeon traveled to North Korea on a mercy mission. He performed hundreds of surgeries so North Koreans with damaged eyesight could see. When his mission was completed, the patients were paraded to a makeshift stage with microphones and cameras. One by one, the patients' eye bandages were removed. Needless to say, they were all overjoyed that they could see! Each patient then robotically praised their Divine Leader for their new vision.

The eye surgeon was not publicly thanked. In the background, looming ominously, hung the photograph of, **The Divine One.** Believing in anyone other than Mr. Divine leader himself, subjects one to torture, imprisonment, loss of everything they own and can even lead to death.

On the lowest rung of the women's prison ladder in North Korea are those who profess a love for Jesus. During assembly, the Christian women are forced to keep their heads bowed. The authorities do not want to afford them the luxury of glancing to the Heavens in hope. The authorities wish to deny them the opportunity to glimpse the return of Jesus.

The authorities must not have read Revelations 1: 7.

> *Behold He commeth with the clouds;*
> *And EVERY EYE SHALL SEE HIM,*
> *They also which pierced him:*
> *And ALL kindreds of the earth shall wail because of Him.*
> *Even so, Amen.*

Parents, who know and believe in Jesus, are cautious in when to share the news of Jesus with their children. Too early, and one of their children may innocently let slip, the word most feared by the throne of darkness which rules their country. That dreaded word they fear is...***Jesus Christ.***

At night, a satellite picture of North Korea will reveal the darkness of their desperation. You will fail to see the sprinkling of lights that decorate other countries. The dawn of day changes nothing, as darkness hangs heavy in the air, making each breath a weighted burden of caution.

Leading a life of piggish revelry, the Divine leader of North Korea, has delegated his citizens to the status of entertainers, there for his amusement and pleasure.

Here today...gone tomorrow, is a saying that speaks the truth of North Korea. Death, starvation, torture, and horrors unimaginable. The constant plague of fear crawls over the hearts and minds of its citizens, like evil creatures, lurking in the cracks and crevices of every thought. That is why a little girl's voice, speaking of God's grace, blinded the authorities with terror. In their terror, they vainly tried to erase the existence of a child, who believed, and her family.

What little girl? What family? Never heard of them.

They have not heard of the other 200,000 or so, who have also vanished from public view, no doubt. Two Hundred Thousand citizen outcasts languish in prison camps or cold freezing cells because they chose Jesus over Juche.

North Korea's shame is openly displayed in the empty lives of its beggar children. These abandoned children are left to roam the land at will, without food, clothing, or care. They fight for scraps of food, or a single crust, that may be dropped or discarded by another. Their wanderings highlight the filth, corruption, and evil heart of shamelessness, carried about by those who rule.

Yet, in their dismal plight, the children are allowed their freedom of struggle for survival to stumble through alleys and side streets. The dirty, unwanted children are given the freedom to stagger in starvation, as long as they refrain from uttering one word, one name.

Do they dare? Should their lips let utter the name of hope, in the land where evil strolls freely, in ruling robes of wickedness?

No! They dare not open their mouths, to say the name of Jesus Christ, or proclaim the grace of God.

One little girl did. Afterwards, she and her family disappeared. They were never heard from again.

Can silence now celebrate a victory? Have the magicians, once more, performed the ultimate vanishing act? With the power of a nation at their disposal, have the wizards of North Korea produced a secret disappearing potion, to *poof* the lovers of Jesus into the unknown? If their ultimate magic show is really a success, then why has the little girl reappeared, here and now?

North Korea will never turn out the light of God, or keep quiet little girls, who proclaim God's Grace. The magicians of hate will be exposed for who they really are. Their shame and filth will not be washed away, when they see the lovers of Jesus returning in glory. Their day of destiny will be arriving soon, and it is not the destiny of Juche. It is the destiny of Jesus Christ.

A young child's voice shames North Korea's cowardly leaders, who fear a name and a little girl's faith.

The little girl **lived in Victory Eternal** *She walked in the Light of God's Greatness*, and that **Light *is* Jesus Christ**, no matter how many leaders, or people in Power, wish it were not.

Ye are the light of the world.
A city that is built on a hill cannot be hid.
Neither do men light a candle and put it under a bushel But on a candle stick;
And it giveth light to all that are in the house.
Let your light so shine before men.
Matthew 5: 14, 15, 16

One little girl gave thanks, She let her light shine.

Her song?!!

This little light of mine,
I'm gonna let it shine!
This little light of mine,
I'm gonna let it shine,
Let it shine,
All the time,
Let it shine!

Then.......
She vanished.

How does your
Light shine?

8

Breath of Prayer
Faith in Action

In the cool of the evening, on the darkest night of his life, a young man fell on his face before his father. His anguished soul cried out in fear, as tears flooded his eyes, and blood seeped from the pores of his skin.

Tomorrow he would be executed. Executed for a hideous, horrid assortment of crimes from murder, rape, and robbery, to a **hall of horrors list** that exceeded the worst tormented **nightmares become real.** There was no crime immune from this young man's charges. It had therefore, been decreed, that he should receive the death penalty. The sentence would be carried out the next day.

And so... here he lay, in the fullness of fear, crying out to his father, who was world renowned and able to stop the execution on his own authority. The intimate intensity of the moment, was flooded with the closeness of two...as one. The cries of a young man, who would face the vilest abuse and execution... before his father. His father's love, for his one son, filled the Heavens with brightness... even as the grip of heaviness and sorrow filled the farthest reaches of his own being. The Father knew, in certainty that justice must prevail. These crimes could not go unpunished. And as he held the tears, the fears and the supplications of his son, in cherished depths of love, he knew there was no other course to follow. The course of condemnation for crimes committed. His son's sentence of death could not be commuted.

How could the father's heart not break, as the pleas of his only son reached up to touch, with tender softness and want? Who could ever come close to knowing, or understanding, the far reaches of feeling that swirled within his being, at this moment in time? Who on Earth, could glimpse into this father's heart, as he heard his only son's pleas, but knew he must be resolute? All crimes must be paid in full. Death was the only choice. The conviction of death must stand.

But the father... looking upon his only son... in his sons darkest moment... was not without the ache of love. And in this naked moment of bare feelings, raw and unclothed, between father and son, they shared the intimacy of perfection. *T*ogether, they shared the **perfection and reflection of beauty, in pure eternal breath of prayer.**

An innocent young man, who feared the suffering to come, but had the courage and power to overcome.

An innocent young man, who despised the wardrobe of shame he would wear, but gracefully removed his own Royal Robe of Righteousness, and set it aside for another, to wear the shame of all.

A son, who allowed himself to be bound by the chains of death, so his father could free the guilty from bondage.

A young man, who was to be King, offering Himself up for the Kingdom.

In this barest moment of private intimacy, between Father and Son, the Son's honesty of the moment, reflected the Majesty of His Offering. A Royal Offering of Sacrifice, so the guilty could go free.

On this night, a young Son's pleas were offered, in honest, humble prayer of fear, in obedient devotion, to his loving Father. The passions felt, flooded the plains of Heaven, as the Eternal Spirit prepared for a sacrifice, **ordained before the foundation of the world.**

He was in the world, the world was made by Him...
BUT tomorrow the world would execute Him.
He went unto His own...
But the next day, His own would ask for that execution.

Tomorrow, a Father would watch, but not stop or hold back, the suffering and shame awaiting... *His only begotten Son.*

For God so loved the world that he gave his only begotten Son that whosoever believeth in him should not perish but have ever lasting life. For God sent not his Son into the world to condemn the world but that the world through him might be saved. They that believe are saved. But they that believe not, are condemned already because they have not believed in the name of the only begotten Son of God. John 3 : 16 & 17

And here in a garden...*a tender plant...a root out of dry ground* ...wept alone, before the Gardener of Love. *Isaiah 53*

The perfection and reflection
Of beauty,
In pure Eternal Breath of Prayer.

Epilogue: (To a new beginning) Hearing His prayer, an angel was sent to strengthen Jesus in His moment alone. Courage then filled His heart, as He rose from His third prayer to meet those, who wished His death. Jesus traveled the dirt road on His way to suffering and death on a cross. But afterwards...He rose from death and walked the Earth for 40 days in victory. He gave hope to many and then...ascended into heaven to become hope.

It was a day of bright beauty, with the Risen Lord, Jesus Christ, shinning in their midst, teaching and sharing with the disciples. And as their eyes beheld their Savior, He was lifted up into Heaven...into a cloud that received Him. And then... He vanished.

After He vanished, the eyes of His disciples strained to follow his disappearance into the Heavens, as if their eyes could capture His destination…if only they could just stare hard enough…long enough.

While transfixed on the cloud on high, *two men in white apparel stood by. Ye men of Galilee, why stand ye gazing up into heaven? This same Jesus which is taken from you into heaven, shall so come, in like manner, as ye have seen Him go into heaven. Acts 1: 10 & 11*

Jesus had prayed with **an honest heart** of fear, but accepted His Father's will, and walked **in an open heart of courage** and of love.

After ascending into Heaven, to sit on the right hand of Majesty, a new, eternal, priestly order was established with Christ as the High Priest. Jesus now reigns from this throne of grace, **on your behalf.**

But this man, because he continueth ever, hath an unchangeable priesthood. Wherefore he is able to save them to the uttermost that come to God by Him, seeing he ever liveth to make intercession for them. Hebrews 7: 24 & 25

For Christ is not entered into the holy places made with hands, which are shadows of the true, but into heaven itself, now to appear in the presence of God for us: Hebrews 9: 24

And when you accepted Jesus into your heart by faith, you were ordained into this Order.

Ye also, as lively stones, are built up a spiritual house, a holy priesthood, to offer up spiritual sacrifices, acceptable to God by Jesus Christ. I Peter 2: 5

As a Priest of an Eternal Order, you are now allowed entrance into the holiest of holies, into the very presence of God, Himself. When you are hurting, feel alone, discouraged, or in doubt, you have an open invitation to enter the royal chambers of grace.

For we have not an high priest which cannot be touched with the feeling of our infirmities; but was in all points tempted as we are, yet without sin. Therefore let us come boldly unto the throne of grace, that we may obtain mercy and find grace to help in our time of need. Hebrews 4: 15 & 16

And is this not still another treasure and wonderful surprise. In the **Amazing Grace...Race**, in the **High calling of God in Jesus Christ,** you have been given a personal invitation directly from God, to appear before Him when you are hurting. A nobody on Earth, you are accepted into the Royal Hall, and allowed to delight in God's very own presence.

As a Priest, who offers up spiritual sacrifices acceptable to God by Jesus Christ, you won't need a butcher's knife, or be required to set up a homemade altar. Jesus, using a wooden cross as His bed, gave the final blood offering, with His own body as the sacrifice.

The offerings of **Thanksgiving** and praise are the spiritual sacrifices acceptable to God. The Lord also desires us, as his priests, to offer prayers in earnest, for our brothers and sisters in Jesus.

Praying always with all prayer and supplication in the Spirit, and watching thereunto with all perseverance and supplication for all saints; Ephesians 6: 18

As a priest of God, in Jesus, we will also vanish one day, as Jesus did, into the clouds, into the riches of everlasting joy and beauty.

For the Lord Himself shall descend from heaven with a shout, with the voice of the archangel, and with the trump of God: and the dead in Christ shall rise first:

Then we which are alive and remain shall be caught up together with them in the clouds, to meet the Lord in the air: and so shall we ever be with the Lord.

Wherefore comfort one another with these words. Hebrews 4:16, 17, & 18.

With these wonderful assurances and hopes, added to our already vast collection, let us rejoice in the Lord, and offer the acceptable sacrifices that delight our God.

By Him (Jesus) therefore, let us offer the sacrifice of praise to God continually, that is, the fruit of our lips giving thanks to His name. Hebrews 13: 15

> Pray in reverence and with humble heart, To so great a
> One, who gave His own Son, Who shed His own blood,
> Who bore the shame,
> Who bound Himself in fear and pain, To die for love,
> To die for gain, Eternally Yours.

> *And...*
> *If it wasn't about you...*
> *Who did Jesus die for?*

For our **Faith In Action,** today, let us obey the word of God that calls us to...

> *Pray without ceasing.*
> *I Thessalonians 5:17*

Prayer is not an early morning, or late night activity, to be engaged in on your...*list of things to do.*

> *Pray without ceasing.*
> ... is our encouragement from the Lord.
> He is always ready to hear and listen.
> And it was Jesus, who wrote the book on prayer.

> *Who in the days of His flesh*
> *When He had offered up prayers and supplications*
> *With strong crying and tears*

> *Unto Him that was able to save Him from death*
> *And was heard in that He feared;*
>
> *Though He were a Son,*
> *Yet learned He obedience by the things which He suffered.*
>
> *And being made perfect,*
> *He became the author of Eternal Salvation*
> *Unto all them that obey Him.' Hebrews 5: 7, 8, 9*

The secret beauty of prayer, is revealed when *one's fear is entrusted to another's care*. Entrusting your fears to the Lord, is a sign of a heart crying out in honesty, obeying the word that encourages us to cast our cares before the throne of God.

Humble yourself therefore under the mighty hand of God, that He may exalt you in due time: Casting all your care upon Him; for he careth for you. I Peter 5: 6 & 7

As we fall on our knees before God, with an honest heart filled with truth, He can encourage and strengthen us.

> *Be strong and of a good courage*
> *Fear not neither be afraid For the Lord thy God It is He*
> *who doeth go with you*
> *And he will not fail or forsake thee.*
> *Deuteronomy 31:6*

With your cares in the hands of God, your hands will become free to handle the burdens of others. Feeling His touch, you can touch another, **in Deed, in Truth.**

With your hands free...you are free.

And In this freedom, you can now begin to lead others to the same. You can fulfill the **Fast** the Lord has chosen, during your **Amazing Grace... Race** in the **High calling of God in Christ Jesus.**

> *Is not this the Fast that I have chosen…*
> *That you undo heavy burdens,*
> *That you let the oppressed go free…*

In addition, as sergeant of a vital supply line to your brothers and sisters in Christ, and now, as the royal army chaplain, know that prayer should be at the center of your strategic planning within your **area**. In prayerful love of heart, we can raise up our family in prayer those on the front lines where the fierceness of the battle rages hot. In and through prayer, we ***can do all things through Christ, which strengthens*** us. Philippians 4:13

Breath of Prayer

Today's Breath of Prayer, Faith in Action, is to…*Pray without ceasing,* all day, and in each moment of the day. In Every pause and, in every action…*Prayer.*

Pray…

> *For a little girl and her family who vanished*
> *For two hundred thousand who live in non-existence*
> *For brothers and sisters who are made to Vanish…*
> *Into dark prison cells…*
> *Cold prison camps…*
> *Into unmarked graves.*

The world thinks they have hidden them well, in the thick darkness of their evil, barren, dungeons and prisons.

They have not.

They are not hidden from God

> *Can any hide himself in secret places that I shall not see him?*
> *Saith the Lord.*
> *Do not I fill heaven and earth? Saith the Lord.*
> *Jeremiah 23: 24*

And in *Deed and in Truth*, as His Spirit leads, in prayerful walk and talk, touch another who is near and…one who is afar.

In everything… prayer. By everything… prayer.

Be careful for nothing; but in everything, by prayer and supplication with thanksgiving let your requests be made known unto God. And the peace of God, which passeth all understanding, shall keep your hearts and minds through Christ Jesus. Philippians 4: 6 & 7

Heavenly Father, Thank you for sharing the depths of your love, that we might know the majesty of your grace. Thank you for forgiveness. I do, here and now, entrust all of my fears to you. I do trust you with them. Please help me walk in courage. Lead me in truth, and guide my every step in your righteousness.

I lift up to you all my Christian brothers and sisters, who suffer in distant lands. Please sustain and strengthen them.

Assure their hearts, Lord, that they have not been forgotten.

And when your children are forced to lay their heads on hardened cell floors, let grace be their pillow.

Today, lead me in your Spirit, and help me touch one who is near… and one who is afar. Allow me to be a candle that flickers with hope, that I may walk in the Light of God's Greatness.

And Heavenly Father, thank you for sharing so personal and intimate a moment of tender trust, between you and your Son, in a garden, so many years ago. Thank you, O Mighty God!

In Jesus name, Amen.

With your prayer, please note the following web sites… *Compass Direct & Open Door* . These sites have comprehensive coverage of what your family in Jesus Christ endures around the world. After you visit these sites, please become a subscriber to the Compass Direct news service when you are able and ready. Their subscription rate is only $25.00 per year, and their service, as a witness of the suffering of the Family of Christ, is a part of God's desire that His children **NOT** be forgotten.

Can the Lord hear the prayer of a Nobody? You were chosen in grace, before the foundation of the world! Your adoption papers, certifying your legal status as a member of a royal family, were filed in the courts of Heaven! He has ordained you as a priest in a royal priesthood! Does a father hear his child?

I love the Lord, because He hath heard my voice and my supplications.

Because He hath inclined His ear unto me, therefore will I call upon Him as long as I live. Psalm 116:1 & 2

By spending the day in prayer...you will have taken the Breath of Prayer. May the Peace of God, in Jesus Christ be with you.

In a garden...*a tender plant...a root out of dry ground* ...wept alone, before the Gardner of Grace.

The perfection and reflection
Of beauty,
In pure, Eternal Breath of Prayer.

In North Korea, darkness trembled when a little girl's voice gave praise to God.

A little light...
... to chase the shadows of night.

How does your light shine?

9

Brothers
Breath of Brotherhood

For ye sometimes darkness But now are ye light in the Lord Walk as children of Light Ephesians 5: 8

Early morning, before the sun could rise up over the horizon, was one of my most enjoyable moments of solitude in life, as one of the homeless. A sense of freedom, hope, and endless possibilities paraded themselves along the avenues of my mind. Although, by the end of the day, most of the parade vanished in disappointments and vague happenings, each morning was still alive in hope.

For we are saved by Hope:
But hope that is seen is not hope:
For what a man seeth, why does he yet hope for?
But if we hope for that we see not,
Then do we with patience wait for it.
Romans 8: 24 & 25

WALKING IN THE LIGHT OF GOD'S GREATNESS

On one morning, as I exited my one bedroom, black Honda Civic, I spotted a man in an old truck parked next to me. He was sitting in his truck reading a bible. Isn't it great that bibles are so easy to distinguish from all other books?

A little joy, like an electric jolt, surged through me. **Here was another believer!**

Reaching into my home, I emerged with a sweet roll and a drink. I tapped on his truck, beckoning him to come out. He raised his head and, with a smile of brotherhood, he stepped out.

He was Hispanic, I, a Gringo, and neither of us could speak nor understand each other's language. I pointed to his bible and then myself, wanting to let him know that I too believed in Jesus. He smiled more.

We embraced as Christian Brothers, a hug of friendship. I offered him what I had a sweet roll and a drink. What did he do? He went into his truck and came out with several oranges that he wanted me to take.

We couldn't talk, but stood in the joy of fellowship, knowing we both belonged to the same family of God. I knew that he too believed in Jesus as his Lord and Savior, and read the bible. He started out his day reading scripture. That underlined where he placed his trust.

He may have had a wife and children somewhere, and could have been here trying to work to help support his family. He was traveling alone, but not…for he put his trust in the Lord.

His truck was old and weary, but his faith was refreshing and clean. And for a moment…we were brothers, standing in front of each other, in the joy of the Lord. There were no words, only God's grace. That was enough.

For where two or three of you are gathered together in my name, there I am in the midst of you. Matthew 18: 20

We were the living, breathing family of Jesus Christ, in Him, and He in us, as one.

There is one body, and One Spirit,
Even as ye are called in One hope of your calling;
One Lord, One faith, One baptism,
One God and Father of all, who is above all,
And through all, and in you all.
But unto every one of us is given grace According to the measure of the gift of Christ.
Wherefore he saith, When he ascended up on high,
He led captivity captive,
And gave gifts unto men.
Ephesians 4: 4 through 8

I love the line that declares **He led captivity, captive,**

because He did! And when He did, He set us free!

There are graduates of theology that recite a different version of scripture than what I have used here. The scripture in this book is based on the King James translation. I believe the King James translation was inspired by God through the writers He used to complete it. For me, the words within reflect a majestic sense of beauty and power, blended together smoothly as no other book could possibly hope to achieve. Today, with so many variations and translations, it is wise to exercise caution when deciding which one you adopt as God's Word. Many groups now edit and print their own version of scripture to fit the doctrines they desire. Scripture was not given to mirror our beliefs, but to give us a new life in truth.

Every word of God is pure, as silver tired in the furnace of the earth, purified seven times.

How can man so casually drop and add words to God's scripture to please himself?

In addition, too often these days, it appears that Bible writers feel the need to use many select Greek words scattered in their scriptural writings to show their own mastery of truth. They then use a half a page, or whole page, explaining what their various Greek words mean, so others will flow with their ideas.

If you are willing to search around, you will inevitably find another theology graduate that will use the same Greek words and write another half page, or even several pages, explaining why they don't really mean what the previous author claimed they meant.

A little bit like President Clinton stating, *it depends on what the meaning of IS, is.*

At times, it may feel as though studying the Bible requires a PhD in Greek literature. *I know Greek, Therefore, I am.*

And what theology did my Christian Hispanic brother and I discuss that morning at the rest stop? Well, we didn't understand any Greek…or Latin…or Hebrew…so we just didn't try to explain the meaning of, *IS*.

It is a good thing that the heart be established with grace and not with meats which have not profited them which have been occupied therewith. Hebrews 13: 9

Two homeless men, who could not speak each other's language, in fellowship, in one space in time, as the world spun by, not caring or sharing our moment in Christ.

Two of us and Jesus. Just Jesus.

Their morning began with the clanging of the bars, as guards proceeded down the prison hallways, to rouse and awaken the inmates. The prisoners, their bones and muscles aching from a restless night, opened their eyes, one by one. It was a new day, but they would not see the sun. The only rising they would observe, was each other, as they were forced to get up and prepare for another day of tortuous labor and abuse.

As their shuffling and worn bodies started to activate, one inmate refused. **This is the Lord's Day, and I cannot work today,** he would tell the guards.

The guards could not believe their ears. Inmates did not tell them what they would, or would not do. However, this man, a man they called **the Preacher**, was insistent. He would not work today.

His reward was a beating and solitude.

Once, this man had been a Youth Minister with an outreach program. He had enjoyed reaching the youth with the message of Jesus, and encouraged them to be courageous.

He once had a beautiful wife and children.

Then he was arrested. He lived in Cuba, as the communists took over. Once in power, the new rulers decided there was no room for the love of Jesus in their country. That is always a central theme of Communism, no Christianity, and no love of Jesus!

After his arrest, the youth minister was tortured with unbearable cruelty, but he would not renounce his faith.

The youth minister's church renounced him. They said they didn't want to hurt their ministry by associating with him. They knew he would understand.

But this man...He could not renounce his faith.

His wife renounced him. She said she could not bear being alone, while he wasted away in prison. She divorced him and married a Communist.

But this man...this servant of Jesus...he could no more renounce his faith in Jesus, then he could cut out his own heart and hand it over to those who beat him, and tortured him.

For twenty years, this man would not renounce his faith. He lived in Christ within the dark prisons of Cuba, daily witnessing the murder and torture of others that also believed. A mind could scarcely imagine the horrors created by the evil that walked those prison halls in the form of men, sent to break and destroy the beating heart of Christ.

This man, who was deserted by everyone he believed had loved him, was abandoned by the church he had once served. Deserted by the half of his heart where stars of love shined bright... shined that is, until his arrest and subsequent extended stay in Castro's home for the hated. That was when she decided she could not wait, said she could no longer be his wife.

This man said that after the beatings, the torture, and the rejection; that in the dark prison cells of his new home, there were no longer any Catholics, Baptists, Methodists, or Seventh Day Adventists. There was only Jesus Christ. Just Jesus and His love.

In tortured moments, where screams the pain...just Jesus

Where shadows lurk, with love disdained...just Jesus

With horrors unleashed for evil gain...just Jesus

In darkened cell, with tears wet stain...just Jesus

For twenty years, he endured the darkened cells of Cuba's prisons. Those, who were entrusted to persecute prisoners guilty of loving Jesus, were unable to extinguish his faith. **The Preacher** became a source of comfort and strength to his brothers in Christ, imprisoned and beaten for love. He became a shining light to prisoners, who did not know the love of Christ, leading many to a saving faith of freedom, which the Cuban Communists could not imprison.

His hand and his heart, reached out daily to those around him, to draw them into the Light. Often, suffering beyond what words could justly describe, he went beyond himself, to ease the suffering of others.

When he was first arrested, he could have renounced his faith, and passed through the prison system without an extended stay. He could have walked free, and passed by the torture, beatings, and brutality that were waiting for him. He could have, but he did not. Because he did not, there are many who would feel the touch of God's grace, in the darkest reaches of hate's grasp.

In the darkness of a Communist prison system, where the guards were encouraged to crush the hope and darken the light of those, who believed in Jesus, they could not douse *his* Light. He shined bright and offered hope to those around him. And his theology? The story of a Savior, Jesus Christ, the Son of God, a Cross on a hill, a sacrifice for sins, and a resurrection from the dead. He taught Eternal Life in Christ Jesus. Even the Communists, who ruled, could not provide that guarantee within their utopia of death and murder.

He was a prisoner of man, a Light of God.

He Lived in Victory Eternal, and walked in the Light of God's greatness, moment by moment, in the majesty of his King.

In the nightmare of evil,
In the deepest horrors of a Cuban Prison,
One man offered hope and love.
He was...The Preacher.
His heart was established in grace.
His love? Just Jesus.

What is your heart established in?

9

Breath of Brotherhood
Faith in Action

One day, a lawyer asked Jesus, **Who is my neighbor?**

Jesus answered. A certain man went down from Jerusalem to Jericho, and fell among thieves, which stripped him of his raiment, and wounded him, and departed, leaving him half dead.

And so…he lay on the sidewalk, a pool of blood seeping from beneath his limp body. It was early morning, as many journeyed off to work, past the dying man. One took a picture. Perhaps he thought this man, breathing his last breaths of life, was famous.

And by chance, there came down a certain priest that way; and when he saw him, he passed by on the other side.

And likewise, a Levite, when he was at the place, came and looked on him, and passed by on the other side.

One by one, two by two, they paraded by in a walk of death, as he lay dying in a pool of ebbing life.

The dying man had been stabbed after trying to help a woman he never knew. The attacker got away. The woman did not stay around either. Thus, here he lay, on a city street in the early morning hours of a bright new day. Alone, in full view, as people rushed by, unfazed by another hopeless, helpless body on the sidewalk. The Breath of Death inhaled…exhaled… walking in the darkness of their own dimly lighted vision.

But a certain Samaritan, as he journeyed, came where he was: and when he saw him had compassion on him, And went to him and bound up his wounds, pouring in oil and wine, and set him on his own beast, and brought him to an inn, and took care of him.

And so… as the Samaritan came by **this** dying man…oops! Sorry. There is no Samaritan in this story. Unfortunately for this man, he was no where near Jerusalem or Jericho. There was no traveling Samaritan prepared to bind up his wounds. This man, laying face down in the concrete arms of death, was only in the Bronx. Whoever heard of a Samaritan riding a beast in the Bronx?

Those in the Bronx, who passed by, did not care to stop. **But we didn't even know him! We didn't let him die on purpose!** It was the shoes. The shoes they wore, walked them past the body of a dying man they did not know. He was all alone, lying in his own blood, on a city sidewalk full of passersby…***passing by***. After all, isn't that what passersby are supposed to do? That is why they are called, ***Passersby!***

Hereby perceive we the love of God, because He laid down His life for us: and we ought to lay down our lives for the brethren. I John 3: 16

One person **did** come close to laying down their life for the dying man. This individual bent down. That could be considered **close** to lying down, couldn't it? The individual bent down to roll the body over enough to see the ever growing river of red. That counted for something, certainly. No one else rolled over the body to see the blood.

And by they walked, in Breath of Death, hearts established in the coldness of the night, as a man's life slowly seeped from his body… a puddle of red beneath him.

People, who did not have the opportunity to pass by the man dying atop the pavement, that early morning, claimed outrage. They were outraged that everyone had passed by the body on the sidewalk. However, how many of them had passed by the body before a knife had been plunged into it? While the man was alive, how many of the outraged, had been **Passersby?**

How many of the outraged had passed him by, before the knife had sliced through his flesh, cutting short his life. How many of the living dead, had offered him a hand without a knife? Perhaps their hands were too cold to offer. Death does that to you. It lowers your body temperature, and your flesh becomes cold. How many, who did not pass by the man in his death, one morning, passed by the man, in their life of death… the day before?

But whoso hath this world's good, and seeth his brother have need, and shutteth up his bowels of compassion from him, how dwelleth the love of God in him? I John 3: 17

How many people had laid down their lives for this dying man before he was…well, before he was face down in his own blood?

Distant family members, and people who knew him, talked about his heroism, and saying that he was just a great guy trying to make it. He was such a **great guy**, that he ended up walking the streets of Brooklyn homeless and alone. He was so well liked by all, that he had no place to stay.

One woman may be alive because he walked the streets that day. I am certain that she also thinks that he is a nice guy, **or was**… until her attacker carved out the man's life for stepping into hers. She probably gives thanks each day now, **Thank you God for the homeless, who are willing to die for others at 5 A.M. on any given morning.**

In the end, he walked the streets as he died, alone. However, at least now everyone likes him! No one can say enough well about him. **Yea, he was sure a great guy! He was a hero!** And off to work… until another greeting of death wakes us, in our early morning walk. Do not worry though, we will not fail with words when the next body drops. Having a vast vocabulary and on-line thesauruses at the ready, we will not be speechless. We love to praise the dead. Just don't bother us with the living.

And now as the **Passersby** pass by, they probably talk often about the one they passed by…who is now dead.

A hero! He was a hero!

Again, a new commandment I write unto you, which thing is true in Him and in you: because the darkness is past and the true light now shineth.

He that saith he is in the light, and hateth his brother, is in darkness even until now. He that loveth his brother abideth in the light, and there is none occasion of stumbling in him.

But he that hateth his brother is in darkness, and walketh in darkness, and knoweth not whither he goeth, because the darkness hath blinded his eyes.

Hey, we didn't hate him. We didn't even know him. *Did you?*

In the darkened light of an early morning, for over an hour, **Passersby** stumbled, unable to see their way…or the blood, beneath the shadow of death that lingered on a city sidewalk. They were blinded by the hardness of cold hearts that told them he was not in their **area.** He was not **their** neighbor. He was not their brother.

What is the creed of **Passersby,** when possible? Always pass by a body **before** the body falls in a crumpled heap upon a city sidewalk. Pass by before the body is stabbed and bleeding and falls in death of early light. This way nobody will blame you for anything. It is **not** your fault!

In the last days…because iniquity shall increase, the love of many shall wax cold. The words of Jesus come to life…or to death… as feet walk by dying bodies that litter the streets of life. *Cold, waxy candles, snuffed out by hardened thoughts.*

An unlit candle, sitting in a darkened room, gives light to no one. It is no more than a useless shape of wax, a lump of paraffin. It gives no light…no warmth…and does not shine. It is just cold wax, a darkened shape of silent death.

Is your life a darkened shape of silent death?

Are you a **Passer-by?**

Does your love, **wax cold?**

Jesus desired to melt the hearts of wax… and began one day with his own.

I am poured out like water,
And all my bones are out of joint:
My heart is like wax;
It is melted in the depths of my being.
Psalms 22: 14

With his heart melted, he poured it out into the souls of those who call on His name. Now, the receivers of His Spirit, can shape and mold the soft wax into candles of light. A little light…**to chase the shadows of night.**

Ye are the light of the world. A city that is built on a hill cannot be hid. Neither do men light a candle, and put it under a bushel, But on a candle stick; And it giveth light unto all that are in the house. Let your light so shine before men that they may see your good works and glorify your father which is in Heaven. Matthew 5: 14, 15, 16

And this *is your calling.* Jesus did not call you to be a **Passerby**. You are not a glass of evolutionary spilt milk, an accident of a big bang.

Ooops, here I am. That's crazy! How'd that happen?

Oh, someone knocked over a glass, and didn't clean up the mess. A Knocked over glass…some spilt milk…and here you are! Just an accident that no one bothered to clean up. Another Passerby, on the great universal evolutionary journey to nowhere!

Wow.!

Has this been your life? Are you simply an extension of a pointless, ongoing selection process, controlled by a mysterious power, worshiped in the realms of adult fairy tales? You are no more than one purposeless part of the great scientific **Ooops Theory!**

This is now your life? A Fairy Tale fabricated in the foolishness of adult childish fantasies. An **Ooops Theory** others dub intellectionalism, to help their made up stories sound brilliant.

Ooops, there you are. Ooops, here I am. The great scientific imagination on the prowl! How did that occur? Oh, it's all covered in the magnificent, **Eternal Theory of Ooops.**

Whatever we do not know can be conjured up through scientific witchcraft and filed away in the **Ooops** file. *It just all happened one day. You know? Yea, sounds scientific to me.*

And…based on the wonderful, mind boggling **Ooops Theory**…I have no brother. Accidents walking around as meaningless passersby have no responsibilities, especially not to other accidents lying upside down atop a pool of blood. Why stop to clean up an accident, a glass of spilt blood, when *you* did not spill it? It is not your fault.

Fortunately, God does not operate on an **Ooops Theory**. God has an eternal purpose for you rooted in Grace, which can reach into every single moment you are alive. Each moment is a potential moment of majesty, with results that can span the ages of endless time. These purposes may seem good, or may appear bad, but they are, no doubt, still eternal.

Jesus displayed this eternal grace when He walked among us. He did not pass us by. He gave ***Himself* as the offering...*that he might redeem us from all iniquity and purify unto himself a peculiar people, zealous of good works. Titus 2: 14***

These are planned works, not ***Random Acts of Kindness.*** God is not a God of randomness. He has works purposely set for you to complete, as He shapes you into the very image of His own Son. And He had your whole life chartered out before you were even born.

For we are His workmanship, created in Christ Jesus unto good works, which God hath before ordained that we should walk in them. Ephesians 2: 10

For whom He did foreknow, He also did predestinate to be conformed to the image of His Son, that He might be the first of many brethren. Romans 8:29

You were chosen to be one of those brethren, as an active participant in grace, not a ***Passer-by.***

That is what our breathing has been all about... is all about. To teach the ***Breaths of Life,*** so you can have one. And in that life, breathe life into another. Let each moment be lived in the ***Majesty of a Moment,*** prepared by God, led by His Spirit.

This experience will not always be illuminated under rainbows or bright lights, so all may see, but in a private moment before the Lord, to touch another life, because he chose you to do so. This may be as simple as giving a glass of water to one who is thirsty or as great as stopping to be with a man lying on the sidewalk, bleeding to death. To stop the bleeding when you can, to give comfort when you cannot. To be there... ***not to pass by. To share Jesus, not keep silent.***

In this ***Breath of Brotherhood,*** within your ***area***, your care and touch can reflect God's grace. Whomever you meet could become your brother or sister. It is the needy and downcast, the unloved and the stranger, the

WALKING IN THE LIGHT OF GOD'S GREATNESS

lonely and the hurting. He has chosen them as worthy of your love. Jesus chose them, **just Jesus.**

If you have never met any of these people, perhaps it is time to move.

Today the Lord calls you to touch a wounded soul. Tomorrow, they will be face down on a sidewalk… bleeding to death.

For our **Faith in Action** in this **Breath of Brotherhood** you will be called to touch the life of one near, and one afar. **To touch one afar,** you are going to write a letter of encouragement to a brother, or sister, who is currently jailed in a foreign country because they love Jesus. And… you will write this letter in a language they can understand, **their own language**.

No, you are not going to have to learn to, **Write in Tongues**. And **No**, you will not be required to purchase a **Rosetta Stone Foreign Language** writing course.

Go to VOM's web site, **www.persecution.com** and follow the prompts for writing a letter to those imprisoned. They have a program where you can pick out selected phrases and scripture. When you do, VOM's program will translate the phrase or scripture into the native language of the person you are writing to!

A person in prison for Jesus, will thus get to read a wonderful letter of hope. If you are a Nobody **walking in the Light of God's Greatness,** here is a place the Lord will allow you to share kindness through encouragement. Your words will lift up, and light up, the heart of a prisoner far away.

If you, yourself, have suffered and received no kindness or encouragement, your pain can be used for good. Because you understand and know how they feel, the Lord may allow your words of understanding the **Power of Love. He will allow your words to carry The Breath of Brotherhood by the power of His grace.**

If you are homeless, you can go online at the Public Library, to write your letter. You, of all people, certainly understand rejection and despair.

You may need some change for the printout, as VOM's program will print your letter and an address to mail the letter. Libraries normally charge for printouts. The cost to mail a letter across the ocean averages around $2.00. A small fee for such a fantastic opportunity to touch a heart in the love of Jesus.

Please do this **TODAY, if you are able. AND** get that blanket off! Skip that TV Show for the night. Be the star of your own Realty Show, where **You** stand before the camera of the Lord, acting on behalf of your Christian brothers and sisters, even if it is only for one night. Turn off your TV for just an hour. It will not take longer. Can you spare thirty minutes for a sister or brother languishing in a prison cell for Jesus?

In your position as a **Sgt. in the Royal Army of Love**, it is good to inspire high moral at the front lines. Here is an opportunity. In your **Amazing Grace...Race**, this is a **Detour** that must be completed. As a member of God's family, write this much needed letter to one of your brothers and sisters, mother or fathers. In God's spiritual house, there is a room that needs a new light. Let it be yours, in the form of a letter. And Remember, we are on a **Fast** the Lord has chosen. Allow a prisoner of the Lord to feast on your encouragement.

Are you currently a member of a **Secret Christian Sleeper Cell?** Hopefully, by now, you will respond with a loud, **NO! I've been Activated!**

Put off the evening fun to get that blanket and mail it out. **That** will bring joy lasting beyond a moment on the town. The moment out will fade away into the dust of the past. **The blanket will fly into the future with you, like a magic carpet ride**. Your joy in the Lord will be eternal.

Write a letter to one of the Lord's prisoners! Your family longs to hear from you.

Your **Faith In Action** for one **Near** is this...to ask the Lord to open your eyes for one day, so that you can see another's need. Ask Him to help you meet it. Ask the Lord to guide you to one, who is hurting, lonely, or in pain, alone and cast out. Ask the Lord to give you a heart of Light, and establish it in His Grace. Ask His Spirit to give you an awareness, to know when to stop and give comfort, instead of being a **Passerby.**

Touching one who is least, is touching Jesus, Himself. **...*for when you do it for the least of these my brethren, you do it for me.***

In our **Breath of Brotherhood,** let us ask for a heart and a spirit that can love and care. For since the Lord has promised us these gifts of goodness, let us make the request.

> *Create in me a clean heart, O God;*
> *And renew a right spirit within me.*
> *Psalm 51: 10*

Breath of Brotherhood

Let us now take our **Breath of Brotherhood.** Jesus said we are all brothers. I'll breathe to that!

Close your eyes for a moment in prayerful grace, with thanks to God and.............breathe.

Dear Heavenly Father,

Open my heart and eyes to see more clearly. Help me touch the lives of my brothers and sisters in need. Help me walk in the family of Jesus Christ, with a gentle and a kind heart.

I lift up my brothers and sisters to you in prayer. I cry out for those who walk the streets of America, without a home, or in another country in darkened prison cells. Please strengthen and comfort them. Lead me to those whom you have chosen for me to touch. Do not let me miss the Moment. Stop me on the walkway of this life you have blessed me with, that another may also taste the grace of God, in Jesus.

Guide me in your will, Oh Lord, and help me with the letter to the one afar you have chosen me to write. And as you prepare my way for the one near, the one you have chosen for me to touch, please prepare the moment, as well.

In Jesus' name, Amen.

Finally, be ye all of one mind, having compassion one of another, love as brethren, be pitiful, be courteous: Not rendering evil for evil, or railing for railing: but contrariwise blessing: knowing that ye are thereunto called, that ye should inherit a blessing. I Peter 3: 8 & 9

During the Cuban revolution, when revolutionaries decided that the name of Jesus would be overthrown, one man decided that he could not be a passerby. He counseled his students to be strong in the grace of Jesus. As a result, he was imprisoned and sentenced to 20 years, because he would not give up the grace of Jesus.

In prison, the authorities tried to beat and torture the grace of Jesus out of his heart. They failed. His wife pleaded for him to choose her grace over God's. She failed. His church stated that the grace in his heart was not as important as was their continued survival. But he knew the grace of God was more important...than survival.

He could have passed by, through life, by going along with all the other passersby, but no, he could not. He believed the love of Jesus was too important...to pass by.

And so, for twenty years, he shared the love of Jesus. He shared it with the beaten, the wounded, and the hardened prisoners of a Cuban prison system. Between beatings, he even shared the grace of Jesus with those who beat him.

His heart had been established by God. It had been established in grace. And the grace of God never passes by a man, dying in early morning light. The grace of God never passes by a man, before he falls to the pavement in a pool of blood. Passersby pass by, but Grace does not hide.

> He walked in the Light of God's Greatness,
> Touching the lives of other prisoners
> With compassion and grace.
> In grace,
> *He led his brothers,*
> To grace.

*It is a good thing that the heart be established in grace
And not with meats which have not profited them
which have been occupied therein.*

*In grace, with God's grace
His heart was established.*

And.......

What is your heart established in?

10

One Eyed Jack
Breath of Fire

But they that wait upon the Lord shall renew their strength; they shall mount up with wings of eagles. Isaiah 40:31.

He had been air lifted to the local hospital in Oceanside, California.

He had been my Rest Stop Area neighbor.

One night, after returning to my **Home Sweet Home** rest stop in Southern California, where I maintained my residence a black Honda I was told that One-Eyed Jack had been air lifted to the local hospital.

One-Eyed Jack had been drinking and smoking as usual, and, in an attempt to light another cigarette, had ignited the oxygen from his oxygen tank. The flames had scorched his face causing third degree burns. He was in bad shape.

One-Eyed Jack had been one of the regulars, who called this rest stop his home. I was one, too. We were the mobile homeless, because we all had cars. Every night, we would pull into the rest area, find a nice spot and spend the night. Over time, one could not help but become acquainted with the other regulars. They are a diverse group of old and young drug users, drinkers, and retiree's. Anyone who could not afford a place to live, but had a car, joined the caravan rest stop community.

What were the advantages? No salesman would call, and no utility bill needed to be paid every month.

My life of nightly rest stop layovers had not been an awful experience. I actually looked forward to them, and enjoyed each night, as I pulled into the rest area to locate the best spot where to park my rolling bedroom. After earning some money, I was fortunate enough to afford a portable propane grill and cooked out, turning each evening into a barbecue!

Each day, rising in the California cool of the early morning, was beautiful! I would start up the car and in no time, be off for a coffee on the beach; bible in one hand, a cup of coffee in the other.

These were special moments for me. Though homeless, the Lord allowed His goodness and peace to comfort me with these simple joys.

On almost any given evening, as I would pull into the rest stop, One-Eyed Jack could already be found leaning against his car, sipping a beer. He kept a well-stocked supply of suds chilled, in a cooler of his car. Other regulars, who knew he had a stash, would hit him up for a brew as their thirst grew. Once he drank a few, he could become quite mouthy. That is why, as he told me, he lost his eye.

A few years earlier, in San Diego, One-Eyed Jack had lived in a Gang infested neighborhood. During one of his drinking binges, he had over-indulged his talking points. Some members of the local hood, who were not amused, stabbed One-Eyed Jack in the eye. At the hospital, the doctors erred and the eye was lost. Instead of an eye, the hospital sent One-Eyed Jack home with a patch.

When telling me the story, One-Eyed Jack lifted the patch over his eye, and there wasn't one, just an empty socket. He let the patch fall back, and opened another can of beer.

Besides drinking and smoking, his lungs sucked up oxygen from a tank he kept next to him. Natural breathing was too difficult, so he needed the boost of an oxygen tank. He had a couple of stickers on his car. They read, **No smoking, oxygen in use.** I guess the day he ignited the oxygen coming out of the tank, he had forgotten to read the stickers. Drinking can do that for you, cause you to forget.

After hearing that One-Eyed Jack was flown to the hospital, I drove off to see him. He had no one else. This showed the state of his life… that I was his last friend, or, at least, the only one willing to go see him. I can safely assume that the other people, who enjoyed visiting with him at the Rest Stop, knew there would be no beer stashed under his hospital bed.

At the hospital, One-eyed Jack looked as though he was agonizing in the hands of death. I did not think he would live long. He was in and out of consciousness. I had brought him a Christian greeting card I had made, but he was not in any condition to read it. I set it on a table for him.

As I watched him sleep, I wondered what would be his fate. One time, when he woke for a brief moment, he stated that they (**The people at the hospital**) wanted to have him committed to a sanitarium-like facility, and he did not want to go. I would not have wanted to go either.

And here this tired old man lay. He was at life's end, his days almost spent, and his face told the story much better than words. A patch over an empty eye socket, on the same side of his face scorched by flames. The rest of his face, a crunched and crowded road map of lines, etched in a display of uncoordinated wrinkles, like an unplanned city where mayhem decided when and where to lay each road. What were his thoughts while alone? Did he watch re-runs of his life play out in the solitude of his nights? Having lost his much valued, immunity in drink, what feelings or thoughts were now free to dance upon the moments of his memory? What regrets or sorrows played with his reasoning?

Once when he woke, I asked him if he wanted me to pray **with** him. I told him God loved him. He said he did pray. I found this statement amazing, so I asked whom he prayed to. My question appeared to irritate him as he answered, *To God. Which God,* I persisted.

The only God, to Jesus, he voiced, his voice inflection underlining the fact that he did not want to discuss the matter further. I did not.

Before I left, One-Eyed Jack asked a favor of me. He wondered if I would mind retrieving his pants from the closet, and checking his pockets. He quietly stated he had some money in those pockets, and was fearful the nurses may have stolen his money. He did not trust the nurses. Could I check it out for him?

Uncomfortable, and uneasy, I went into his closet and withdrew his pants. In one pocket, my hand felt the bills folded up in a thick wad. I pulled out the bills. It was a roll of hundreds! I held the money up for him to see.

It's still here. They did not steal it. I tried to reassure him, but by this time, he had already drifted back off to sleep, leaving me with his hundreds gripped in my fist. I did not steal his money either. I put the money back in his pocket, replacing his pants in the closet.

Looking upon this burned and tired old man, I did not think he would survive, but I would never know. I said a silent prayer, left, and did not see him again.

He lived to drink, spoke in the brash language of a drunk, and lay dying in a scorched life of ruin, alone. I could have been staring at my own end, had not the grace of God discovered and grabbed my life from imprisonment, and a bottle of lies. One-Eyed Jack could have been me.

A drunk, dying in the despair of darkness…or so it seemed to be. His flight, on the wings of death, into the clouds of darkened thoughts…into the unknown, was booked from a bottle of useless hope.

She was airlifted beyond the stars of Heaven, to paradise!

She was airlifted after her father had cut out her tongue. She soared, after her father had chosen to set her on fire. Yet even though he tried, her father could not burn off the wings that lifted her beyond his reach.

As her body burned, he had watched her die. He was a policeman in Saudi Arabia, one of America's Middle Eastern allies. In his country, his action was not Child Abuse. It was an act of righteousness afforded the Religious Police that patrol the streets, seeking out evil lovers of Jesus.

There will be no news media coverage, no outrage. She was only a Christian in a Muslim country, a nobody.

The teenage girl had learned about Jesus and His love on the internet and had accepted Him into her heart by faith. She had no church to attend, no Christian friends to run with. All she had was her faith and happiness in knowing that Jesus loved her and a father who would kill her, after cutting out her tongue. She was a nobody, who would be resigned to obscurity had her name not found its way out of Saudi Arabia.

However, like Jesus rising from the grave, so did her life.

Her father had been seeking justice for Allah. He cut out her tongue, so she could not share her love of Jesus with anyone else. In Saudi Arabia, the love of Jesus is outlawed. Their religious police are ever vigilant, on the lookout for anyone not adhering to the law of the land. Their righteous goal of killing all who convert to the love of Jesus compels them to murder even their own children.

And so, she was murdered by her father. Nobody really cared, except perhaps, a few odd Christians whom she met on the internet, and those who would take her story out of a desert land parched by hate. There were no TV crews, roving reporters, or rolling cameras to capture the story of a teenage girl that was set aflame because she burned with love.

She was not an outraged Muslim in a Christian country, one of many who had been searched at an airport and thus received National News Media coverage. She was just a Christian in a Muslim country, who was murdered because she was...a Christian.

Our White House recently declared that America is no longer a Christian Nation. However, the White House does not have the authority to make those types of declarations. The White House cannot declare that we are not what we choose to be.

In every other country around the world, where the name America is mentioned, our country *is* considered a Christian Nation. As a Christian Nation with freedoms others cannot hope to receive in their own lands, they flock to our shores.

If Islam is bliss, why do so many Muslims hold deep desires to live in America, a Christian Nation, rather than in one of their Allah dominated countries? Is Islam and the rule of Islam no more than a religion of terror, accompanied by the fear of Allah, so get out the rug?

Currently, there are no Islamic ruled countries where Christians are treated as equals. Where Islam rules, Christians do not enjoy the freedoms or protections afforded Muslims, but are subject to persecutions, beatings, and degradation. Even when laws teach equal protection, they are often ignored by those in authority, who are frightened by the thought of Islamic retaliation. The daily Christian beatings, murders, and rape of Christian women are ignored by the Arabic press and more often than not, receive no more than a shrug from the authorities.

And even now, as the world watches angry men and women flood the streets of Egypt and other Middle Eastern countries crying out for freedom, their cries are not for those they persecute, shun, beat and murder. Their cry is a cry for Muslims. The greatest force behind the demonstrations are the Muslim Brotherhood. It is not the Brotherhood of Freedom. It is not the Brotherhood of Mankind. It is a Muslim Brotherhood that wishes the rule of Islam. It desires submission to Allah, not freedom for all.

The Muslims who have taken to the streets, seek only their own, not the welfare of their Christian Arab Brothers, who have been given the garbage heaps of Egypt to dwell in.

A religion of threats and fears, Islam holds many of the countries in which it prevails in the madness of its religious Imams. The wilder and more radical the Imam, the greater his sphere of power and his influence to control.

In America, a Muslim wants to go on strike because the company he works for does not want to allow him his prayer rug and prayer time at sundown.

In Saudi Arabia, a teenager has her tongue cut out and is set aflame, because she doesn't want a prayer rug and has no wish to offer prayers to Allah at sundown.

The only countries where moderation in Islamic beliefs and practices are preached and regularly practiced, in mass, are those countries where Muslims are a minority and do not rule.

> **In deserts fire**
> **Where rages hate and madness**
> **With evil sword**
> **The righteous do they slay.**
>
> **Their glistening blood**
> **In rivers of forgiveness, Flows from their wounds,**
> **God's Grace in life displayed.**

The righteous perisheth and none taketh it to heart. The merciful men are taken out of the way, none considering that the <u>righteous are removed from the evil that is to come.</u>

They think they have destroyed and killed Jesus, when they kill a Christian, but how can you kill God?

They did not know her Lord. Yet, when one teenage girl returns with Jesus, in the glory of the **Father,** accompanied by all the mighty angels, what will they say?

Is her death a rare, isolated incident by a deranged dad doing the unnatural?

In the religion of Islam, a child is branded a Muslim upon birth. There is no choice or freedom involved. The newly born are ordained Allah's by parental and religious decree. If then, when they grow up, these children decide they do not wish to drag around the torturous mandate of Islam, they face hatred and violence from their family and friends and possible death by the governments that rule over them. If a Muslim converts to Christianity, he or she signs their own death warrant. This is the faith of Islam.

And in America it appears that extreme radical progressives and Radical Muslims have banded together to promote harmony. Why would extreme radical progressives, who mouth freedom, be holding hands with Radical Muslims? Hard-Core Islam is one of the most intolerant and violent religions operating at ground zero and on and in, any other ground it can occupy and force its' will upon.

Do not be fooled by the talk of those who would confuse you as to their intent. They complain about a Christmas display of Bethlehem, but stand up to fight for a Mosque at or near ground Zero.

They will go to court to prevent anyone from mentioning the name, **_Jesus,_** in public, but publicly finance an Imam's trip to the Mideast to promote good relations with Muslims.

They scream and yell about America's intolerance and bigotry towards Muslims, because someone wants to burn a Koran, but are silent when a child is burned because she chooses to open a bible.

Do not be fooled by the riots in Islamic countries, stoked by hatefilled Imams. They will hate you no matter what you say or do. Burn a book, have a riot. Burn a child, praise Allah!

So what is this love affair between the radical progressive elite, and hardcore Islam? It has nothing to do with fairness and tolerance. Despite our flaws, there is no other country on the face of the planet that has afforded more freedoms to more people, irrespective of their faith or religion, than America. Americans have no need to prove they are tolerant. Even Muslims in America enjoy far more freedoms than they could ever hope or imagine in any country ruled by the name of Allah.

When they band together against Christians, it is not the Christians they hate. It is the name, *Jesus* that is their common bond of fierce rejection.

If the world hate you, ye know that it hated me before it hated you. If ye were of the world, the world would love its own: but because ye are not of the world, but I have chosen you out of the world, therefore the world hateth you. John 15: 18 & 19

And what of one courageous teenage girl in Saudi Arabia?

The love of God glistened in the blood she shed for His glory. Pray that God will use this love to open the heart of her father, and many others in a country hard with hatred.

After being set on fire, there was no helicopter ride rushing her to the local hospital for emergency care. But God's grace was available, and He provided a...

Flight for Life.

For surely, the angels her Lord sent to carry her into the Heavens of peace, filled her with giddy abandonment and joy in her Lord and Savior, Jesus Christ!

And they shall enter into peace, and rest in their own beds, each one walking in their own uprightness

A nobody in the glory of God...is no longer a nobody. She shines bright, walking in her own uprightness! To walk in the *Light of the God's Greatness*, we pray...*that we may.*

A man at a rest stop, on his last act, in his final scene, could only peer through one blurry eye, in drunken loss, as he staggered in the night, alone and afraid. The flight he boarded had no plans to land in glory, but departed just the same, carrying him to the dark abyss of hopelessness. His was a flight of death.

A girl in Saudi Arabia was learning to see through the eyes of Jesus. She was **Living in Victory Eternal** and walking in the **Light of God's Greatness**. Though her tongue was cut from her mouth, and her body set on fire...her faith in Jesus burned brighter and her voice sang louder. All that could be heard were her words...*JESUS LOVES YOU! You cannot silence love.*

And when her passage to heaven was booked, her eternal destiny secure, she flew with the angels of God, on a flight to paradise.

What flight are you on?

10

Breath of Fire
Faith in Action

The Middle East is the Flash Point of History.
It is here history will be decided.
It is here the war will be won.
It will be won by the Lord,
Not by man.

Today, the flames of hate are roaring throughout the Middle East. These fires of madness consume the innocent and non-violent with savagery. Yet, within this burning mass of violence, the Spirit of God is waking up Arabs to truth. As they sleep, the Word of God appears in righteous dreams of life. When dawn arrives and they wake, they are His! They believe!

But as many as received Him, to them gave He the power to become the Sons of God,

> *Even to them that believe in His name.*
> *Who were born, not of blood,*
> *Nor of the will of the flesh,*
> *Nor of the will of man,*
> *But of God.'*
> St. John 1: 12 & 13

And they are soaring high over desserts night, In love of God, His Grace, His might.

And in this transformation, these Arab Christians are walking **in the Light of God's greatness.**

As others strive to destroy the image of Jesus as Divine King and Lord, investing in the ideology of hate, Christian Arabs walk in grace. They often suffer, but hold fast their freedom under constant threat of death. Once found, they will not be turned away from the Truth of Jesus Christ found in the gospel of Salvation.

In the truth of Allah, Arab Christians are routinely beaten, persecuted and treated as less by their Muslim compatriots. In the majority of Islamic countries, simply converting from a Muslim to a Christian is a death sentence in itself.

A baby born of Muslim parents in the Middle East is christened a Muslim at birth, with no choice or ability to say, **hey, wait a minute, I am not sure I believe all this Allah stuff.** This christening is the chain of slavery that binds the rest of their life to the religion of Islam.

If, once an adult, they open their eyes and do not like what they see, do not like the ball and chain of Islam that they have been forced to drag throughout their life, they face a dire choice. They may continue in the slavery of the religion they did not choose, or face the hatred and violence of family, former friends, and their own government, many times under penalty of death. This is the faith of Islam. It is a faith that robs infants of choice and freedom. It is a faith that teaches their young to hate. It is a faith of fear.

Islamic children are schooled in hate at an early age. Jews, Christians and America as a whole, fall into the acceptable realm of revulsion, which they learn to carry with their warped sense of justice. As the Twin Towers came crashing down and people were crushed under the rubble of steel and cement, in the Middle East, they cheered in the streets.

At birth, these Arabs were shackled to the chains of Islam. From infancy, they were ordained, **Slaves**, forced to bear the ideology of Allah throughout life under threat of death. But the God of Truth and Grace has decided that they should not remain slaves and has begun His own cause... the cause of freedom. The Lord of Mercy visits them while they sleep, and as they roll about in fitful twists and turns, Jesus proclaims peace.

I create the fruit of the lips; Peace, peace to him that is far off, and to him that is near, saith the Lord; and I will heal him. Isaiah 57: 19

The Sword of the Spirit, which is the Word of the living God, cuts away the bondage of slavery as they lay upon their beds, healing them in the Light. In the morning, as they wake, they are no longer Islam's slaves, but instead, have become God's **Freemen.**

This is why their brothers and sisters wish for their death. Those who choose to stay enslaved do not wish to see others freed. Those that wander around in the dark cannot stand under the brilliant glare of the light. Thus, they deem the Arab **Walkers in Light** enemies who must be killed lest others also be converted. Hatred has no room for love.

But Christian Arabs shine on. Even in death, their light shines bright. The blood they shed glistens with the love of God, whose love also beckons them to courageous heights, as they brave the dark motives of those who hate them. When their bodies fall on the desert sands, slain by the Muslim Faithful, God simply raises them up. From the dessert floor, they ride the **Flight of Life** into the Heavens!

They will return. And when they do, they will return in glory, not in the shame of empty shoes thrown by the shameful. The enemies of the Light can throw their shoes as often as they like, but the shame they wish to cast on others remains their own.

Islamic Terrorists are not engaged in a political fight for freedom, as reported in the news. This is not a cause of Palestinian freedom. This is not a jihad that began because of the re-establishment of Israel in 1948, and the Demon Infidel country known as the **United States of America**. The adherents of Islam butchered and slaughtered their way across the desert sands of Arabia, into North Africa and the southern reaches of Europe over a thousand years before America was ever established as a Nation. Over one thousand years before Israel was once more able to reclaim its homeland, Mohamed was leading murderous raids to kill any who would not submit to Islam.

Over 500 years before the Catholic Church instigated the Crusades, Mohamed led his own crusades, in a march of bloodletting, to conquer and overthrow all who would not bend a knee to Allah.

They marched into Spain, pillaging and murdering all who resisted, then moved on into France. They were stopped in 732 AD by Charles Martel, whose army faced off 40,000 to 50,000 Muslim Calvary and defeated them. And thus ended the Muslim Attempt to force submission upon all of Europe through an onslaught of death and destruction.

The claim of Palestinian Freedom is nothing more than a Propaganda Branch of the Islamic lie. The Islamic terrorists and Arab States care nothing for the Palestinians. They care about continuing their expansionist agenda of conquering Europe and forcing it into the submission of Allah. Their two fronts are, **The War of Peace** through mathematical multiplication, by increasing the Muslim population in Europe until they have a majority, and through **Blood Letting**, killing and terrorizing any and all who stand in their way.

Terrorists do not care about Palestinian freedom. There is no freedom in Islam. Terrorism is the cause of darkened minds that desire to destroy God's nation, Israel, and kill Arab Christians for the glory of their Allah. Kill and force submission, is the truth of Islam.

But they will not annihilate Israel no matter how boldly they profess their intent. God will not allow it...unless they have now devised a plan to overcome God.

Their efforts to destroy Israel and murder Christians, is but a feeble attempt to overthrow Jesus, Himself. However, Jesus will not be overthrown.

They can murder them, beat them, and cut out the tongues of their own children, but they will not stamp out the love of God in Christ Jesus. They can set their Christian Arab brothers on fire, but they will not be able to douse the flames of passion...*the passion of the Christ.*

This is the story of the Middle East, a story that is being written in blood. But they will not re-write the history of life and death according to their own desires. God has already finished the story line and proclaimed victory.

> *For I am God, and there is none else;*
> *I am God and there is none like me,*
>
> *Declaring the end from the beginning,*
> *And from ancient times the things that are not yet done,*
> *saying, My counsel shall stand, and I will do all my pleasure.*

The epic has already been scripted by God, and Israel is God's declaration of intent. Over 2,500 years ago, these days were revealed so we might know the truth and power of God's Word.

The burden of the word of the Lord for Israel, saith the Lord, which stretcheth forth the heavens, and layeth the foundation of the earth, and formeth the spirit of man within himself.

Behold, I will make Jerusalem a cup of trembling unto all the people round about, when they shall be in siege both against Judah and against Jerusalem.

And in that day will I make Jerusalem a burdensome stone for all people: all that burden themselves with it shall be cut in pieces, though all the people of the earth be gathered against it. Zechariah 12: 1, 2, & 3.

As long as Israel is a nation, the word of God is true and the faith of all who believe is steadfast. That is why Muslims hate Israel and Christians.

Muslims cannot rid themselves of God, until they rid themselves of Israel and Christians, who walk in the Truth. Muslims cannot get rid of *Jesus* until they annihilate every Arab Christian and Jew.

Even now as TV cameras record thousands marching through the streets, crying for freedom, their cries are distinctly quiet when it comes to the suffering and murdering of their Christian Arab brothers.

The Middle East is aflame in anger and hate, and the fires that stoke their rage will not end until the day Jesus returns.

When Jesus returns, Egypt, Assyria and Israel will live in peace, forming an **Axis of Grace.**

In that day, shall there be a highway out of Egypt to Assyria, and the Assyrian shall come into Egypt, and the Egyptian shall come into Syria, and the Egyptian shall serve with the Assyrians.

In that day, shall Israel be the third with Egypt and Assyria, even a blessing in the midst of the land: Whom the Lord of hosts shall bless, saying, Blessed be Egypt my people, and Assyria the work of my hands, and Israel mine inheritance. Isaiah 20: 23 & 24

Christian Arabs will walk in peace, hand in hand with the Israelites.

One day, the Nation and people the United Nations loves to condemn, will be exalted above every Nation and people who condemned it.

And it shall come to pass, that as ye were a curse among the heathen, O house of Judah, and house of Israel; so will I save you, and ye shall be a blessing: fear not, but let your hands be strong. Zechariah 8: 13

Thus saith the Lord of hosts; It shall yet come to pass, that there shall come people, and the inhabitants of many cities:

And the inhabitants of one city shall go to another saying, Let us go speedily to pray before the Lord, and seek the Lord of hosts: I will go also.

Yea, many people and strong nations shall come to seek the Lord of hosts in Jerusalem, and pray before the Lord.

Thus saith the Lord of hosts; In those days it shall come to pass, that ten men shall take hold out of all languages of the nations, even shall take hold of the skirt of him that is a Jew, saying, We will go with you: for we have heard that God is with you. Zechariah 8: 20 through 23

The Middle East will see true, lasting peace. But this peace will only be possible when *the times of refreshing shall come from the presence of the Lord.* **This Lord will be, Jesus Christ.**

Until then, courageous **Arab Christians** will continue to walk in the Light of God's greatness, proclaiming Jesus their Lord and King. They are the **Walkers of Light** in a dark and desolate land of madness.

They have the breath of fire. Without it, they would faint under the cruel and violent forces that seek their destruction. In their breath of fire, they are crowned with courage and lifted in strength by the God of strength and courage. In their breath of fire, they hold their hope in the embers of love, glowing in God's grace.

They are ***our*** brothers and sisters. They are Arab Christians, who bear witness of Jesus Christ in a land that worships the name of Allah. They bear witness, sacrificing their own lives in the truth of love, that the gospel of Salvation may be heard by all. They breathe the breath of fire in a land of flames. They do not send their children into the streets to blow up their enemies while they hide safely away in caves. Those are the tactics of their foes. These Arab Christians offer themselves as a sacrifice of love, to show love and to teach love...the love of Jesus Christ.

Now, as the history of the world unfolds, in the final stages of its production, the **Stars** are performing in the glory of their Christ. With the breath of fire, they speak their lines clearly, unfazed by the carnage around them. As they **walk in spirit**, in the grace of God, their heroic feats of love and self-sacrifice are the stories of legend.

When their director, Jesus Christ, cries, **"Action,"** they are ready. And as their loved ones are beaten and murdered, the tears they shed on the desert sand, only water the story of Salvation, allowing the love of Christ to bloom and flower in a garden of glory to God!

The love of God glistens in the blood they shed for His glory.

There is no small part here. They all have leading roles and star in the feature of a lifetime. There is no question as to how this epic ends. It ends in the Kingdom of God, when Christian Arabs return with Him in the victory celebration. When the revues are in, the critics will rave...and... **the standing ovation could last for ages.**

The question to ask will not be **what is the end of all things**, but what will be your end? Will you be left in the wreckage and ruins of meaningless wasted moments, or rise to become a **Walker in Light**, one of the stars in the Royal Production of Heaven?

Will you soar across the Heavens in **Light of Grace**, a celebrity in the Majesty of Jesus Christ, or stumble upon a gravel road going nowhere?

The Lord desires to cast you as one of His leading men or women. Wouldn't you like to rise to the occasion? Wouldn't you like to stand on the stage of eternity and live out the drama of love in Jesus, for all to see?

We are in the final **Act**. There may be very few scenes remaining. Your time to walk in the Light of God's Greatness is upon you. You can have a leading role as a **Walker in Light, by trusting in Jesus and allowing**

His spirit to fill you with passion. Alternatively, you can fall by the wayside, caught up in the drama of wasted moments promised by second-hand production companies.

One Teenage girl in Saudi Arabia starred in a story of love and joy. She rose up for the occasion, believing in the promises of Jesus Christ and Salvation. While she burned with love, her father burned with madness. Her performance as a **Walker in Light** on the stage of history, defied the second hand producers of hate. And in her role, there was no acting. She needed none. She burned with the **Passion of the Christ,** and had no problem living in that passion... ***and dying in it.***

It is now the time for us to seek this passion and step up on the stage of Christ's love. We need to shine in our roles as **the Walkers of Light,** that the production of Salvation in the Grace of God may be revealed in our words and in our deeds. We need... **The Passion of the Christ, in the Breath of Fire.**

<u>**Faith in Action.**</u> Our Faith in Action for this **Breath of Fire**, is to speak up with passion on behalf of our brothers and sisters in the Middle East, who are being beaten and murdered.

They are scorned and hated, beaten and burned, as Arabs with no value. They could convert back to the storied lines of Islam. Thus, they could be accepted once more and spared persecution. Yet... they could not. They would rather continue their walk in the role of a lifetime, knowing they perform in the love of an Eternal Kingdom, then be relegated to a walk-on-extra, in a b-rated production, conjured up by second-hand screen writers.

Blessed are those who are persecuted for righteousness sake, for theirs is the kingdom of Heaven.

For our Breath of Fire, we must be aware that as we witness the rise of thousands marching in the streets demanding freedom throughout the Middle East, that their demands do not include their Arab Christian brothers. If we do not speak up for them no one else will.

If beginning a conversation is awkward for you, try getting a T-shirt from V.O.M. They have an assortment of T-shirts that speak out for your persecuted brothers and sisters. Wearing a T-shirt can speak louder than any words you might have to say. In silence, as you go about your day, others will see and wonder. The Spirit of Christ can move deep within a heart, in the silence of a moment. In that silence, as the heart is moved, one may ask you what your T-shirt means. This is your opening. Keep your answer simple and truthful. It is the Spirit of God that opens a heart, rather than a loud, boisterous and argumentative debate.

Many who **are not** Christians may ridicule you and mock you. When they do…rejoice and remember Jesus own words.

Blessed are you when men revile you and persecute you and say all manner of evil against you falsely. For great is your reward in heaven. For so persecuted they the profits who were before you.

In our Breath of Fire, we must ask for the passion of the Spirit to fill our hearts and minds with the desires of Jesus. This is the **evening… of the dawn**, and we need an eternal desire. The alarms are sounding and our brothers and sisters in the Middle East need their family in Jesus to stand up for them, to stand up with them. And this is our **Breath of Fire, Faith in Action.**

It **will** take courage. However, **be of good cheer**, as Jesus would say. You are just a nobody anyway. **No one ever listens to anything you have to say; thus, why not say something important that they refuse to listen to.**

If you are financially able, I would suggest a special gift of love. A donation offered from a hand of love to **The Joshua Project.**

The Joshua Project is a project that reaches out to persecuted Christians in the Middle East. In this **Breath of Fire, let the fire of our passion reach those at the front lines.**

The **Joshua Project** can be found on line simply by googling the same. This web site can also become a valuable tool in your Worldwide

Missionary Project. Become a voice for your suffering Christian Brothers and sisters on the world stage.

And this is your **Faith in Action** for this breath. But beware. This may be the hardest **Faith in Action** yet. Many do not want to hear about how others suffer for Jesus. Many Christians want to feel the joy of Jesus, but they do not want to feel sad.

They want the joy... but they do not want the nails.

Within your **Breath of Fire,** be ready for rejection. In **Their Very Best Moment Now,** many who walk as Christians do not wish to be burdened with the burdens of others. **It is not their fault.** When you go out to share the stories of your brothers and sisters who suffer for Jesus, you need to know that you may only get a patronizing pat on the back.

Yea, what a horrible shame, they may say. If they do, ask them this. **Would you have patted Jesus on the back as He stumbled, weak and in pain, down the rocky road to Calvary and said, "Oh, what a shame?"**

Would you have patted the bare back, shredded by whips and commented, "Oh what a shame?" Ask them that.

When on a journey for the Lord, make sure you take your Dream Team with you when you go. Your Heavenly Father will watch over you. The Holy Spirit will guide you and Jesus alongside you.

With your Dream team, you can soar in moments of Majesty, through clouds of uncertainty, across the Heavens of hope.

Never catch a flight without your Dream Team and in everything, Prayer!

And so...are you ready for the Breath of Fire? You will need it when you go out into the world and talk about Christians who suffer. You may feel isolated and alone, as people begin to distance themselves from you. I hope not, but it would be wrong not to warn you. If you have the Breath of Fire, if the flame of the Holy Spirit is lit within, it will help.

Breath of Fire

Okay, prepare yourself... Close your eyes for a minute, and in the embers of Christ's love, allow the fan of His Passion to flame up within...and Breathe!

With two breaths remaining, what can you do that you have not yet done? Isn't it time to put Jesus first? I knew you would agree. Don't pout... smile!

A young girl in Saudi Arabia learned about Jesus on the internet.

Her joy at His love and Salvation overwhelmed her,
And filled her,

Before she was silenced by the hate.
She walked in the Light of God's greatness.
And though darkness surrounded her,

Her witness burned brighter than a thousand candles!
When her father decided to snuff out the candles,
there were too many.

Two flights. Two destinies.

A drunk, at the end of life, caught a flight of emptiness.
His flight crashed on a bed of hopelessness and despair.

One Saudi teen caught a flight to Heaven,
And soared above the clouds, Beyond the stars,

In the company of angels,

To where grace reigns and joy thrives.

What flight are you on?

11

The Voyage
Breath of Hope

For we are saved by hope,
But Hope that is seen is not hope:
For what a man seeth, why doth he yet hope for it?
But if we hope for that we see not,
Then do we with patience wait for it.
Romans 8:24, 25, & 26

I slept the night on the ground by an exit ramp. It was cold in the crispy night air. I tried keeping warm under my tattered, silver, emergency blanket, but the cool air had other plans, slipping in through the tears and open spaces. I was kept well chilled and was thankful when the morning came.

I was on highway 15 North, just outside of Beaver, Utah, hitching from Oceanside, California. This was my third day on the road. The drive in a car to where I lay, unshaven, cold, and tired, was less than one day. I walked to an Open Mart and using what change I had left, purchased my morning coffee.

The greatest creation ever, (**In strictly earthly-wanting something terms**) is a cup of black coffee!

The greatest moment in time, (**In a strictly, a selfishly-awakening moment**) is drinking that coffee in the early morning!

Coffee in hand, I walked back to my exit ramp to continue my voyage.

After coffee, the wait was short. A semi-truck pulled onto the exit ramp and stopped. The trucker got out and approached me, asking where I was headed. After telling him I only needed to go up the road to the highway exit leading to Denver, he opened up the back of his truck.

The back of the semi rig was no more than a long space of emptiness. A large shipping container designed to carry a heavy load, today, it carried me. I hopped in and he closed the back door. Darkness engulfed me. I could not see my hands in front of my face as I felt the truck begin to move off down the highway. That is when my mind really had fun playing the game that only a mind can play.

Was the trucker a serial killer, who would take me to his ranch somewhere…in the middle of nowhere…then force me to work or kill me and bury my body in a barren field…to be forgotten by all? Who was this man, and was I safe, or in danger? I placed my life in the Lord's hands and sat back. What else could I do? I was forced to trust the ride offered by this stranger.

Had I been in Eritrea, a coastal country on the eastern edge of Africa, the container that I would have been placed in would not have taken me down the highway. The containers in Eritrea that house Christians do not move. They are set in the desert and are normally unventilated. This is where Christians in Eritrea catch a ride…a ride to nowhere.

They are forced into Huge Shipping containers, as make-shift prisons, for believing in the love of Jesus. The heat bakes them in the day and the cool dessert air chills them at night. They are not provided thermal emergency blankets, not even ones with holes and tears.

They live in dysentery, sick and weak, treated worse than cattle, in the shipping containers of their imprisonment.

Their ride is stationary. My ride was long and quiet, only the hum of the semi as it rolled along.

Soon, the truck slowed and pulled over onto the gravel byway, alongside the highway. The back door opened, and there stood the trucker. He did not kill me or force me to work on some obscure ranch without pay.

The trucker waited for me to climb down, then asked what I was going to do when I got back to Denver. I told him that I was going to try to get a job and begin again. I briefly shared how my family had lost everything, how I had traveled to California, and was now on a new journey back to the Mountain State.

He was very kind in thought, as he listened. Then he handed me a fifty-dollar bill. I was shocked. Quite often, many American Christian's like to pat a person on the back…love to pray for, and with them…but beyond that, it's all fog…gone before the morning is over. There are many American Christians, who seem to believe that only sinners roam the streets as beggars. When they see a homeless person, they see a failure in need of Salvation. When they see the poor, they only see those who need a lesson in finance. It is the American Christian version of India's Caste System. Those on the streets, the untouchables, are there for a reason. It is always their fault.

When Jesus sees the poor and observes beggars, He sees those He… **_raiseth up from the dust …and lifteth up from the dunghill to sit them among princes, to make them to inherit the throne of glory._**

Jesus has great plans for the poor. That is why God has chosen them to be…**_rich in Faith._ Jesus has designs to take those who have nothing, and give them everything. He will take them from rags to riches. In fact, He has already made the travel arrangements.**

I can safely guess that we will be seeing a lot of one-time beggars in the Kingdom of God. Will they, once there, talk of your kindness and how, after losing everything, you helped re- kindle a spark of hope...or will they only talk of others?

> *God's hand is NOT shortened that it cannot save.*
> *Nor His ear heavy*
> *That it cannot hear.*

If the Lord chooses to lift a person up, the person will be lifted, with or without you. If you become a mere *Passerby*, a meaningless follower of the *Ooops Theory*, the Lord will not be confused or unable to act.

God's hand was certainly not shortened that it could not help me. He used many non-Christians to help me in my time of need. But here, as I stood there before this Christian trucker, on the side of the highway, sharing my ordeal, new hope rose up within me. The trucker was my encouragement. He was a spiritual lift from the Lord. We prayed, and he left on his way. When he comes up within me for remembrance, I pray for him and his family, and give thanks for the Lord's hand of love towards me that day.

This trucker traveled across the country in the **Light of God's Greatness**. His desire was to serve Jesus! One day, he allowed the Lord to book passage for a homeless man, who needed to be carried up the road. He not only obliged the Lord, but reversed the charges. The Trucker of God paid the homeless man $50.00 for accepting the ride.

> *"...when you do it for the least, you do it for me." Jesus.*

That night I slept inside, in a homeless shelter in Grand Junction, thankful for a bed and the generous gift from the trucker. The world of tomorrow was filled with unknowns, but today, the Lord had helped me on my way and allowed hope. He had led me in kindness, and in His mercy, had moved the heart of a trucker to carry a heavy load up the highway.

I was a nobody, but I was the Lord's nobody. Moreover, I knew that and was thankful that He had kept me in His Light. I was trusting in Jesus, and he was preparing my way. He had made the travel arrangements, booked my stopovers, and secured my reservations.

As I lay down on the bunk bed provided by the shelter, the hope of tomorrow filled my heart. I was on a voyage, being carried upon the currents of life, riding the tide, but it was all under the divine, watchful, guiding will of the Lord.

Oh Lord, thou hast searched me, and known me.
Thou knowest my downsitting and mine uprising,
Thou understands my thoughts afar off.
Psalm 139: 1 & 2

Day 133... *The ship rocked gently in the rising waves of the Pacific Ocean, riding the current eastward. The young 14 year old tried to reorganize his thoughts from afar. However, no matter how hard he tried, they would not remain on their proper shelves. He attempted to carefully place each thought here or there, up and away from his moment of confusion. But when the boat rocked, everything would slip off their assigned shelves, to land in a jumbled heap upon his reasoning.*

The young boy tried again, to place a thought here, place another one there, and stuff them into the cubbyholes of forgetfulness. Store them away, so they would leave him alone. **Time to cook. I'm a cook!**

He did not want to end up as some of the others. One had jumped from the boat and disappeared into the vast waters stretching off in all directions ... **endlessly...day after day...forever...a ship of ghosts...a ship of...Stop!**

The young boy forced himself to cut off the ever-reaching madness of eternity, for a brief moment of escape, into the present. He tried to get up from his seated position, but fell back. A large wave lifted the boat high into the sky then, dropped it back down with rude detachment.

The boy, using the sides of the boat to stabilize himself as he rose, stood up once more and staggered over to a pot. He had been hired on as a cook, and it was the one activity he was able to take solace in. The preparations kept his mind occupied and his wandering thoughts at bay. He poured a little sake into the pot, added some rice and set it over a make-do fire. The fire had been built from wood chips taken from the ship's mast. The sailors had cut down the mast during the typhoon.

As the boy watched the rice boil, he had no way of knowing that soon, in his homeland, people would begin dying for want of rice. The boy had no clue that, on the Japanese mainland, the rice held in his drifting cargo ship, would be worth more than its weight in gold. One of the greatest famines ever to hit Japan was edging closer to the country that now ...was so far away...so far behind the 14 year-old boy and what was left of a 14-man crew.

While the remaining crew of a Japanese cargo boat drifted in uncertainty, on land in Japan, they would soon begin starving. Even the Japanese rich would die of hunger, their wealth of no more value to them than an empty porcelain bowl *(of which the boy's boat also had a nice supply.)*

On dry land they would starve whilst here, on the vast Pacific Ocean, with no land in sight, he and his fellow sailors, adrift in a wooden cargo ship with a 150,000 ton load, had more rice than they could ever hope or want to eat. But this young boy knew nothing of this tragedy, could not know, as the currents of the Pacific Ocean carried a Japanese cargo boat ever eastward.

They that go down to the sea in ships,
That do business in great waters:
They see the works of the Lord,
And His wonders of the deep.
For He commandeth, and raiseth the stormy wind,
Which lifteth up the waves thereof.
They mount up to the heaven,
They go down again to the depths:
Their soul is melted because of trouble.
They reel to and fro,

THE VOYAGE...BREATH OF HOPE

> *And stagger like a drunken man,*
> *And are at their wit's end.*
> *Psalm 107: 23 through 27*

Day 179...The rocking boat felt as if it would rip apart at any moment. The new storm had attacked with a disdainful lack of care or concern for those who were passengers, on this Trans-Pacific crossing.

Up...up...and up. Taking off on flight of soaring wave, only to fall down...down...down, to lose one's stomach and the little rice within it.

The new storm tormented the creaking ship, but could not break it. This storm did not mirror the terrible Typhoon that had begun their odyssey. That is what started it all, the Typhoon. It had turned a three-day trip to deliver a barge of rice, into the Voyage of the Doomed, out into the wilds of the Pacific Ocean.

Without a rudder or a mast to guide or steer them, they were at the mercy of the winds and the seas.

Hope was no more a reality, only a distant memory. Hope belonged to those who walked on land. Aboard this boat, hopes were replaced by daily staggering...from one side of the boat to the other. Each day...held in constant drone of nothingness, with nothing to do, nowhere to go. Stagger from this side to that. Stagger from that side to this. Except for the man who had jumped overboard. He no longer staggered. He had gone to stroll in the oceans' depths.

They had survived the Typhoon...for what? To rot slowly, lost at sea? Would they decay, riding the waves of death forever, as spirits with no rest? The young boy shivered and looked at his brother. His brother did not look so good. Pale and weak, his eyes were rolling around in his head, even as the ship was rolling around in the storm.

Day 213...They had to struggle to lift the body up over the edge of the boat. A tremor shimmied through the young boy's flesh, before the body fell into the ocean.

As the body rested, for one brief moment, on the ship's edge, the dead body's face filled the boy's vision. A clammy, gray mask that once was the face of a youngster, who had talked and laughed. That was when the tremor of fear filled him like a graveyard chill.

The young boy believed that he witnessed his brother's ghost, in distant reflection… from somewhere deep within the glistening pupils that met his. In the silent stillness of lifeless touch, his brother's eyes revealed a ghost, in quiet flight of death…but ***just for a moment***.

Then they let go and the body fell, splashing into, and disappearing under, the waters that ruled their destiny. Tears welled up in the young boy's eyes, his brother now dead, so far from home. His thoughts returned home, to images of his family, his parents. He thought of his mother, always so loving. He felt her gentle hand against his cheek, as he squeezed shut his eyes.

Tears started streaming down his face in damp streaking lines, as rivers of sadness. His soul screamed within, but without…only silence…silence and the watery streaks that highlighted his face.

No one attempted to comfort the young boy. The remaining survivors were too weary. Others had also died. The smell of the corpses had torched their senses with the evil odor of death. Their solution was to dump the odor over board. And they did, one by one…from under the setting sun.

Day 280... The young boy could not force his eyes away from the man in front of him, stuffing his mouth with rice. As the man shoved rice in, his efforts were laborious and agonizingly slow.

Above the man's left eye, blood dripped from a wound received during the night of the typhoon. The man did not seem to care. His fingers were an odd purplish color, mingled with the pink of blood from his gums, where loose teeth wobbled. Two teeth had fallen out.

What a horrible night! The waves had tossed the ship wildly about as nonchalantly as he once enjoyed tossing a frying fish. With a flick of the wrist, the fish would fly high, perform a perfect mid-air summersault, and land back again, into the pan.

THE VOYAGE...BREATH OF HOPE

In front of him, the wounded man continued his struggle and fitful fight to eat. Each time he stuffed his mouth, the rice would re- emerge in a pinkish drool.

The young Japanese became transfixed on the show acted out before him. The rice began as a fluffy white mound of edible nutrition, but came out as a pinkish saliva of disgust. **Stop,** someone shrieked, **Stop!** The screeching voice hurt the young boy's ears. **Who had screamed,** he demanded in silent irritation? **Who?!! Oh... it was me. I was screaming... screaming at me.**

Then, as the man attempted to raise his arm one last time, it fell limp to his lap, and he stopped eating. **Was he full,** the young boy wondered, straining his thoughts to understand? **Was he full?**

The man did not move again. His arms sagged lifelessly at his sides, his pale face but a wax candle in a heated room, melted and sad.

*Sad in death. Sad in life...sad in death...*the young boy drifted off to sleep.

<u>Day 345.</u> A salty ocean spray layered the deck in a fine mist of seasoning, dampening those who sat in thoughtless disarray, in the noon day cool of a moment. The young boy's eyes skimmed across the waters, like a flat stone skipping across the ocean waves. The water shined in a million little sparkles of light, each mirroring the heated rays of the sun. As the ship rocked on, atop the roving waves, only three survivors remained of the original 14.

The ship did what it wanted to do, or was it the ocean...the ocean led the ship along...along the paths and currents of empty space and time...and three of them remained with barely breath of life. The young boy's soul sank into the depths of hopelessness, as his mind fought the ravaged thoughts and incoherent syllables that bobbed about in his thinking... even as the ship bobbed about in the waves.

<u>Day 400 and???...</u> **Land,** cried a voice from somewhere distant. The voice filtered into the young boys mist shrouded mind. **Land!**

The young boy, weak and unsteady, raised himself up, to look over the edge of the boat. **Yes…it was land!**

The crew and their hopes rode the cresting waves to shore, where their ship beached itself on a chilly day in January 1834. They had landed at Cape Alva, on the northwestern coast of Washington State. They had drifted over 5,000 miles from off the coast of Japan, to the beaches of America. They are the longest known castaways to survive at sea.

Yet, as their boat made shore, and their spirits began to rise, how could they know that soon, they would be begging for their very lives?

A tribe of Indian seal hunters called the Makah, would discover a young man and two boys as they made their weak and wobbly way ashore. The survivors would plead for mercy, once discovered, and end up becoming slaves of the Makah Indians. But how could they know that, here and now, aboard their drifting ship, as they watched the land grow ever closer? How could they know that their hope would come crashing down, like the waves breaking upon the shoreline?

Their voyage began as a simple commercial trip to transport rice up, along the coastal waterway, off the coast of Japan, when it was interrupted by a typhoon. After the typhoon, they were carried on by the currents with no control or ability to do anything other than hope. When they no longer hoped, they existed…when they could not bear to exist, a few gave up and embraced the ever beckoning voice of death. Of 14, three remained.

And here, at the end of their ocean voyage, with land looming as a beacon of light, signaling salvation, they would soon stagger from one nightmare to the next.

This was only the beginning. They would endure A brief span of time as slaves to an Indian tribe. A rescue by British agents sent from Fort Vancouver, a fur trapping enclave on the Columbia River. Those at the fort would hear about their capture and decide to free them.

Then a stay at the Fort, to learn English from a missionary, who also taught them about a God banned in their own country. In Japan, in the

THE VOYAGE...BREATH OF HOPE

early eighteen hundreds, teaching Christianity was a crime punishable by death.

God had planned a sea voyage across the Pacific, in a cargo ship designed for Japans' local waterways. He had booked the young boy's passage, before the great famine of Japan fell upon those left behind. Later He delivered the boy to a tribe of Makah Indians for safe keeping.

Even as a captive, the Lord had the boy's freedom secured and his course set. Before the Japanese boy ever knew or heard about Jesus, His love and Salvation, God was saving the boy... before the boy could ever think to save himself.

> ***But God commendeth His love towards us***
> ***In that while we were yet without strength,***
> ***In due time, Christ died for the ungodly.***
> ***Romans 5: 6***

In due time, the Lord had plans for one Japanese boy to go from Japan to America, into captivity and then freedom, and on to the island of Macao in Indonesia. From the Macah Indians and slavery, to the island of Macao and freedom, where the Lord had a missionary who needed to learn Japanese.

Once on Macau, the Japanese boy, now a little older, would help this missionary translate the Gospel of John into Japanese. After the translation, the Japanese boy would change his name. He would change his Japanese name to John, after the gospel book he would help translate.

He would never return to live in Japan. Once, as he and his two fellow castaways tried returning to Japan aboard a British ship, the Japanese shore batteries fired upon it, warning it away. In the early 1800s, Japan isolated itself from the world. Even Japanese sailors who would be carried away by force, through storms or drifting seas, would not be welcomed back. They were tainted, banned for life, unable to return, except under penalty of death.

The Japanese boy, exiled by typhoon, saved from famine, and then freed from captivity, would have a journey through life packed with adventure and the unknown. He would eventually have an illustrious career as a translator. Fluently speaking several languages, he would assist the British in a treaty with Japan, and finally settle in Singapore with his family, a son and a daughter, to live in a colonial estate. He would be granted a British citizenship as a reward for his services.

But on this day, in January of 1834, the young Japanese boy knew none of these things. His family far away, his brother dead at sea, landing in a strange country, he would feel the pangs of hope begin to rise, but only briefly. Strangers adorned in whale bones would soon discover him and make him a slave. Hope would be packed up and crammed back into a cellar of despair.

How would his hope survive then? After a year drifting on the endless waves of gloom, to land ashore in a fresh moment of promise, only to be enslaved. How would he cope…with hope? Could he even summon up the strength or will to hope once more?

His hope would be held by God, held in Christ Jesus. God held the Japanese boy's future in the Breath of Hope, *in the certainty of God's own will.* God reserved a place for this young boy in the *Heavens of His Will, and had already made the travel arrangements.*

> *For He spoke and it was done.*
> *He commanded and it stood fast.*
> *Psalm 33:9*

A 14-year old Japanese boy was on the journey of a life time. His journey was well planned, with all travel accommodations secured prior to his departure. On this course, throughout his voyage, his *Breath of Hope* would be held in the gentle, loving hands of the Lord, a Lord he had yet to meet.

But God who is rich in mercy, For His great love wherewith He loved us, even when we were dead in sins hath quickened us together in Jesus (made us alive in Jesus) for by grace are ye saved.

THE VOYAGE...BREATH OF HOPE

And hath raised us up together and made us sit together in Heavenly places in Christ Jesus that in the ages to come He might show the exceeding riches of His grace in His kindness towards us through Christ Jesus.

*For by grace are ye saved, through faith
And that not of yourself
It is a gift of God
Not of works, lest any man should boast.
Ephesians 2: 4 through 9*

A Japanese boy, a castaway on a drifting ship, accompanied by the smell of death, rode the currents of fear, to the beaches of uncertainty. There he found salvation. And he sailed again, in Heavens wind, willed by God, into a new life. Jesus became a young boy's **Travel Agent,** and booked his passage throughout life, long before the boy ever stepped foot...off dry land.

He sailed on wings of Grace,
In morning light of hope,
Across majestic oceans.
With Heavenly winds and Breath of Hope
From God.

Who's your Travel Agent?

11

Breath of Hope
Faith in Action

Are you on a voyage of uncertainty?

Are you adrift aboard a ship of endless time?

Day in, day out,

The rocking motion making your walk difficult.

Are you caught in a typhoon? Are the winds and darkness tossing you about in storm's laughter?

Does your hope, like an ocean wave...Crest? Hope rises high... wave of strength and power.
Only to crash against a rocky shore.

To become...nothing.

WALKING IN THE LIGHT OF GOD'S GREATNESS

Jesus was sleeping when the storm hit. His disciples were not. They were awake and wide-eyed, pulses pounding, fear throbbing within. This was the day of their doom!

Wave after wave rose up in taunting heights of death, threatening to swallow them whole, falling upon them with wicked revelry, drenching their clothes and their very souls in the waters of fear. Their boat was tossed about like a toy, kicked aside by unthankful children. Surely, this was the **Day of The End.**

> *Then they cry unto the*
> *Lord in their trouble...*

The disciples, crazed out of their minds with fear, shook Jesus to waken Him. **Lord, save us! We Perish!**

Jesus opened his eyes. **And He saith unto them, Why are ye fearful, O ye of little faith.**

Then He arose, and rebuked the winds and the sea; and there was a great calm.

> *And He bringeth them out of their distresses.*
> *He maketh the storm a calm,*
> *So that the waves thereof are still.*
> *Then are they glad because they be quiet; So He bringeth them unto their desired haven.*
> *Oh that men would praise the Lord for His goodness*
> *And for His wonderful works to the children of men.*
> *Psalm 107: 28, 29, 30, 31*

But the men marveled saying, "What manner of man is this that even the wind and the seas obey Him?" Matthew 8: 24 through 27

And so it is still, as He whispers to you,

> *Why are ye fearful, Oh ye of little faith.*

Have you cried unto the Lord in your storm? Did you know that He secured your passage and booked your ocean voyage even before you started to believe in Him? As your Travel Agent, Jesus has determined your walk, to guide your feet, even while your brain fumbles around with directions. Even if you are unable to make sense of the map you are trying to unfold, in the cramped compartment of your interior, you will find your way, as He will make sure of it.

> *A man's heart deviseth his way:*
> *But the Lord directeth his steps.*
> *Proverbs 16: 9*

What a marvelous verse of encouragement in the simplicity of its truth! When the Lord is your Travel Agent, He directs your steps. When you allow the Lord to guide you, He does!

In your **Amazing Grace...Race**, it is the Lord Jesus Christ, your boss, who is helping you reach the front of the pack, to make sure you are in the winners' circle. He has given you victory over Death and the Grave, and forgiveness from all sins. He has dressed you in the finest tailored Royal Robe of His own righteousness. You have God as your personal partner. Your Heavenly Father shelters you under the feathers of his wings, **(Psalms 91:4)** as the Spirit of Christ dwells within, guiding you on the voyage of a lifetime! Can anyone say, **Breath of Hope?!?**

Even when you stumble, even when you trip and fall, He is ever faithful. He will never desert you.

> *For the Lord is a God of knowledge*
> *And by Him actions are weighed.*
> *The bows of the mighty men are broken*
> *And they that stumble are girt with strength...*
>
> *...He will keep the feet of His saints.*
> *I Samuel 2: 3,4 & 9*

> *For the just man falleth seven times And riseth up again.*
> *Proverbs 24: 16*

Your unique and awe inspiring Travel Agent, Jesus Christ, having planned your voyage before the foundation of the world, knows where to set up the aid stations and help centers. Jesus knows the pitfalls and moments of stumbling fear. **He knows! That is why you can trust Him to book your passage, make your reservations and set up your itinerary.**

He knows the troubles you are in, or will face tomorrow, and has already resolved them today. You may not see the resolution yet. You may ride the waves of uncertainty, in a drifting ship with no mast, but do not fear. Jesus is in control of the currents and is **Master** of the wind and the waves. No wave is too high, no splash too minor.

There will be storms, perhaps typhoons, but nothing can overcome the will of the Lord. The Lord may use a typhoon to re-direct your course. The Lord may allow your captivity for a brief moment in time, but has also planned for your freedom.

So great is your God, that He promises to use, even the **worst** nightmares of horror, to your advantage! That is why Jesus can confidently proclaim Salvation to the uttermost, to all that come to God by Him. He asks you to call out to Him in trust, even when you are at the uttermost, farthest point possible, *especially then*. He delights in rescue!

> *The righteous cry, And the Lord heareth*
> *And delivereth them out of all their troubles*
> *The Lord is nigh unto them that are of a broken heart;*
> *And saveth such as be of a contrite spirit.*
> *Many are the afflictions of the righteous:*
> *But the Lord delivereth him out of them all.*
> *Psalm 34: 17 18 19*

The Lord states boldly that **Many are the afflictions of the righteous...** He does not state that, **silk pillows and a cushy lifestyle are the life of the righteous. Especially if they can afford it!** He states, **Many are the afflictions. BUT EVEN STILL,** He promises to deliver you out of each and every one! And that is a promise you can bank on. That is a promise worth investing

BREATH OF HOPE...FAITH IN ACTION

in, with returns that are beyond any earthly measures unless one is wise enough to measure eternity, and the wealth of a universe and beyond.

A 14-year-old Japanese boy woke up one morning, almost 200 years ago, believing he would go on a short boat hop up the coast of Japan. His job, to cook for the crew as they transported rice to a neighboring community. A three-day trip on the waters of life. How could he have imagined the voyage that was waiting? Not even in his wildest dreams, if his ship had never entered the typhoon of terror, could he have sat down and scripted out such a journey, or planned it in detail of determined thought. He was under a **Divine Wind**. That Wind, was the will of God.

Had the Lord not intervened in this young boy's life, would he have languished and died from hunger in a country that was soon to be gripped by starvation? Would he have perished without hope? If it were not for God intervening with a Typhoon, and a 400 day voyage upon the rolling waves of the Pacific Ocean, to the shores of America, what would have been the fate of one boy?

The Lord booked his passage on the voyage of a lifetime. The Lord allowed a typhoon to lead a young Japanese boy across the great expanse of the Pacific Ocean, all the way to...***Himself.***

The Lord carried this young 14-year-old boy, weak and without strength, in a rudderless ship, over 5,000 miles via the currents of the Pacific, to a fort of outback fur trappers, in the wilds of Washington. Here, the Lord had a missionary who could tell him about Jesus and Salvation.

> *For when we were yet without strength,*
> *In due time, Christ died for the ungodly.*

In the ***Amazing Grace...Race***, the Lord guided a 14-year-old, who had no strength or direction.

Why so much drama for one young boy to hear about salvation?

> *Hast thou not known? Hast thou not heard,*
> *That the everlasting God, the Lord,*
> *The Creator of the ends of the earth,*
> *Fainteth not, neither is weary?*
> *There is no searching of His understanding.*
> *Isaiah 40: 28*

And because **He is**...the everlasting God. And because we **cannot** begin to search or understand His ways, He counsels us **in Trust**, and in **how to Trust**. We then secure our hope, by trusting. **Which hope we have as an anchor of the soul, both sure and steadfast. Hebrews 5:19**

> *Trust in the Lord with all thine heart*
> *And lean not in thine own understanding*
> *In all they ways acknowledge Him*
> *And he shall direct thy path.*
> *Proverbs 3: 5 & 6*

Jesus Christ is the ideal and supreme travel agent, available to any and all, who are willing to place their trust in Him.

If a typhoon is rising in force, threatening to carry you away from home, you need to know that the Lord directs the winds and the sea. Cling to the Lord in your hope, and if your hope begins to fade, close your eyes and do not let your trust in Him fade away too.

And I was with you in weakness, and in fear, and in much trembling. And my speech and my preaching was not with enticing words of man's wisdom, but in demonstration of the Spirit and power:

That your faith should not stand in the wisdom of men, but in the power of God. I Corinthians 2: 3, 4, & 5

Allowing your faith to stand in the power of God, assures you of victory. God's weakness, being stronger than men, can hold you upright, even as others observe you flat on your face. If everyone around you looks upon you as a failure, or a fool, their eyesight is of little value. God has already secured your place in the winners' circle, in the **Amazing Grace...Race.**

Hearken unto me, ye that know righteousness, the people in whose heart is my law; Fear ye not the reproach of men, neither be ye afraid of their revilings. Isaiah 51: 7

Too often in America, we conclude righteousness based on the eyes of a world addicted to the rich and famous. Those adorned in rags, are obviously failures and sinners to be pitied. We revile them, walk around them, and keep our distance from them. We set up aid stations far from the front doors of our magnificent cathedrals, built by men, to display our glory to God. However, God is neither interested in, nor moved by, our own, self-perceived glory.

Thus saith the Lord, the Heaven is my throne, and the Earth is my footstool: where is the house that ye build unto me? And where is the place of my rest?

For all these things hath my hand made, and all those things have been, saith the Lord: but to this man will I look, even to him that is poor and of a contrite spirit, and trembleth at my word.

It is not our glory that God desires. It is our contrite hearts and our trust in Him. Our glory is little more than spittle in the wind. God's glory is eternal.

Oh, that men would praise God for His goodness
And for His wonderful works to the children of men.

Our Breath of Hope is not based on our acceptance in the world, or approval from the world, that **we have arrived.** We do not hope, because we see land.

For we are saved by hope
But hope that is seen, is not hope:
For what a man seeth, why doeth he yet hope for it?

> *But if we hope for what we see not,*
> *Then do we with patience wait for it.*
> *Romans 8: 24 & 25*

Our Breath of Hope is taken in the promises of a faithful, loving God. We Breathe in the hope of the riches, assured us and waiting for us by His kindness in Christ Jesus. We will enjoy them in a Kingdom of Joy and love, not a fantasy Kingdom of legend and lore.

Our Breath of Hope is based on our knowledge that He has promised us deliverance from each affliction. That even when we receive more than we can handle, **we will never receive more than He can handle.**

Our Breath of Hope is taken in knowing that all we do in His name, is done in the Greatness of the power of the One who does not fail.

Our Breath of Hope, is based on our faith in Jesus as our Lord and Savior, and in the knowledge that He dwells in our hearts by faith. As His Spirit dwells within, He reigns over us and directs our steps. He controls the raging seas and promises to bring us to a safe haven, **our Haven and Hope, Jesus Christ.**

At times, on our voyage, He will have those He has set aside for our well-being waiting for us in rest stops, aid stations and medical outposts to strengthen us and help us heal. There will then be moments He will ask us to set ourselves aside, for the care and well-being of another.

He may choose you to comfort a wounded heart, to warm a cold hand. He may desire for you to spend, but a moment, with one who needs an ear, or a hug. He may call you to dry another's tear, without asking questions, **or providing answers.** He may move within you, so that your voice can share the truth of Life and the way of Salvation. He has so many good and wonderful plans, with an eternal purpose, **and all for you! You do not need to understand each one, just trust Him and follow.**

He will then be your hope, that you might also encourage the hope... of another.

The Breath of Hope

And now, with Hope in a heart of trust, let us take our Breath of Hope, in Him...Breathe!

Faith in Action:

Try marking off the next free day on your Calendar. Give it to the Lord. Let it be His day, for you to do... whatever.

A quiet day of prayer...A walk through the city street, where the less fortunate meet, to watch and seek...His will.

A drive along a country road, a moment singing under load, the love of Him to one you'll show... being in His will.

Or just a moment, one on one, with you and Him, God's dear Son, to know Salvation He has won...for you...are in His will.

And now count all the money from your very first Missionary Mug, or Pocket Ministry, and send this money to VOM. You may not think it much. Perhaps you could only afford a dollar or two. But it is a great gift, a gift to God, for His children. If you feel your gift is small and meaningless, let us hear what your High Priest and Boss, Jesus Christ, has to say about this.

And Jesus sat over against the treasury, and beheld how the people cast money into the treasury: and many that were rich cast in much. and there came a poor widow, and she threw in two mites, which make a farthing (less than two cents) and he called unto Him His disciples, and saith unto them,

Verily I say unto you,
That this poor widow hath cast more in,
than all they which have cast into the treasury:
For all they did cast in of their abundance;
But she of her want did cast in all that she had,
Even all her living.
Mark 12: 41 through 44

What a wonderful thought to cherish, that your Lord holds dear the love in your heart, over the wealth of the world. What you offer, no matter how insignificant it may appear, to Him, matches and exceeds the wealth of the richest. So give in celebration to a God, who is rich in His love towards you!

You can get a Money Order or, if there are only a few bills, fold them up in a white piece of paper, put the paper in an envelope, and send it off as is.

V.O.M. P.O. Box 443, Bartlesville, Ok. 74005-0443

Dear Heavenly Father,

Thank you for so rich a hope, in troubled seas and drifting currents of uncertainty. Thank you for our security in the hope of knowing that each of life's storms will be used for our safety. Thank you for reassuring us that even the winds that blow so hard, are guided by your divine hands and will carry us into your loving arms. That is your promise to us.

Thank you for looking down from Heaven upon us, who feel a little less than nothing and desiring for us to be something. Thank you for the voyage you have charted, through trials and Moments of Majesty lifted high, upon the wings of faith.

Thank you.

Please accept our hope in you, as a treasure of our faith, and let us stir up hope in another, that they may also know of your great love and Salvation.

Please bless this Missionary Offering for the aid and comfort of your children who suffer for love. Let it be their aid and a light of hope in the dark storms they endure, for the faiths sake. Let your name be magnified in all the Earth and let us all Praise you, O mighty God, for your goodness, and for your wonderful works to us, the children of men. In Jesus' name. Amen.

The Voyage of a lifetime...
On waves that bide His will,
Tho drifting oft uncertain,
In hope, and praise, and thrill,

Tho storm and thunder rally,
And lightening strike with fear,
We take our Breath of Hope in life,
Because we know He's near.

Now the God of Hope fill you with all joy and peace in believing
That ye may abound in hope,
Through the power of the Holy Ghost.
Romans 15; 13

And who... is your Travel Agent?

SECTION THREE

After a short stay
In the Grand Junction Homeless Shelter
I returned to Denver.

There, I headed a Fugitive Recovery Unit
For a major Bail Bonding Company.

My job was the investigation, apprehension
And transportation
Of all their fugitives.

I was aided by a young 19 year old
Whom I trained and was blessed to have help me.

He was the only original, Hood, I ever met.

Then I re-established my Fugitive Recovery School and taught
Fugitive Recovery

12

Out of Control
Eternal Breath

And take heed to your selves, lest at any time your hearts be
overcharged with surfeiting, and drunkenness, and cares
of this life, and so that day come upon you unawares.

For as a snare shall it come upon all them
that dwell on the face of the whole earth.

Watch ye therefore, and pray always, that ye may be accounted
worthy to escape all these things that shall come to pass,
and to stand before the Son of man.
Luke 21:34, 35, 36.

They were out of control, brandishing guns…holding people hostage… forcing their way into homes.

They were out of control…***and they had been my students!***

A Private Individual does not have the unlimited right to run the streets, making arrests for quick cash. However, a bail agent does have the right to make an arrest on any individual that they bail out of jail. They can also transfer their, **Power of Arrest,** to a private individual that acts as their agent to make the arrest for them. This person is known as a **Fugitive Recovery Agent**, or, as the TV show, **The Dog**, has made famous, the term **Bounty Hunter** can be used.

These individuals investigate, track down, and arrest those who have **jumped bail. Jumping BAIL** is the act of fleeing from a bail agent, because one does not want to go to court or go back to jail.

Although the rulings of the U.S. Supreme Court, dating back to the 1800s, have upheld a Bail Agent's right to arrest his or her defendant and or hire others to track down and arrest the fugitive for him, each State typically adds rules to the game, which must be followed.

In Colorado, an individual must complete a **Fugitive Recovery Course** by a **Provider** registered with the State. In 1998 I established a school and was certified as an Approved Provider. Those who wake up one morning deciding they want to become Fugitive Recovery Agents are a rough and tumble bunch. They have many colorful reasons for wanting a job that is long on hours and small on pay. Very few ever have great success, or make any money at it.

But across America, hundreds of fugitives **ARE arrested** weekly, without fanfare, safely and quietly, by these unseen hands of justice. Unseen, because most Fugitive Recovery Agents will never make the news. They go about their business with cool efficiency and work in the quiet of the shadows.

In late 2007 and early 2008, two individuals contacted me. Each wanted to set up Fugitive Recovery and Investigative Teams to work in the State of Colorado. I agreed to teach the classes they set up.

One of the individuals would later be arrested for cheating those same students that she paid me to teach. Apparently, she made promises she could not, or did not want to keep, depending on whom you talk with. Eventually, she was arrested for fraud. She is, at the writing of this book, currently in prison.

The second individual that contracted with me was a hard working guy, with sights set on achieving his own investigative company. Unfortunately, his concept of Fugitive Recovery was straight out of Hollywood. He and his crew fell for **the thrill of the hunt and the adrenalin rush, rushing out of control.** I do not know why he got out of control so quickly, but he is fortunate that he is not also currently sitting in a prison cell.

Having a Fugitive Recovery School, other bail agents call me from time to time, asking if I know of anyone able to catch a fugitive. Once in awhile, I'll take the case myself. Other times, I will pass it off to a team I have trained and certified. In this case, I received a call from a General Manager, who said one of his agents wrote a bad bond on a defendant and they would take a hit of $66,000.00. That is the amount of cash the bail agent would lose if the defendant were not caught. This was a great case, because an informant had disclosed the defendant's location.

The most daunting task of Fugitive Recovery is **not** the arrest. The task that holds the value is **the locating of the defendant**. Finding the defendant is always the key. If the defendant can be found, the arrest can take place.

In this case, the General Manager actually **knew where the defendant was staying**. The General Manager wanted to know if I had anyone available to stake out the house for a couple of days. The purpose of the stake-out would be to organize the circumstances of an arrest, whereby the defendant could be surprised and safely taken into custody.

I called the individual that had contracted with me to teach his team of hunters. He, himself, had also been through my course. I handed the case off to him, believing it would be a smooth and simple operation.

WALKING IN THE LIGHT OF GOD'S GREATNESS

The next day I learned how terribly wrong I was.

Instead of quietly placing two individuals in the defendant's neighborhood for surveillance, as I had stated, the Group Leader formed a pack of heavily armed boys and headed out to meet the bail agent. The bail agent, lacking any paper work or a defendant photograph, took the gang straight into the neighborhood for a drive by. That is when the Fugitive Team turned into the Keystone Cops.

As they neared the home, they saw the defendant in his vehicle, at the residence. Seeing dollar signs instead of common sense, they slammed on the brakes and barreled out of the truck they were in. Their leader, after picking himself off the ground, (**He fell getting out of the truck**) raced up to the defendant's vehicle, gun drawn.

The defendant, safe and secure within his vehicle, reacted like anyone might, which saw heavily armed men approaching quickly. He fled. He sped off to elude capture.

The fugitive team stumbled back to their vehicle and took pursuit. Now, with adrenalin flowing, full of bravado, they were off on a high-speed chase. They raced after the defendant, tailing him toward and onto the highway. On the highway, they tried to attract police by calling in an anonymous **DUI SPOTTED call**.

Why didn't they call 911 and tell them plainly that they were following a wanted fugitive, who could be armed and was considered dangerous? As they were racing down the highway, at a high rate of speed, they were fearful of any trouble they might receive for an illegal, high-speed pursuit. Fugitive Recovery Agents have no legal authority to engage in high-speed chases through the city streets, endangering innocent citizens.

A midday DUI call may not have seemed credible to the police that are constantly operating at full capacity, answering calls for criminal matters throughout the Denver Metro Area. The chance of a patrol car conveniently passing by to answer the call was unlikely. And so, they raced on, weaving their way north, in and out of traffic.

The defendant finally shot onto an off-ramp. At the end of the ramp, sitting quietly, minding his own business **was** a police car. Had the Fugitive Recovery Agents called in a **Dangerous Wanted Criminal** spotted, along with a name and license number, this chase may have come to a quick and tidy end. With the police involved, the odds of the fugitive stopping were significantly higher, then that he would voluntarily stop for an SUV loaded with gun-toting, good-ole boys, out on a Hunt. The fugitive was actually able to pull up next to the police car, exit into traffic and speed off. The Fugitive Recovery agents, who said nothing to the police officer sitting there as they drove by, lost the defendant.

After losing the fugitive, the Agents returned to the location where it all began. This time, they forced their way into the home the defendant had been staying at, and began to intimidate and harass the defendant's girlfriend. Forcing their way into her home, knowing the fugitive had left, was criminal. Inside the home, they cornered the girlfriend and began to interrogate and threaten her.

Over the next few weeks, these same gunslingers ran the gauntlet of house raiding and gun waving. They even strutted into one bar, like a picture out of the Old West, armed and loaded, looking for the bad guy.

Their actions may have made them look tough. They probably even felt tough, but they accomplished nothing. And that was what they got, nothing.

That they are not all currently sitting in prison for an array of charges is a merciful blessing that I hope one day they understand and are thankful for.

Shortly thereafter, this motley posse disbanded, ceasing their new found, short-lived career.

What happened to the dangerous fugitive they failed to capture? After this gang of keystone cops finally terminated their efforts, a tipster called in the location of the fugitive. The General Manager arranged for the police to go to the residence indicated, and the fugitive was arrested, safely and expediently.

WALKING IN THE LIGHT OF GOD'S GREATNESS

Very few ever have much success at Fugitive Recovery. It is a hard, dangerous business. The goal of an efficient fugitive recovery team is the safe apprehension of their fugitive. To catch **one**. Sometimes, they just cannot count that high.

> **Jesus loves me this I know.**
> **For the Bible tells me so...**

They were out of control...breaking down the door, brandishing clubs, and beating people up. They were members of the local Mosque.

> *Little ones to Him belong...*
> *They are weak but He is strong...*

With voices of hate, hurling threats, they stormed into the building hosting a Vacation Bible School, a riotous mass of violence.

> *Yes Jesus loves me...*

The children ran screaming.

> *Yes Jesus loves me...*

The pastors, who were teaching the school, were caught and beaten.

> *Yes Jesus loves me...*
> *The Bible tells me so.*

Their bibles were torn and ripped apart.

It was the students of insanity, against little children. One group, adults who foamed at the mouth, spewing vile chants of darkened hate, chased the little children, students who were learning about the love of Jesus.

The rioters of hate left behind a wreckage of ruin, fear, and terror. The pastors, beaten and bruised for teaching about love, tried to pick up the pieces.

The rioters had not taken the time to learn about the love of Jesus, as their blood lust flowed through veins of madness.

The trials that followed were a mockery of justice. They resembled the mockery of justice given Jesus, before he was nailed to the cross.

Jesus suffered for our sins.

These children in Pakistan and their families? They **fill up that which is left behind of the afflictions of Christ in their flesh for the body's sake which is the church. Colossians 1: 24**

In Pakistan, it only takes a rumor for certain Muslims groups, formed out of hate, to rise up like a plague from the dark side and swarm, a lust for violence boiling in their blood.

An Imam incites and ignites the flames of hate with cunning rumors. **The Koran is burned by Christians**, he declares. And the mindless masses follow in step, hordes of angry madmen marching for glory. The glory of Madness.

Yet, when terrorists or the Taliban set off bombs, murdering their own women and children…blowing little ones into a million pieces of flesh and bone…these same righteous marauders are silent. The blood of their own family members, at the hands of terrorists and the Taliban, barley causes a stir among these same rioting individuals. And why should it? Terror fulfills itself in terror. Why should darkness care…that darkness has arrived?

This violence occurs frequently in Pakistan, **a Muslim Dominated Country**. It actually happens frequently in many Muslim Dominated Countries. However, this event at the Vacation Bible School happened in Pakistan.

It is a beautiful summer's day! The children are up and ready. It is the first week of summer vacation and they are excited. They are going to Vacation Bible School. They will have fun there, playing games and learning about the love of Jesus. Perhaps they will get to do some arts and crafts… maybe even…**sorry, not today. Today, is a day for screaming and terror.**

This is life for Christians in the countries of Allah.

The West is virtually silent, like beggars on the side of the road, begging for acceptance from Muslim Marauders. Meanwhile, the Marauders dance the dance of death upon the lives of those they hate. Only in the west, where Muslims do not dominate, are Christians afforded equal standing and protection.

Young Christian children in Pakistan are aware that an afternoon of fun in the sun, can easily turn into a day of beatings and mockery by Muslim Youth. At an early age, Muslim youths are instructed in the fine arts of hate for Christians, Jews and the United States, by their local Madrasahs. These are the accepted norms of life in Pakistan, where even playgrounds can become war zones for innocent Christian Pakistani Children.

The Muslim right in Pakistan, is the right to rape, beat and burn out of house and home, those who choose the love of Jesus, over the veiled madness of their Allah.

There will be no mass street demonstrations over the blood they spill. You will not see many Pakistani Muslims standing up for justice, when their fellow Pakistani Christians are herded to slaughter. Burn a book and die. Rape a child and live. And what is the response of the Pakistani Christians? They learn how to count to one. Using an advanced mathematical formula taught by Jesus, they count one day at a time.

> *Take no thought for the tomorrow:*
> *For tomorrow shall take thought for the things of itself.*
> *Sufficient unto the day is the evil thereof.*
> *Matthew 6: 34*

And daily, they know that they may be savagely hunted down and murdered. How do they fight back?

They do not strap on explosive belts and send their enemies into oblivion. They fall on their knees and pray, asking God to allow them the strength to forgive those who hate them. They may also cry and weep at the suffering and torture inflicted by Muslims, under the approving eye of the authorities. They may have outrage at the savagery their children suffer, while their young daughters are taken at will, by those who claim to fulfill Allah's will.

Pakistani Christians may mourn the loss of their loved ones, as they are dragged off to prison for sharing the love of Jesus with others, or are falsely accused of insulting Mohamed. Pakistani Christians may be denied their rights and cursed for their faith. Pakistani Christians may be considered the dregs of their society, but Pakistani Christians stand bright in the eyes of the Lord Jesus.

They are His brethren and He will not leave or forsake them, as they continue to share the love of Jesus, even with those who beat and murder them. They live one day at a time, one moment at a time. They do not know if they will have another.

In Pakistan, Christians are sounding off the alarm. The marchers of Madness are coming. The rulers of darkness are stretching forth their shadows of death, stalking those who would choose love. They hunt for those, who would choose Jesus over Allah.

Yet, when recent natural disasters from earthquakes to floods ravaged their lands, it was a Christian Country that reached out to give aid. America stretched out its hand to show mercy to a country that appears to know none, and offers less.

The Light of Jesus began in the Middle East 2000 years ago. It began with Jewish men and woman. It began with Arabs. Arabs became Christians long before Mohamed ever raised an army to spill their blood. Christianity is **not** a Western invention. Christianity was born in the Middle East and spread to Asia. Christians were first called Christians in Turkey. Turkey, a country that defines its heritage as the heritage of Islam, had Christians spreading the good news of Jesus and Salvation, six hundred years before Mohamed ever took step one.

They were first called Christians in Antioch, present day Antakya, in southeastern Turkey.

Hundreds of years before the European Crusades, Mohamed was leading his own crusades, slashing and murdering his way across the Arabian peninsula, and on into India, across Asia, and finally invading Europe. The mass conversion of Arabs to Islam was not completed with love and truth, but with a sword dripping in the blood of those who would not submit.

Yet, in these lands where Christianity was born, **which at the first began to be spoken by the Lord, and was conformed unto us by them that heard Him. God also bearing witness, both with signs and wonders, and with divers miracles, and gifts of the Holy Ghost according to His will. Hebrews 2: 3 & 4.** The alarms are sounding. *It is the evening…of the dawn*, and death is getting out of bed to walk the dessert lands of fire, bringing the tidings of hell. Will we hear in time, or go back to sleep?

In Pakistan, a ticking time bomb of instability and hatreds, which are injected into their youth by their local Madrasahs, it is clear. Their goal is not peace, but war. They are raised to rise up and walk in the glory of death. After death, they are promised an eternal orgy of sexual pleasures. This is their spirituality. Murder and death today, over 70 virgins and continuous, eternal, sexual pleasures in paradise, tomorrow. This is the spirituality of Islam, promised to those coddled by their Imams to strap on a belted bomb and blow themselves up.

If the glorious death of Martyrs is to be cherished above all acts, why don't those who lead, do so by example? Why don't the cowards, who hide in caves and send young boys to die for the cause, get out and strap on a belt? They are not courageous and brave warriors, neither are those who chase little children, rape women, and kill others because their victims have chosen love, over madness. It is easy for cowards to incite fear. They just attack those who cannot fight back. They slink around in the alleys like rats.

It is only in countries where Muslims do not rule, reign, or have a majority, that passiveness and acceptance are taught as pillars of Islam.

In Pakistan, Christians know this law of Allah that allows rapists and murderers to act with impunity. Yet the same law imprisons and burns out of house and home, many who choose the love of Jesus, over the darkened halls of hate.

That is why Pakistani Christians have learned to take One breath at a time. Pakistani Christians hold onto their hopes in *Eternal Breath of Christ,* one day at a time. As fast as Jesus haters cut them down with savagery befitting barbarians from hell, Jesus just raises them back up. One day they will return with Jesus, when Jesus comes in the glory of His Father with all the Holy Angels. **What do you think those who hate the Light will do then? The bible tells us.**

And the Heaven departed as a scroll when it is rolled together; and every mountain and island was moved out of their places. And the kings of the Earth, and the great men, and the chief captains, and the mighty men, and every bondman, and every free man, hid themselves in the dens and in the rocks of the mountains; And said to the mountains and rocks,

"Fall on us, and hide us from the face of
Him that sitteth on the throne,
And from the wrath of the Lamb: For the great day of
His wrath is come; And who shall be able to stand?"
Revelation 6: 14, through 17

Who indeed!

One day, a **Day of Real** is coming. On the **Day of Real**, when Eternal destinies are revealed, Pakistani Christians will **not be hiding** in caves and dens. They will not be begging for an avalanche, their fear and trembling shaking the very mountainsides that provide their hiding place. On the **Day of Real**, Pakistani Christians will be in the Glory of Jesus, appearing with the King of Kings, riding the wings of Grace in Victory. They will have no fear.

> *When Christ,*
> *Who is our life, shall appear*
> *Then shall ye also appear with Him in glory.*
> *Colossians 4:11*

And... that day is **not** an illusionary day made up in dreams and drifting clouds. That day will be as real as you are, right now reading this page and your hands holding this book. That day will be the **Day of Real**. **And that Day will come soon!**

> *Be ye also patient; stablish your hearts:*
> *For the coming of the Lord draweth nigh.*
> *James 5: 8*

On a day of sacrifice 2,000 years ago, on a hill far away, the Son Of God, a person ridiculed, laughed at, beaten, whipped and mocked, was nailed to a tree and left to die. He did, but then, He rose. He rose from the grave in Eternal Victory over death. The same victory He promises to anyone who looks to Him for **Eternal Breath** in Salvation.

> *Look unto me, and be ye saved, all the ends of the earth:*
> *For I am God and there is none else.*
> *Isaiah 45: 22*

> *I, even I, am the Lord,*
> *And beside me, there is no savior.*
> *Isaiah 43:11*

> *Neither is there salvation in any other.*
> *For there is <u>None Other Name</u>*
> *under heaven given among men,*
> *Whereby we must be saved.*
> *Acts 4: 12*

No other name. Just one. Just Jesus. Can you count that high?

He was a Nobody, they thought. Now He is King of Kings.

*The children of Pakistan attend Vacation Bible school
Under threat of death.
They want to learn about Jesus.
Once they learn about Jesus,
They are beaten on the playgrounds.
They are chased and menaced while attending
Vacation Bible School,
But they still believe.
They know how to count to One.
One day at a time.
They do not know if they will live beyond it.*

Can you count to One?

12

Eternal Breath
Faith in Action

On the edge of Eternity...

Each thought...each moment...

Holding eternal weight of gold...

Or Eternal loss...

Every man's work shall be made manifest;
For the day shall declare it,
Because it shall be revealed by fire;
And the fire shall try every man's work of what sort it is.
If any man's work abides which he hath built thereupon,
He shall receive a reward.
If any man's work shall be burnt, he shall suffer loss,
But he himself shall be saved;
Yet so as by fire.
I Corinthians 3:13, 14, & 15.

WALKING IN THE LIGHT OF GOD'S GREATNESS

During the reign of Hitler and the rise of Nazi Germany, **Evolutionary Grandeur** cooked in the ovens of a country determined to rule the world. The elite and powerful determined that people of Jewish heritage should be extinguished and the Germanic race exalted. As the evolutionary cream of the crop, the Germans would define perfection in selection.

As ovens burned the flesh of the unwanted and helpless, one man's eyes looked beyond the world of thought. He rejected the ideas presented by the propagandizing, evolutionary team of scientists and rulers, who deemed the annihilation of the Jewish Race its highest calling.

One man defied the odds and surrendered his life, so that others might escape death. He used his wealth, charm and cunning to help Jewish people escape the madness of the Murderers. He stepped into the darkness of the night, and with **eyes of sight**, became their light. His arms opened and hands reached out, grasping for every Jewish man, woman and child he could afford, one at a time.

The wealth he sought for Earthly gain became the wealth of each life he paid for. Under the clouds of war and darkened uncertainties, he chose the **Breath of Life** over the panting desires of golden coins and the neon lights of fading glory.

Schindler's List, a true story, was a provocative and inspiring movie. However, I was most deeply touched by the movie's ending. For after this man had given all his wealth to help the Jewish people, after he risked his own freedom, spending his last dime to save as many Jews as he could from the nightmarish evil of the Nazi Death Camps…when it was all over, as he walked to his car, he was hit hard in the gut.

I could have sold it, and saved ten more, he whispers to himself. Those he saved are standing around him trying to comfort him. He refuses to be comforted. At the end, as he walked to his car, a very nice sedan, a sedan of the rich and mighty, it hit him. Was the value of the car he was going to ride in, his last possession, more valuable than the lives of others he might have saved had he sold it? **Ten other people perished in a gas chamber, so I could have this car.** This was the thought of horror that flared up within his being. And he could find neither comfort

ETERNAL BREATH...FAITH IN ACTION

nor rest. As the car pulled away, for all he had done and sacrificed, he could find no comfort.

He had started out as a selfish man, intent on creating wealth beyond measure. He had prepared to leave Germany with three suitcases packed with hard currency, and would return home within the victory and celebration of his success. He did return, but not with the wealth that he first intended to acquire.

He traded his worldly fortune for over 1000 Jewish men, women, and children. These people became his riches. But even in this living wealth of human souls, he could gather no comfort, as thoughts of those he might have saved, rose up to claim his peace.

Will you also find no comfort one day soon when you face the Lord? Do preachers tell you; your first appearance with the Lord will be all sunshine and lollypops?

In America, we know how to count into the millions and billions, but have we forgotten how to count to One?

In America, are we too often so busy about the things we see and want, that we tend to pant like dogs on a hot summer day? We reach out to grasp the things we see, and fail to see the things we do not.

> *For the things which are seen are temporal;*
> *But the things which are not seen are eternal.*
> 2 Corinthians 4: 18

Do we focus on our daily assigned tasks with tunnel vision? Have our spiritual eyes become blinded in the wanted desires and or, miseries that fill our being?

As we rush about, do we block out the lighted rays of Heavenly mist, shining upon a soul in need? Do we miss the **Majesty of the Moment,** in the mayhem of the rush? In the riotous needs of the day, do we allow ourselves to take time for an, **Eternal Breath,** in the **Light of God's greatness?** Do we know how to pause, for just a moment, to take an **Eternal Breath** with **Eyes of Sight?**

Do we prefer to sleep-walk as a **Passerby** in life, dropping by a church each Sunday so a pastor can open our bibles for us? We like it when others open our bibles. After they open them, we want them to read to us as well, like a bedtime story. After they read to us, we can go back to sleep without counting sheep.

> *Wherefore He saith, Awake thou that sleepest*
> *And arise from the dead,*
> *And Christ shall give thee light.*
> *Ephesians 5: 14*

In America, too often, do we complain about the light? **Turn off the light! I'm trying to sleep!**

Are we out of control?

It is the evening...of the dawn, and soon the dawn will rise over the horizon, and a **Day Of Real**, arrive.

> *For it is written, "As I live," saith the Lord,*
> *"every knee shall bow to me,*
> *and every tongue shall confess to God."*
> *So then, every one of us shall give account of himself to God.*
> *Romans 14: 11 & 12*

When it is your turn to account for your life, will you have the joy of one whose life is filled with eternal treasures and wealth beyond measure? Or will all your wealth have been left behind, in the rubble of your past?

Will you suffer anything on that day? I know that many preachers claim that there will be no suffering. But what about the suffering of regret? Haven't you discovered that in life, regret can be one of the greatest pains to suffer? Regret is the torment that keeps on giving. Regret could outlast the Energizer Rabbit.

> *Whoever's work shall be burned shall suffer loss*
> *Yet he himself shall be saved yet so as by fire.*

After the war, this man Schindler, who suffered the loss of all for a few, lived with a failed marriage and failed businesses. How long did he carry the burden of regret around in his heart? **If I had only sold the car...I could have saved ten more!**

He was a brave man, who gave all he had to purchase a future for as many lives as was possible. And the seed of hope he planted in each heart of everyone he saved from the horrors of the Nazi Death Camps, became the seeds of life. For those he saved and their children, and now... their children's children, received life because of his sacrifices. But his sense of regret, rightly or wrongly...did it linger in pain, within his heart? What will linger in your heart when you stand before Jesus, who gave His life **for you?** Right now...in this living moment of truth, **think...what will linger?**

And so it is, here and now, in this **Eternal Breath**, that you must decide for who and what will you live. Will you live for the temporal, that will perish with the world... or the eternal that will last forever.

> **For it is written, "As I live," saith the Lord,**
> **"Every knee shall bow to me**
> **And every tongue shall confess to God."**
> **So then we see that every one of us will Give account of himself**
> **To God.**

Many of the defendants I post bail for, believe that **Real** is running the streets doing as they please, acting up when they want, and living how they want.

If I tell them that what they are doing, the fun they are having and the things they believe in, are meaningless, they fail to hear.

> **He that hath ears to hear,**
> **let him hear what the Spirit saith to the churches.**
> **Revelations 3: 22**

If I counsel them that their freedom and future will end in loss, they do not understand.

> *But the end of all things is at hand:*
> *Be ye therefore sober and watch unto prayer.*
> *I Peter 4: 7*

When I explain to them that on the day they are caught and sent to prison, they will know what **Real** is, they cannot picture it enough to see.

> *I counsel thee to...*
> *Anoint thine eyes with eye salve, that thou mayest see.*
> *Revelations 3: 18*

Then the **Day of Real** arrives and the accounting begins. They are sentenced to prison. And as they are transported, cuffed and shackled, aboard the prison bus, away from home, family, and friends, all they now feel...*is the loss.* This is the day of understanding what **Real** is... *but it is too late.*

As you walk the streets of life, will the day of **Real** come upon you unannounced? Will the Lord come as a thief, when you are unprepared, and take away the wealth you thought you had secured?

> *For all that is in the world,*
> *The lust of the flesh, And the lust of the eyes, And the pride of life,*
> *Is not of the Father, but is of the world.*
> *And the world passeth away, and the lust thereof: But he that doeth the will of God abideth forever.*
> *1 John 2: 16 & 17*

In America, are too many Christians lulled to sleep by the bedtime stories of those who walk in the grandeur of their own glory, *those who preach under neon lights, for golden coins?* Do we prefer to snuggle under the blankets of electrified warmth, to wait for the Lord, hiding from the horrors of the world and the suffering of our brothers and sisters on distant shores? In our irritation at being disturbed, do we knock the alarm clock off the night stand, across the room, to silence the ringing... to shut out the voices crying out in pain? The suffering we do not see, cannot touch our hearts, upsetting our perfectly planned moment of self, our very own, special, **Best Moment Now?**

> *And whether one member suffer,*
> *All the members suffer.*
> *I Corinthians 13: 26*

Have we forgotten the greatness of our calling? Have we relinquished our **Area** to others?

In North Korea, a young girl disappears after praising God. ***In America, how many Christians disappear after church and a Latte each Sunday?***

In Sudan, a boy, who refuses to give up his faith, is thrown into the fire. ***In America how many Christians don't mind trading their faith... for a little fire here...a little fire there?***

In Saudi Arabia, a girl's tongue is cut out, so she cannot speak about Jesus and a wooden cross he was nailed to for our sins. ***In America, how many Christians are too embarrassed to speak the name of Jesus and share the story of a cross?***

In Pakistan, Christian children are chased in terror by the Muslim Fanatics of hate, those who claim Allah as their god. ***In America, how many Christians prefer to chase American Idol?***

In Bangladesh, Buddhists chase down and beat those who have left their empty, meaningless lives of chants and idol worship, to become Christians. ***In America, how many Christians prefer an empty, meaningless lifestyle?***

In India, where a Hindu Caste System holds the masses in the slavery of religious servitude, the lowest rung, the Untouchables, are being touched by God and freed from slavery as pre-ordained nobodies, to walk in the Freedom and Grace of God. Though they are brutalized by Hindu fanatics, their homes invaded by the violent hordes of Hindu Faithful, who drag them into the streets for beatings and burning, they hold fast their standing in Christ Jesus. They have chosen life and freedom in Jesus, over the six-armed deities and endless array of gods and goddesses, envisioned in the minds of their tormentors.

In America, have Christians replaced their freedom in Christ, for a Christianized Caste System? A system of human gods and goddesses, as they worship Mega Marvels and Late Night Beggar Preachers, who claim the authority of God over them? A caste system that forces them to dig into their pockets and pay off the ransom demands of gilded orators, assuring them of wealth and prosperity, if they will first surrender theirs?

How many Christians have bartered their freedom in Jesus, for imitation spirituality, trading **charity, the bond of perfectness,** for a chance to roll down the aisles in babbling laughter, bound and drunk in a spirit they **claim** is Christ.

As they mimic animals, or faint like groupies, **slain in the spirit**, have they determined that **life in the spirit,** is not as much fun? Have they finally discovered true enlightenment in a Caste System where their leaders, who revel in the mystical mist of self-adorned glory, use pointed fingers to appoint them as minions, as they forget the Cross that points them to Heaven?

How many ministries have forsaken the name of Jesus, to impose the name of **Self** upon their glorified works? Do great Christian leaders now name ministries after themselves, just to make sure God knows who is supposed to get the credit for anything good that may happen?

Jesus said, **He who is greatest among you shall be your servant.**

The American Christian Caste system says, **He who is greatest among you...well, he IS really great, isn't he?!!**

As the glamorous and beautiful prance and dance across their stages in holy refinery, proclaiming their divine standing with God, the lower Caste members are relegated to worship them with awe, paying a sin tax before they can return to their empty lives. At home and alone once more, they return to bed until the next summons arrives. Until the next Bright and Beaming Apostle calls them forth, they can return home to slumber under the religious covers purchased from Hollywood's Religious **Bed, Bath, and Beyond.**

Do we slumber, snuggling under the covers of electrified warmth, as if it was Heaven itself? It is not.

And…it is time to wake up and do the works of Him while it is day… *for the night cometh when no man can work. John 9:4*

It is the evening… of the dawn. But before the Dawn rises over the horizon of hope, the night is coming and the mountain we now walk atop in the day, may soon crumble. Shortly, our life's way of security, may be a walk…*through the valley of the shadow of death.*

In the night, will you *fear under deaths shadow, or shine under the Eternal Light?*

We have been given an **Eternal Breath**, to allow us the courage to shine in the darkness. To shine in the Eternal Light of Jesus Christ, not in the man-made, glimmering halo of those claiming the voice of God, in order to subject others to their voice. We are called to walk in the Light of God's Greatness, not slink beneath the shadows of men and women draped in their own religiosity.

We are called to Greatness.

We are called to touch one life that is near…and one life afar.

We are called to touch.

Jesus said he would leave the 99 to find the **One** that is lost. While many Christian Leaders appear to revel in their own glory, as they stand like immaculate towers of light, before audiences of thousands gathered together to hear their next words of wisdom, Jesus would be out looking for the One who was lost. In America, we count Greatness in the millions and billions, but we have forgotten how to count all the way up to… **One.**

We revel in great revivals when thousands attend, and hundreds come forward. But who will go outward, to find…the **One?** Who is willing to leave the spotlight of glamour, with **Eyes of Sight,** to see the **one,** afraid and alone?

Who will offer a hand of fellowship to the **One,** others claim is not in their **Area?** Who is willing to learn a little Heavenly math? Whose heart can become a mathematical calculator in the hands of God, programmed to add, divide, subtract, and multiply by the number, **One?**

You may require a new position for this numerical journey, as you venture out into unknown lands and foreign territories. But worry not, for early this morning your boss notified us you have one.

Now, I know what you're going to say...

Hey, I'm already a sergeant in the Royal Army. I have a position in the High calling of God in Christ Jesus, am in the middle of the Amazing Grace...Race, am on a Fast the Lord has chosen, as a Priest offering up sacrifices acceptable to God by Jesus Christ... am currently adrift on a ship with a lot of rice... and...

Slow down. Relax. This new job is another step up into divine greatness...and the offer? You have been offered an Ambassadorship!

> *Now then we are ambassadors for Christ...*
> *2 Corinthians 5: 20*

From His Royal Palace, Jesus has appointed you an Ambassadorship, to go forth and represent His Kingdom. As a royal ambassador, you represent the **Kingdom of Salvation, Forgiveness and Love**, in the gospel of Jesus Christ, crucified for the sins of the world. Your duties as an ambassador are to share the wealth of the kingdom, in **Deed and Truth.**

In **The Amazing Grace... Race**, you are now representing **the Kingdom of Heaven, as a Royal Ambassador.** In America, these positions are usually reserved for the political faithful and large money donors. In Heaven, these positions are handed out to **Nobodies**, **Failures (*Soon not to be*)** and **Christians in Sleeper Cells**, who can be activated. The only requirements are Faith, the love of Christ, and a little math. You must know how to count as high as **One.** On the voyage of a lifetime, across oceans, through storms, tossed in the waves of life, you have been honored with a **Royal Ambassadorship,** to represent the Kingdom of Heaven, in the **Majesty of a Moment** and walk in the **Light of God's Greatness!**

For a Nobody, I would say you have come a long way in only 11 breaths. You have gone from nothing, as a failure in life, to a noble standing in a **Royal Family,** by adoption. Having lost everything, you have become heir to greater riches than man could ever comprehend.

> *But as it is written, eye hath not seen, nor ear heard,*
> *Neither hath entered into the heart of man,*
> *The things which God hath prepared for them that love Him.*
> *I Corinthians 2: 9*

From a homeless vagabond of no account, to a guaranteed seat among princes, with a mansion built by the greatest carpenter ever to walk in Heaven *or* on Earth.

From rags and second hand clothes, to a **Tailor Made, Royal Robe of Righteousness.**

From poverty and nothing, **to having it all!**

> *Therefore let no man glory in men.*
> *For all things are yours; Whether...*
> *the world, or life, or death,*
> *Or things present, or things to come;*
> *All are yours;*
> *And ye are Christ's; and Christ is God's.*
> *I Corinthians 3: 21, 22, 23*

It *is* about you.

You are the reason Jesus walked to that hill, The hill of Calvary,

To die.

He died for you.

Jesus did not want you to continue stumbling around in the woods alone... and lost.

And now that you have been found, Jesus would like you to help another who is lost. **You do not need to be a woodsman, or an outdoor expert at survival.** You do not need to be an expert on Theology, or understand the forty variations of each Greek word.

Jesus said, **My Yoke is easy.** I cannot find the verse that says, **Hey, look out! Christianity is a real rat race!**

You simply need the Breath of God, His Spirit, to fill you with His love, desire, and guidance and to be continuously washed in His Word, the Bible.

You do not need to wait for the next proclamation of one, who claims a supernatural, secret hotline directly to God. God, in His infinite wisdom and love, desires you to come directly to Him, **yourself !**

For through Him (through Jesus) we both have access by one Spirit unto the Father.
Ephesians 2: 18

With direct access, you have the same line of open communication to God as those, who may boast that **they walk on clouds at His beckoning. Or... that He trails them at their demand.**

You are allowed into the very presence of God through prayer. No man-made appointed intermediary, or public confessional booth is required.

Through Him, (Just Jesus) through One Spirit, you have access to One God, the only true and living God!

Just One. Touch just **One.** Reach just **One.** Help just **One.**

One near... and one afar.

As an Ambassador who represents the Royal Kingdom of Jesus Christ, you are called to the religion of God, not of man. You are called by the Spirit of God, to a **Pure Religion**, to touch just **One**.

Pure religion and undefiled before God
And the Father is this,
To visit the fatherless and the widows in their affliction,
And to keep himself unspotted from the world.

James 1: 27

And you thought religion was counting beads and lighting candles.

As an ambassador of a **Kingdom of Light,** can you shine a little light on one who is afflicted?

Can you, as **Christ's Ambassador,** reach across an ocean, to touch one life burdened, beaten and brutalized, carrying a heavy cross?

If you do, perhaps one day while you are walking in the brightness and joy of a beautiful, Heavenly moment in paradise, you will hear a voice.

Hey you, wait up! As you turn to look, the voice will be adorned by a smile of gratitude. **You were the one who gave money to help after I was thrown into a fire. When they asked who would pay for my burns, you paid the bill. I just wanted to thank you. I told Jesus about you, but He said he already knew.** How will you feel then?

As you stand before Jesus, awed into silence at the presence of the Lord, unable to speak, what will you feel if an excited voice blurts out, **Jesus, this is the person who sent money when my family was burned out of our home. While we wandered in despair, a gift they sent allowed me to feed my children.**

How will you feel then?

What if, while attending the dinner feast of the Lamb, you overhear a conversation about one who spent time in prison for the Lord. ***And so, one day after being tortured and throne back into my cell, I felt lost and abandoned. That's when this other guard slid an envelope under the door. I'm telling you, I couldn't believe it when I opened it up. It said, "You are not forgotten." I cherished that letter the entire time I stayed in prison...all 15 years.***

As he talks, the Lord's eyes look into yours. You and the Lord both know that the card, slid under the cell door so long ago, was a card you had mailed. **How will you feel then?**

It is really not too difficult to count up to One. And if you begin having a hard time with your spiritual math, just ask Jesus for help. The indwelling of His Spirit, your Dream Coach in the **Amazing Grace...Race**, can calculate any problem in the blink of an eye.

The rich and the famous count in billions. Jesus wants us to learn to count all the way up... *to One.*

The rich and famous use bulldozers to move mountains. God likes to use Nobodies. Can He use you?

To touch one who is near, and one who is afar.

In the **Majesty of a Moment,** will you see the one who needs you, or will you leave them face down, bleeding on the sidewalk? **Will you leave them to die alone in a pool of blood?**

Each moment in Jesus Christ, is a **Moment in Eternity**. Each moment in Jesus is the **beginning of Eternity**. Will you remain in the death of the world, in the Breath of Death, or...**will you learn to count to One, in the Majesty of an Eternal Moment?**

> Jesus said, *Behold, I stand at the door, and knock: If any man hear my voice, and open the door,*
> *I will come in to him.*
> *And will dine with him, and he with me.*

Have you opened the door yet? Who are you having dinner with tonight?

The Eternal Breath.

The ***Eternal Breath*** will be the ***Breath*** you take each moment you walk in the ***Spirit of Christ.*** *The **Eternal Breath*** is the breath you will take when you live for the ***Day of Real, the return of Jesus,*** in the ***Majesty of a Moment with spiritual eyesight.***

The Eternal Breath is the breath you will take, when you trust your Travel Agent to book your passage…on a ship adrift in the Pacific.

Even the winds and the sea obey Him

If your ship sinks beneath the icy depths of oceans deep, leaving you alone, adrift in a life raft, your ***Eternal Breath*** is knowing that your life raft is what it is ***A Raft of Life, not death.***

Because Jesus did not want you to go down with the ship, he provided you a life raft. He will not let you drift forever, bobbing on the waves like a fishing lure. You are His chosen, chosen unto life, chosen by God to walk in the Light of His Greatness. That's a pretty great thought all by itself!

The ***Eternal Breath*** is **Living in Victory Eternal, each day, every day, by abiding in Jesus Christ.**

It is better to walk in the Truth… than be slain in a lie.

Faith in Action: **Our Faith in Action for this, our last breathing exercise, is to share what we have learned with one other.** After finishing this book, place a five-dollar bill in the cover and give it to another. As you go about your daily tasks, ask the Lord to touch your heart when he is ready. Then, when you see a person alone, sitting or sleeping in a doorway, offer them hope in **Deed and Truth**.

Maybe the Lord will allow you to see one on the side of the road, a person walking slowly down the street, shoulders sagging from the weight of their load. In your Eternal Breath of life… always be ready to share yours.

If you wish to keep the book to review the **Faith in Action steps**, and you can afford it, buy another book. Put a five-dollar bill in the second book and keep it handy. When the Lord prompts your heart, hand it out.

If you are homeless, and have lost everything you own, you will have a greater blessing. For you can place a one dollar bill in the book when you are done. Wrap the one-dollar bill in a note that says the following:

Hi. I am homeless but really enjoyed this book. I have put a dollar in it, because that is all I could afford. You will need the dollar for your first, Faith in Action. I hope this book helps you cheer up a bit.

After you write the note and place a one-dollar bill in the book, ask the Lord to guide your walk and introduce you to societies finest. Ask the Lord to reveal one who **has it all**, including the tears that run down their cheeks because, all they have…is nothing. When you believe you have spotted the right person, go up and offer them the book. Explain there is a special message in the book just for them, and you hope they enjoy it. Hand them the book and walk away, asking the Lord to open their heart and their life to His blessings and His truth.

On this day, in this one act, you will have completed our breathing exercises. There will be more to come, more to do and yet more breathing, but your first session will be over. Being over, you will have a new beginning. A new beginning in Jesus.

Life and Death are happening now. All around you, Eternal Destinies are being shaped and formed. **What shape is your**

Eternal destiny?

> The wicked shall be turned into hell,
> And all the Nations that forget God.

In Pakistan, a nuclear time bomb, in the madness of darkened grip, with hands of hate, they are out of control, chasing little children in the shame of their foaming rage.

And in America...? You will help determine that...in your eternal breath.

> **The wicked shall be turned into hell**
> **And all the nations that forget God.**

> *Are we, in America...forgetting?*

Jesus told Abraham He would not destroy the cities of Sodom and Gomorrah, if ten righteous people could be found. There were not ten.

> It IS about you

> Everyone else is too worried about their image.
> You and I have no worries there. *(Smile)*

> If you can learn to count to one,
> You will know that what you do... *counts!*
> If not...what you do not do...?

Thank you for Salvation, Lord. Sorry I didn't get around to waking up, but you know, I didn't really think that...I mean heck, I had so many things to do! I wanted to make a difference. Really!...I mean....I wanted to count....but you know... I wasn't good at math and that carnival ride was so long...heck, how was I suppose to know that before the last ride was over, I would die? I wasn't expecting it. How could I have known that I wouldn't live to see the morning?!

> But you know now, don't you?

> How high can *you* count?

This Is Only The BEGINNING!

And now, as we stand at the edge of eternity...*you need to know that this is only the beginning!*

As you gaze into the eternal moment of tomorrow...you should allow each breath you take today, to hold the eternal hope of a life without end.

As long as there is yet breath

There is yet hope...

And within the riches and treasures of your hope, is the beginning of life.

This is only the beginning.

A beginning to wonders and miracles and life in Jesus Christ! An abundant life! The life He promised you!

It does not matter if you walk the streets alone, broke and wearing second hand clothes. Jesus has you walking streets of Gold in His hand tailored **Royal Robe of Righteousness!**

It does not matter if you are a beggar, unwanted and unnoticed by those who pass you by each day. Jesus has you sitting among Princes and has prepared for you to inherit the *Throne of Glory*.

It does not matter if you are not in **their** area. Jesus has given **you all areas**! In Jesus, you **are** a conqueror.

It does not matter if you are in prison. Jesus has secured your freedom.

And it does not matter if you are laying atop deaths bed. Jesus has you walking streets of gold.

If you have followed the suggestions within these pages, then I am humbled and I pray that His Light is growing within your heart as you begin to understand the wonder of being a **Nobody in the Greatness of God!**

If you were unable to complete all **Faith in Actions steps** for any reason, do not lose heart. Were you able to complete One?

And after your **One,** try another, one at a time. If not a **Faith in Action** listed within the pages of this book, ask the Lord for your own, personal **Faith in Action, one He can help you complete.**

And so, this day **IS** only the beginning!

It does not matter your age. Even at 103, you are a mere babe within the time-scape of Eternity!

Whether you are Male or female.

Whether all hate you or despise you.

Whether anyone knows you at all! **He knows You! He chose you!**

The King of Kings stands by you and states, **This is only the beginning.**

So do not stop. Even though by the end of the day, you may fall, without strength, in a heap of depression and loneliness, a failure once more, your doubts rising up like Alexander the Great. This is Prime Time for your Lord. Let His words carry the moment. He says to you…

THIS IS ONLY THE BEGINNING!

> *... my strength is made perfect in your weakness.*
> *Corinthians 12: 9*

You see, Alexander the Great, is great no more. He is dead. The lands he conquered are now in the hands of others. All he had is gone. Trust in Him who conquered death and He will help you conquer your failures and subdue your sadness. Trust in Him to comfort you when you are lonely. He will and He can.

And then...the morning will rise once more. Your hope will be restored, and you will see...that this is only the beginning.

And God said, Let there be light: And there was light.
And God saw the light, that it was good: And God divided
the Light from the darkness. And God called the light Day,
And the darkness He called Night.
And the evening and the morning were the first day.

This *IS* the evening...of the dawn
He whispers to you...*I am here.*

On a hill far away stood an old rugged cross,
The emblem of suffering and shame;
And I love that old cross where the dearest and best
For a world of lost sinners was slain.

So I'LL CHERISH THE Old rugged cross,
Till my trophies at last I lay down
I will cling to the old rugged cross,
And exchange it some day for a crown.

O that old rugged cross, so despised by the world,
Has a wondrous attraction for me;
For the dear Lamb of God left His glory above
To bear it to dark Calvary

So I'll cherish the old rugged cross;
Where my trophies at last I lay down;
I will cling to the old rugged cross;
And exchange it some day for a crown.

In that old rugged cross, stained with blood so divine,
A wondrous beauty I see,
For twas on that old cross Jesus suffered and died,
To pardon and sanctify me.

So I'll cherish the old rugged cross
Where my trophies at last I lay down;
I will cling to the old rugged cross
And exchange them some day for a crown.

Written in 1912 by George Bernard

FOR Christ sent me not to baptize,
But to preach the gospel: Not with wisdom of words
Lest the cross of Christ be made to none effect.

For the preaching of the cross is to them that perish foolishness;
But unto us which are saved it is the power of God.
I Corinthians 1: 17 & 18

And so...this is only the beginning.

Prayer of Salvation

You are not an accident.

You are not an evolutionary glass of spilt milk.

You were not given the Breath of Life to stumble around in a haze of confusion, hugging trees, claiming a mound of dirt as your mother. You are not a byproduct of an Evolutionary **Ooops Theory.**

You are unique, designed by God.

Before I formed thee in the belly, I knew thee:
And before thou camest out of the womb I sanctified thee.
Jeremiah 1:5

God loves you and has great plans for you.

For I know the thoughts I think toward you, saith the Lord,
Thoughts of peace, and not evil...
Jeremiah 29:11

How precious also are thy thoughts unto me, O God.
How great is the sum of them!
If I should count them, they are more in number then the sand:
When I awake, I am still with thee.
Psalm 139: 17&18

He also has a gift for you.

The greatest gift one could ever hope to receive. He has the gift of forgiveness and Eternal life.

For God so loved the world that He gave His only begotten Son.
That whosoever believeth in Him,
Shall not perish but have everlasting life.
John 3 : 16

It is not a gift that can be earned.

It is not a gift that can be bought.

It is free.

God does not charge for forgiveness.

And He does not charge for love.

If you have never been forgiven for the sins of your heart and life, now is your opportunity to present yourself to the court of God, for clemency. Today, you live in a season of God's grace and forgiveness.

Whosoever shall call on the name of the Lord shall be saved.
Romans 10:13

Tomorrow, it may be too late. ***It is the evening...of the Dawn.***

One day, two thousand years ago, a man, Jesus Christ, the Son of God, created a bail bonding business. He decided that His operation would expand on a global scale and began appointing agents to work on His behalf. His business plan was simple. His agents would post bail in His name, for anyone accused of any crime.

The people He wanted to free were all condemned and waiting for the **Court of Death**. They were all guilty and set for execution. That is when *He* showed up.

PRAYER OF SALVATION

He presented himself in their place, accepted the guilt, the shame, and sentence of the court, the sentence of Death. He offered himself as a replacement for each and every one imprisoned, for each and every crime committed. For each and every sin.

He was God in the flesh, walking among men, **anointed to preach the gospel to the poor;** Jesus was sent to **heal the broken hearted, to preach deliverance to the captives, and recovering sight to the blind, and to set at liberty them that are bruised. To preach the acceptable year of the Lord.** Luke 4: 18 & 19

And Jesus has not changed His message. This is still the acceptable year of the Lord, a season of grace… but it will not last forever.

The seasons are changing and **Fall** has arrived. Soon it will be **Winter**. Now is the acceptable year of the Lord, tomorrow may be too late.

Are you in need of redemption? Do you desire forgiveness? God is ready for both and has prepared your way before you, for you. He only asks of you to accept Him, to embrace His forgiveness, and the gift of life in His Son, Jesus Christ. There is no other.

For there is none other name under heaven given among men Whereby we must be saved.

*For there is One God
And One mediator between God and Man
The man Christ Jesus
Who gave Himself a ransom for all
To be testified of in due time.*

One God and One mediator. One name under Heaven.

The name, *Jesus Christ.*

Won't you now accept this name into your heart and allow yourself the forgiveness God longs for you to enjoy? Today, won't you allow yourself to walk in the freedom of God's grace, and the security offered by His Son? He established His bail bonding company in His own blood, on a cross, 2,000 years ago. He established it for you. The company services are free, provided in the Breath of Love, the love of Jesus Christ.

He that hath the Son hath life.
He that hath not the Son, hath not life.

For by Grace are ye saved, through faith,
And not of ourselves,
It is the Gift of God!
Not of works, lest any man should boast.
Ephesians 2: 8 & 9

Grace is simply *Undeserved Love.*
Undeserved, but offered as a gift of God.

Won't you take a moment to unwrap this most precious gift of God to secure your future and eternal well-being?

The word is close to you, even close at hand, even the Word of Faith that the bible teaches.

That If thou will confess with thy mouth, the Lord Jesus Christ And believe in thy heart, that God hath raised Him from the dead thou shalt be saved. For with the heart man believeth unto righteousness And with the mouth, confession is made unto salvation. Romans 10: 9

So just ask…and be saved!

Jesus waits for you to allow Him into your life.

If your girlfriend or a boyfriend were standing outside your home, knocking on your door, how could they enter, unless you opened the door for them? If the door stayed shut, even though they waited outside patiently, despite knocking, they would never enter.

PRAYER OF SALVATION

*Jesus says, Behold I stand at the door and knock,
If any man hear my voice, and open the door,
I will come into them, and will sup with them,
and they with me. Revelations 3: 20*

Won't you open the door? The door to life!

While He hung, nailed to a wooden cross, his body battered and bruised, his heart melting within, and his lifeblood oozing from the wounds where nails pierced his hands and feet, he thought of you.

Beside him were two criminals, also nailed to crosses. He also thought of them.

One mocked him continuously. The other, in a breath of hope, confessed his sins and rebuked the mocker. *Here we are suffering for what we deserve. This man is suffering but doesn't deserve it.* Then, in whispered breath of prayerful want, he cried to Jesus. **Lord, remember me when you come into your Kingdom.**

What do you think Jesus said?

No, not unless you do 10,000 Hail Mary's. And I really do not see how you are going to accomplish that with your hands nailed up as they are.

No... that is not what Jesus said.

Jesus simply said, *Today, you will be with me in Paradise.*

That was it! That was His answer.

A dying sinner condemned to death, asked for life. A dying Savoir, with the power of life, granted his request.

That is the love of God. Are you dying now?

While there is yet breath…there is yet hope.

But do not put this off. God's word says,

*While it is said, "Today if you will hear His voice,
Harden not your hearts…"
Hebrews 3: 15*

And again

*… He limiteth a certain day saying…
"Today after so long a time,
As it is said,
Today if you will hear His voice
Harden not you hearts."
Hebrews 4: 7*

*For the wages of sin is death
But the gift of God is eternal life
Through Jesus Christ our Lord.*

*For all have sinned
And come short of the glory of God.*

Won't you seal your eternal life with hope by this prayer
On this very day?

Jesus said, *I am the Resurrection and The Life. He that cometh to me, though he were dead, yet shall he live. And whosoever liveth and believeth in me shall never die.*

*While there is Breath…there is yet hope.
But do not let the breath of life escape you,*

Without asking for… the Breath of Life

Those who plan to ask for life tomorrow…
Often die today.

PRAYER OF SALVATION

What will you do?

Here is a prayer of forgiveness and life.
Won't you accept life?

A prayer of salvation.

Dear Lord God of Heaven and Earth, I bow my head and heart before you and ask for salvation. I ask for forgiveness for any and all the sins of my life and believe that by the blood of Jesus Christ on a cross 2,000 years ago, there is forgiveness. I believe that He, as your son, came to die for me and all like me, so that we could have forgiveness and eternal life.

I believe that after He died, He rose again from the grave, and by His rising, overcame death for all who believe. And now, being justified, not by my own actions, but by the actions and life and death and resurrection of Jesus Christ, I ask you to dress me in the gown of His salvation, and the robe of His righteousness, that I may have life.

I hereby open the door to my heart and ask you to come in and be my Lord. And I thank you for this gift. This gift you have given freely, and for your son, whom you offered freely, as my sacrifice for death and sin that I may live forever in your Eternal Kingdom.

Thank you for the cross and for life. In Jesus name I pray.

On a Hill...

Far away...

Stood an old rugged cross.

The emblem of suffering and shame.

Yet I love that old cross...

Where the dearest and best,

For a world of lost sinners was slain. *(by George Bernard 1912)*

And on the third day...

He rose again,

Promising to raise up all those, who would believe in his name.

For by faith are ye saved through grace,

And **NOT** of yourselves.

It is a gift of God.

Not of works, lest any man should boast.

A gift of God.

May His peace be with you...

...and His spirit fill you.

Resources Used

The following resources were used in the research and development of each story involving those, who suffer, and have suffered for believing in Jesus.

VOM Voice of the Martyrs web site, persecution.com

VOM Voice of the Martyrs monthly magazine

Compass Direct News

Juche....by Thomas J. Belke

Rogue Regime....by Jasper Becker

Eyes of the Tailless Animals...Soon Ok Lee

Jesus in Beijing....by David Aikman

Stories from China...Luke Wesley

Marx & Satan....by Richard Wurmbrand

Extreme Devotion...VOM The Costly Call

The Costly Call Book Two....Emir Fethi Caner & H. Edward Pruitt

The Overcomers....by Richard Wurmbrand

Walking from East to West....by Ravi Zacharias

Iran Desperate for God...Living Sacrifice Book Company

Voices behind the Vail...Ergun Mehmet Caner

Islam and Terrorism....by Mark A. Gabriel, PH. D.

The Unfinished Battle; Islam and the Jews...by Mark A. Gabriel, PH. D.

The Truth about Muhammad....by Robert Spencer

The Battle for the Last days Temple....by Randall Price

If I have left out any source that should have been noted, I humbly apologize and pray that the end cause, the cause of Salvation, and the Grace of God in Jesus Christ, may be magnified.

As the world around us dissolves into hate and madness, the events, as they are unfolding, clearly outline and highlight the declarations proclaimed in the Word of God. This was the irrefutable source by which all materials used in this book, were measured for accuracy. All scripture is taken from either the King James or the New King James version.

This book was written in grace, that those who read it might find grace.

www.ingramcontent.com/pod-product-compliance
Lightning Source LLC
Chambersburg PA
CBHW032101090426
42743CB00007B/198